Scheherezade in the Marketplace

ELIZABETH GASKELL
AND THE VICTORIAN NOVEL

Hilary M. Schor

D1457720

New York   Oxford
OXFORD UNIVERSITY PRESS
1992

Oxford University Press

Oxford   New York   Toronto
Delhi   Bombay   Calcutta   Madras   Karachi
Kuala Lumpur   Singapore   Hong Kong   Tokyo
Nairobi   Dar es Salaam   Cape Town
Melbourne   Auckland

and associated companies in
Berlin   Ibadan

Library of Congress Cataloging-in-Publication Data
Schor, Hilary Margo.
Scheherezade in the marketplace : Elizabeth Gaskell and the
Victorian novel / Hilary M. Schor.
p. cm.   Includes index.
ISBN 0-19-507388-6
1. Gaskell, Elizabeth Cleghorn, 1810–1865—Criticism and interpretation.
2. Women and literature—England—History—19th century.
I. Title.
PR4711.S36   1992
823'.8—dc20   91-42287

1 3 5 7 9 8 6 4 2

Printed in the United States of America
on acid-free paper

Acknowledgments

This book began as a dissertation under the generous direction of Barbara Gelpi, Ian Watt, and Regenia Gagnier; to their kind and intelligent readings, I owe much. Along the way, other readers and colleagues have given me always welcome assistance in the form of editing, information, and forums in which to present work in progress, and I must especially acknowledge Cathy Gallagher, Christopher Herbert, Kelly Hurley, John Jordan, James Kincaid, Donna Landry, Jayne Lewis, Sylvia Manning, David Miller, Tania Modleski, Robert Polhemus, Tita Rosenthal, Richard Stein, and Sue Zemka.

My deepest debts are to those who, at one stage or another, read the entire manuscript, and offered the kinds of readings that make revision a challenge and a pleasure: they are Deidre Lynch, Garrett Stewart, Peter Manning, Robert Patten, and Jay Clayton. To them, and to the other friends whose encouragement allowed me to finish this at last—particularly to Elinor Accampo, Eric Mallin, Robert Newsom, and Laurie Novo—I owe more than any formal acknowledgment could make clear or begin to repay.

To my family, whose support (intellectual, financial, emotional) has seemed, in these years, limitless, I owe another kind of debt, especially to my dear sisters, Barbara and Renée, and my parents, Arthur and Judith, who began my education early, and from whom I never cease to learn about the intricacies and the joys of reading, of writing, and of teaching. To my grandparents, Dora and Ben Saltz and Kathryne and Joseph Schor, whose courage and capacity for love are the most profound lessons of my life, this book is dedicated.

Portions of this book appeared elsewhere in different forms, and I am grateful to the editors of *Novel* for permission to reprint portions of

Chapter 3, which appeared in 22:3, Spring 1989 (288–304), and to Macmillan Press and Indiana University Press for permission to reprint portions of Chapter 2, which appeared as "The Plot of the Beautiful Ignoramus: *Ruth* and the Tradition of the Fallen Woman" in *Sex and Death in Victorian Literature*, edited by Regina Barreca, Macmillan Press © 1990, and Indiana University Press, © 1991.

Contents

Scheherezade in the Marketplace

A Klee painting named "Angelus Novus" shows an angel looking as though he is about to move away from something he is fixedly contemplating. His eyes are staring, his mouth is open, his wings are spread. This is how one pictures the angel of history. His face is turned toward the past. Where we perceive a chain of events, he sees one single catastrophe which keeps piling wreckage upon wreckage and hurls it in front of his feet. The angel would like to stay, awaken the dead, and make whole what has been smashed. But a storm is blowing from Paradise; it has got caught in his wings with such violence that the angel can no longer close them. This storm irresistibly propels him into the future to which his back is turned, while the pile of debris before him grows skyward. This storm is what we call progress.

WALTER BENJAMIN, "Theses on the Philosophy of History"

Women and fiction might mean, and you may have meant it to mean, women and what they are like; or it might mean women and the fiction that they write; or it might mean women and the fiction that is written about them; or it might mean that somehow all three are inexplicably mixed together and you want me to consider them in that light.

VIRGINIA WOOLF, *A Room of One's Own*

Never mind! it is a very pretty *naive* little thing, and we can't always be high flown and moral in our stories. If you like you may adopt a sentence out of Mary Wollstonecraft to this air.

ELIZABETH GASKELL, letter of 24(?) April 1848

Introduction

The Scheherezade of my title is borrowed not only from the Arabian Tales but from the salutation of a letter to Elizabeth Gaskell from one of her more illustrious contemporaries. When Charles Dickens wrote to Gaskell in 1851 and addressed her as "my dear Scheherezade," he conjured up a curious figure: Scheherezade, the manipulator of male desire, the designer of endless narrative, the woman storyteller telling stories to win her husband and save her own life. But Dickens's offhand editorial flirtation has a more ambiguous side: in this vignette of authorship, the male storyteller captures the fabulist princess for himself; it is his stories that he wants her to tell. She is there to seduce him, and he to publish her tales—a curious encounter of fiction and the market, of desire and its containment, of female power and male anxiety, of the seductive "publicity" of Victorian fiction. I have appropriated this tale not to give Dickens the last word but to point to a problem in Victorian authorship: the difficulty, one we are still far from understanding, of the woman writer, and her relationship to the forms of Victorian fiction.

It is no accident that I begin with the invocation of one of Gaskell's more famous contemporaries: the easiest place to begin addressing the question of "Why a book on Elizabeth Gaskell?" is with the reminder that she wrote at a time of incredible activity in fiction, and that from the publication of her first novel until her death she was perceived as (and lionized as) one of the foremost novelists of the day. Even more central to the reputation her novels have built is her participation in a wide range of social transformations that we now recognize as "Victorian England": she lived in Manchester at the height of its industrialization; she wrote novels on such controversial subjects as prostitution and working-class politics; she was a woman of considerable intellectual sophistication, at home with the most important issues of her day. But she has also come to represent for critics a kind of domestic fiction (and domestic virtue) summed up in her nomination as "Mrs. Gaskell," the most conventional and soothing of the major novelists; she has also been seen as politically tame, where others were radical, and intellectually frail, where others were experimental, and it is *against* these notions that this book has been written. For those reasons, while I will continue throughout to stress the indeed crucial connections between Gaskell and her contemporaries—and important strains in contemporary thought—my primary focus here will be on the specific struggle of the woman writer with the literary plots she has inherited, and the forces of the marketplace she must confront; it will be on the ways in which Scheherezade may have had to reimagine her own story.

To begin here is to begin with some of the contradictions of Gaskell's career, and of her fiction; this has not been the starting point of most Gaskell scholarship. Contemporary criticism has made of her a more conventional, if not less divided, figure: the Unitarian minister's wife from the South of England who moved to the North during the industrial revolution and described what she saw. When Elizabeth Gaskell came to write fiction, the (critical) story goes, she did so out of a sense of social outrage; her novels trace the history of that outrage, and, as transparent and naive literary creations, allow us to imagine what a typical Victorian woman, looking around her at the transformation of English life, thought and felt. For these critics, as for social historians and the many nostalgic readers of novels like *Cranford*, Gaskell herself is a curiosity—in various ways a museum piece of Victorian culture, her novels mere curios, whether of lost rural life or the painful changes of industrialization.

Gaskell's own stories about herself as a writer have a very different—and more powerful—energy: "Women" she once wrote to her friend, the painter Eliza Fox, "must give up living an artist's life, if home duties are to be paramount." For women, she wrote, the "hidden world of art" is at once a "shelter . . . [from] . . . daily small Lilliputian arrows of peddling cares" and the "work . . . we are sent into the world to do." In this tension between "art" and "duty," between "woman" and "artist," we see both her frustration at trying to manage a household, support a husband, live a proper life, and write fiction, and the power that Gaskell saw in her art, her "appointed work to do, which no one else can do so well." But she exclaimed to Fox in another letter, "Nature intended me for a gypsy-bachelor"; as she asserted midway through her career, when describing her friend Charlotte Brontë after the publication of *Jane Eyre*,

henceforward Charlotte Brontë's existence became divided into two parallel currents—her life as Currer Bell, the author; her life as Charlotte

Brontë, the woman. There were separate duties belonging to each character—not opposing each other; not impossible, but difficult to be reconciled.
When a man becomes an author, it is probably merely a change of employment to him . . . a woman's principal work in life is hardly left to her own
choice; nor can she drop the domestic charges devolving on her as an
individual, for the exercise of the most splendid talents that were ever
bestowed.

Those "difficult" "oppositions," "duties," "reconciliations," "exercises"
are the donnée of Gaskell's authorial presence; their traces are at the
center of this study.

In studying the tension between these visions of what the Victorian
woman novelist was to be; how she was to write; how she could read and
be read by those around her, this book in turn constructs its own
narrative of Elizabeth Gaskell's fiction. I begin with the assumption that
Gaskell was intensely interested in publication and in acquiring a public
voice, and that her attempt to write the fiction of those denied a voice
within Victorian society led her to an awareness of her own silencing, a
sense of the ways that literary and cultural plots shape our understanding
of the world and limit our ability to describe it. Her experiments with
literary form led her to examine the central stories of her culture, particularly the inscription of woman as the (silent) other. Writing at a time of
intense social upheaval, Gaskell sought in and through fiction what she
called "a permanent state of change," fiction that would allow for possibilities beyond those that looked absolute to Victorian readers, beyond
what one of her characters describes as "planning marriages and looking
forward to deaths." This book, then, tells two parallel stories: the difficult
evolution of the woman novelist, and the "story" of the heroine across the
progress of Gaskell's work.

The romance plot (the heroine's progress toward or through marriage)
has been much neglected, even scorned, by critics, who have dismissed
the marriage plot as either politically suspect (tending toward preserva-
tion of the status quo) or as literarily derivative; neither of these supposi-
tions seems true to me. The lessons of feminism suggest that these private
plots are (particularly for a woman novelist in a time of intense social
change) *more* likely to be the centers of political critique; I will be
arguing here that the politicizing of the heroine's plot is intrinsically
linked as well to the literary transformations Gaskell's work carries out.
It was through her attempts to write the woman's story (to rewrite its
social conventions, to imagine for it a different ending) that Gaskell came
to her most radical challenges to the conventions of literary plotting.
Although in a novel like *Mary Barton*, the heroine's plot is made to do

much of the work of political reconciliation within the novel, by the time of *North and South* that link between political and domestic resolutions is the most vexed issue in the novel; similarly, if *Ruth* traces the passive heroine's progress into the plot of the fallen woman, *Sylvia's Lovers* examines the tensions between the heroine's sexual desire and the plotting of *male* identity in the historically complicated world of Jacobin England. That is to say, the political economies so easily seen at work in these novels translate into and intersect profoundly with both sexual (or domestic) economies and the fictional plots that enable them—plots that are increasingly put into question. Even such seemingly conventional works as *Cranford*, with its benevolent female community, and *Wives and Daughters*, with its vision of quiet village life, carry out social and narrative critiques, again through the heroine's plot. In *Cranford*, a novel without a heroine, we see the formation of a model of collective heroineship (and of a nonlinear plot); in *Wives and Daughters*, with its Darwinian hero, its two heroines, and its play with plots, secrecy, conspiracy, and gossip, we see Gaskell's most relativist fiction, her most self-conscious revision of a marriage plot, and her final questioning of the relationship between novels, readers, and culture. For the neophyte novelist, writing *Mary Barton* in 1847, these questions were far from abstract; questions of female authority, of the heroine's freedom, of the forms her story (and I mean here both Gaskell's and Mary's) could take are everywhere in Gaskell's approach to authorship, and everywhere in the novel. The interdependence of these questions and their formal and thematic implication for Gaskell's fiction will be the subject of this book.

For this reason, this book is committed to a wide range of material: each chapter has at its heart a set of variations on the conventions of narrative, on the conditions of publication, on the authorial questions that confronted Gaskell in writing these novels. That is, I read the early works as literary apprenticeship, primarily through the romantic inheritance from Wordsworth. The second section focuses largely on the problems of publishing and the marketplace, and the influence of (and Gaskell's rebellion against) her editor, Charles Dickens. The third and final section moves into questions that are more purely formal, the problems of closure and relativism, as shaped by the cultural forces of Darwin and others, and the growing awareness of women novelists (Gaskell, Eliot, the Brontës) of one another, and of the different complexities of women's fiction.

The question of female authorship will be present in several different forms in this book, and the critical vocabularies I utilize will shift similarly. I have learned greatly from Marxist and feminist critics, and this study tries to connect these methodologies; perhaps the best way of describing what I am after here is to explain my relationship to psycho-analytic feminism, particularly in its French, Lacanian forms. Although I am intrigued by the notion of a female language, and the question of writing like a woman is certainly at the heart of this project, I have assumed throughout that any answer to that question must be phrased in terms of the specific cultural languages available to the particular woman writer. Gaskell, for example, was fascinated by the relationship of the daughter to her dead mother, and of the possibility of a separate female realm, and this vision (which will recur throughout this book) is easy to discuss in the terms made familiar by French feminists: the semiotic, the uncanny, the disruptive. But in the terms of this study, to ask what a maternal language (an exclusively female language) meant within the domestic structures of Victorian England makes of this a less abstract, and less easy, question.

That is also to say that my assumption throughout is that narrative is a social, and socially determined, act; since this is primarily a study in fictional form, my attention is focused on what makes for a coherent narrative, what one form of fiction endorses or rejects, what happens at those moments when narrative ceases to cohere and fictional forms begin to crack or shift under various strains. Two other implications of this argument must by now be clear. The first is my conviction that the form of "the Victorian novel" was still very much in flux at the time Gaskell was writing. While Gaskell is usually treated as a practitioner of a kind of transparent realism, a naive reporter, an untrained sympathizer, I see her novels as both complex and self-conscious, and as part of a larger debate over form, over the relationship to one's audience, over realism, at play in Victorian fiction. I see Gaskell's progress—both her own formal innova-tions and her relationship to the literary marketplace—as representative of central issues in the formation of the genre we loosely call "the novel," and as highly suggestive (in her movement toward relativism and self-awareness) for our understanding of the relationship between Victorian and Modernist novels.

This is a very different view of Gaskell's career—and of her importance in the history of the novel—than has been argued before. It is an argu-ment about the merit of her fiction, but (and here is the other implication of my theoretical assumptions) one not based on the valuation of any one work over another. I have resisted the move made by other recent critics who try to save Gaskell; the impulse of this study is to carry out the "reassessment" critics are always about to perform for her not through a piecemeal recanonization of one or two preferred novels but through a treatment of the career as a whole. The concept of authorship and heroineship—of voice and plot, as they might be labeled within this study—gives structure not only to my treatment but to her oeuvre. Other critics have occasionally attempted to rescue one novel or another, but this has always resulted in a slighting of other works, the privileging of one strain or another in her fictional repertoire. I have resisted the temptation to prefer the "social novel" to the "pastoral" or the "document" to the "sketch," the impulse to "love her heroines" or "admire her technique" exclusively. An examination of Gaskell's works leads one to see as arbitrary the divisions between the problem novel and the nostalgic idyll, between gothic romance and urban realism, between the development of character and the intricacies of plot. Victorian fiction looks very different when these boundaries, distinctions no Victorian would have made, begin to break down.

At the most abstract level, the critical questions raised by this discussion range from the debates over the relation of ideology and narrative form to those over the (social) construction of desire; the individual details (the narrative history) of those desires will be the material of this book. But I will be reading those questions as inflected by issues of publication and authorship, issues like changes in circulating libraries, in serial publication, Gaskell's complicated relationship with other writers, with editors and publishers and readers—that is, I will be focusing on the text as a cultural production. To connect questions of literary form to the languages of class and gender in Victorian society, to problems of how plots were read, to questions of intentionality within the history of forms and genres seems to me the challenge that faces feminist critics today. The finest critics of Gaskell (Raymond Williams, John Lucas, Catherine Gallagher, Rosemarie Bodenheimer) begin with these questions of the play of social tension, ideological structures, and fictional variation; feminist criticism leads us to rewrite these questions to focus on women both as writers and as figures, as sites of meaning within the text. Victorian novelists believed in the power of fiction to transform society; increasingly, criticism of the Victorian novel has focused on the social functions (and constraints) of the text, on the contradictions, gaps and silences, the "discontents" of Victorian fiction. Feminist criticism has had little to do with the grit of culture (trains, factories, evolutionary biologists), and in its privileging of the heroic, romantic woman artist has sacrificed some of the particular achievements of novelists like Gaskell: the connection of the female plot with social transformation, of cultural marginality with narrative experimentation, and the myriad varieties of realistic fiction that female authorship engendered.

In these contexts, to read Scheherezade's story is to reinvent it: to imagine it as a story with the power to transform. Scheherezade, of course, had to tell stories to live; she lives to tell stories of storytelling. Here we can ask not only which stories she told but which was she not free to tell; which stories spoke through her; and which stories she, through imagination and courage, managed to make new. A Victorian Scheherezade, writing her own endings to a story she inherited, would be a storyteller worth knowing.

I

THE NOVELIST AS LITERARY DAUGHTER

1

"I Have Tried to Write Truthfully": Authority and Authorship in *Mary Barton*

From the time of its initial, startlingly successful publication in 1848, *Mary Barton* has owed its fame to its depiction of the sufferings of the working class, its careful and sympathetic realism, and its political engagement. The novel has largely been read as John Barton's novel, and everything that has distracted from the story of the visionary worker, his losses, his anger, and his pathos, has seemed exactly that to critics—a distraction. Included—indeed, central—in that critical impatience has been Mary Barton's story, which has seemed to most critics a weakening of the strong material of her father's tragedy, a conventional way out of the complexity of the social dilemmas his novel represents, as—in Raymond Williams's tidy summary—"the diversion . . . [to] the familiar and orthodox plot of the Victorian novel of sentiment."[1] Mary Barton's plot, in short, has seemed subordinate in subject, in political import, and in authorial skill.

That last is not quite a coincidence; the other myth that has plagued criticism of Elizabeth Gaskell's first novel is that of the amateur author, directed by her affectionate husband to submerge her grief over the death of her infant son into the project of a novel. The novel here becomes both therapeutic and social work but could not—given the myth—ever be read as reflecting authorial ambition or as more serious social critique; its success in *either* field, then, becomes purely accidental.

I begin with these two myths both because I wish to make a more serious case for the novel's success (as it is, not as it fails to become *John Barton*) as political critique, and because I think the novel's success is precisely linked to what these myths elide. The same political critique that marks the "John Barton" plot informs Mary Barton's plot, and I will be arguing here that it is a critique of received languages and received plots, of the inability of workers and of women to speak for their own experience in industrialized Manchester. But it seems to me further that the political critique of the heroine's plot—the novel's understanding of the connections between sexual and economic exploitation, of the limitations of female autonomy—grows out of Gaskell's own experience of suppression, and her coming to authorship in the late 1840s—not a single, chance occurrence but the cumulation of a deliberate progress toward publication, one about which she was very canny, and very far from amateurish. The narrative of the grieving mother is indeed central to *Mary Barton*, but as a story about female authority and power, in much the same way that, on closer examination, the novel that is *Mary Barton*'s story reveals its own powerful critique of existing structures of authority in Victorian England—and, more crucial to our purposes here, to Gaskell's revisions of existing forms of fiction. In this revisioning, it is specifically the woman writer who has the power to transform the novel's form—and its readers.

i

> The Chartist who denies the suffrage to women, is a Chartist only because he is not a lord; he is one of those levellers who would level only down to his own level.
>
> HARRIET TAYLOR MILL, "The Enfranchisement of Women"

> This speech . . . was so different to all she had planned to say, and from all the formal piety she had laid in store for the visit; for this was heart's piety, and needed no garnish of texts to make it true religion, pure and undefiled.
>
> *Mary Barton*

In her important essay "Desire in Narrative" Teresa de Lauretis points out that "love interest" can denote both "the singular function of the female character, and then, the character itself."[2] To put it even more boldly than that, the love interest refers to both the heroine and her plot in the conventional hero's narrative; in Dorothy Sayers's *Have His Carcase*, the mystery novelist Harriet Vane, frustrated in her efforts to make her new novel conform to her editor's instructions—and to convention— wires back a furious message: "Tell Bootle I absolutely refuse introduce love-interest."[3] Such dissatisfaction has marked critics' responses to

Mary Barton's love plot—and to its heroine, who seems flat, conventional, "romantic," in the light of the heroic realism of the Chartist plot.

Gaskell herself offers some comfort for those critics who, like Raymond Williams, argue that the move to *Mary Barton* must have been a relief; in her letters she declares that "John Barton was the original title of the book. Round the character of John Barton all the others formed themselves; he was my hero, *the* person with whom all my sympathies went."[4] But it is a long step from that to Stephen Gill's assertion that the move of the novel into *Mary* Barton's story is a "change [in] the direction of the novel" that leads the reader "into a fiction in which there are no problems of form or content because its content has been the staple of fiction ever since minstrels began to tell stories."[5] As Gaskell suggests in another letter, "I am glad you like Mary, I do: but people are angry with her just because she is not perfect."[6] Williams himself writes, "If Mrs Gaskell had written 'round the character of Mary Barton all the others formed themselves', she would have confirmed our actual impression of the finished book."[7] And as Gaskell's commentary suggests, the "finished book" is most important for its *im*perfections.

My point in this chapter is that the novel we have *does* pose "problems of form [and] content," and that far from constituting a "diversion" from the more serious, socially critical plot of *John Barton*, Mary's plot both echoes the questions of the more explicitly political novel, and questions the politics of the heroine's story, precisely through its innovations in form, its critique of narrative and social authority, its jumbling of public and private, through the very romantic plot dismissed by these critics. To interrogate the love plot, reinserting it into the political plot, to reinsert further into that "staple of fiction" the politics of form, seems to me to create a very different novel. What the two plots share most clearly is a sense that power is linguistically motivated and enabled, and if the "political" quest of the characters is largely for an effective language of representation, for words to change the world, no less is the heroine's plot shot through with these questions of language, speech, and power; the question of the heroine's right to confront the fictions that write her life. The heroine's movement toward speech, her ability to "own" her story, is as significant as her father's need to have his petition heard. Woman's speech was a politically charged question for contemporary readers, and the novel's critique of the restricted lives of women makes her speech itself a political act.

I will return in the next section to Gaskell's own concern with woman's speech and particularly with authorship, but it is worth rehearsing the plot of *Mary Barton* here to point out how difficult it is to separate

Mary's and John's stories—and worth investigating further what links them, to locate, in Rosemarie Bodenheimer's phrase, the "politics of story" in *both* plots. The double-plot account of *Mary Barton* takes roughly this form: the political story is that in which John Barton, Chartist worker, goes to London with the Petition, comes back disillusioned, and, during the heat of a strike, joins a "Political Union" and assassinates the arrogant Harry Carson, son of a factory owner; the domestic story is that in which lovely, motherless Mary Barton is nearly seduced by the handsome, rich Carson but realizes in time that she loves Jem Wilson, the worker who loves her, only almost to lose him to the gallows when he is arrested for the murder her father has committed, an accusation from which she must exonerate Jem without revealing her father's guilt. The lines between the plots already blur on so brief an investigation: the equation the novel makes (that the sexual villain, Harry Carson, is also an oppressor of workers) requires a blurring of the violence as well, for the common enemy must appear to be assassinated by the unhappy lover, only to have the workers' plot revealed again at the novel's end.

But the blurring between the two plots goes deeper than the assassination plot, or its doubled motivation. Throughout the novel, scenes of public (political) action are interrupted by private (domestic) pathos; more, one narrative is constantly being substituted for the other. To take only the most obvious example, when John Barton returns from London, having been part of the group delivering the Petition, he refuses to tell his story—the tale that *should* be the centerpiece of this novel of desperate Chartist assassins and their starving families. Precisely what happens is that a tale of family life takes the place of the political centerpiece; Job Legh tells a heartbreaking story of *his* journey to London to see his daughter and her new baby, and arriving to find her and her husband dead, and of leaving them (as dead as John Barton's hopes, we might interpolate) in a strange cemetery, returning with the baby girl he then raises. A similar substitution takes place when Jem Wilson visits the Bartons to continue his wooing of Mary, only to have her leave the room and John Barton begin a tale of laborers' injuries after working overlong hours. What is a reader to make of this exchange of explicitly political and domestic scenes? At the least, we can say that one plot never quite advances, or advances only at the (again, explicit) cost of the other; more, the continuing juxtaposition of the two leads to a denser feeling of working-class life, in which organized politics and domestic details live side by side. The substitutions not only push forward the revolutionary domestic content of the novel (Gaskell's claim to be writing a "novel of

Manchester life," a work that goes beyond other condition-of-England novels precisely through its feeling of being written *within* that life) but encourage us to see the politics of that domestic life.

But what, then, links these two sides of "Manchester life"? What both John and Mary Barton seek is a way *out* of Manchester and the limits on them—John, out of the poverty and starvation of working-class life; Mary, into the upper-class life she fantasizes will be hers if she marries Harry Carson. It is true, as Rosemarie Bodenheimer points out, that what the characters have in common—the escape that both seek—is not connected to "politics as such,"[8] but it is also worth remembering how much "politics as such" was connected to what seems to me the novel's question, that of speaking out, of finding an adequate language to represent one's desires—a desire that is, at any level, political.

A critique of language is at the heart of the social movements of the day. Gareth Stedman Jones has suggested that the Chartists were largely motivated by a sense of the fictionality of government. In his essay "Rethinking Chartism" he traces the political rhetoric of the Jacobin movement, with its emphasis on law as a fiction, through working-class radicalism, into the thirties.[9] Workers, he argues, believed they needed to capture power politically, to control what they saw as fictions of wealth and value, linguistic counters. John Barton's sense of power is akin to this: the wealth is out there but is kept from workers who lack authority to move fictional profits back to those who produced the real goods. Because he is cut off from the structures that "invent" these profits, he is unable to place himself in the political system: Parliament will not hear the workers, as he says, "No, not now, when we weep tears o' blood."[10] More, the language of political economy, which Gaskell ironically states she does not understand, is equally inaccessible to John Barton: critics have continued to try to prove, in one form or another, the logic of the master's thought, but they ignore Gaskell's main point, that the logic is never explained to the workers. Neither can John Barton—or his friends—find an adequate political label that will explain him to the masters; the novel, significantly, responds by calling him merely "a visionary." By contrast, the speeches the workers deliver make sense to them—and to us—because they mirror the experience we have been witnessing. When starving workers explain their poverty in terms of dying children, readers who have watched children die for two hundred pages will be moved; the empty talk of foreign markets lacks validity for us, as for them. What we share with the workers, then, is a sense of the manipulation of their (our) experience, at the expense of a fiction of government (the distant London indifference) we cannot believe in, either.

Critics have made much of Gaskell's own division between the workers' "truth" and the narratorial interventions that represent the middle-class hesitation ("we," she suggests, looking at the "uneducated" see a "Frankenstein" and share a fear of "combination"), but those interventions strike us as precisely that; the "truth" John and Mary Barton fight to speak is linked not to what is added by the narrator, a question to which I will return at the end of the chapter, but to the individual truths spoken by the characters themselves, and to the struggle for an adequate language that is thematized throughout the novel.

In *Mary Barton*, what characters crave is what Gaskell calls "heart's piety," a language apart from what they term "speechifying"—public, political language—that would be a speech powerful enough to convert, to transform, to redeem experience. That such a language cannot exist in a separate realm, any more than could domestic space exist apart from the larger political or social structures around it, is the novel's most profound point, one that critics who dwell on the novel's domestic (for which, read quietist) solutions seem to have missed. There are moments in which characters do speak from the heart, seeming (and perceiving themselves) to escape, however briefly, the larger structures in which they move and speak: when John Barton gruffly blesses his daughter; when Mary "in many tears . . . told him her repentance for her faults"; moments when characters who "do not know how to speak" "gulp down their pride" and "hold out their arms." But many of those are moments *before* speech—like Carson's forgiveness of Barton—and a significant number of moments of real understanding in the novel come precisely from (or in) silence: John Barton's inability to tell the story of the trip to London; Margaret's hesitation at telling her grandfather she has gone blind; Aunt Esther's lies about her desolate life; Mary's inability to tell Jem Wilson she loves him. This inability to speak directly, the silences and secrets at the domestic fireside, the inability (even in private) to find a language for expression gets to the heart of the novel, and to the centrality of *Mary* Barton's plot.

The work of the novel is to move its heroine from her upper-class to her lower-class lover, and, more interesting, to move her into public, which is where she finally (when a witness at his trial for the murder of Harry Carson) tells Jem of her love. This movement of speech can be read as essentially "private," but I want to begin to stress its public (and political) import. The Gill-Williams line on this novel depends on the idea that women (and their romances) are exempted from the larger political questions of the time, and that novels exist outside a politics of discourse—one such as *Mary Barton* foregrounds.

The concern with speech that marks early Chartist debate (the debate over the Stamp Acts, which William Lovett called "one of the most important political movements that I was ever associated with,"[11] or the attention to publication that Bronterre O'Brien stressed, arguing that "to accomplish a revolution we must have an *instructed* as well as a united people"[12]) extends to their concern with women's rights. The Chartists kept Mary Wollstonecraft's *Vindication* in print; R. J. Richardson wrote a pamphlet on *the Rights of Woman* in 1840 that both recalls Wollstonecraft and anticipates John Stuart Mill.[13] The concern with the desecration of the home, the transformation of the female worker, female enfranchisement (though the latter was not part of the *Charter*) all seemed equally men's and women's issues; more, it was possible for women to speak out in public on these issues. A contemporary report of a "Miss Ruthwell" who addressed a Chartist assembly in 1845 begins with much the same hesitation as *Mary Barton* admits on this issue:

> In addressing a meeting composed of hundreds of thinking men, she keenly felt her situation and was aware that among the ranks of the middle and upper class she would obtain the unenviable epithet of a bold and forward girl: but, should that be the case, they who would thus charge her should remember that the blame lay at their own door. The persecution of herself and her family had caused her to reflect and that which was a mystery and buried in obscurity was now clear and plain before her mind's eye.[14]

But the "bold and forward girl" goes on to use her platform to speak up not only for "her class" but for other women, and their role in the political movement:

> While she had a tongue to proclaim the wrongs of sisters in slavery; while a drop of British blood flowed in her veins she would strive for the emancipation of her class and ere long they would find that the female workers in Bradford would be a powerful auxiliary in the onward march to a fair day's wage for a fair day's work'. Miss Ruthwell sat down loudly cheered.

For Miss Ruthwell, as for Mary Barton, it is easier to speak in the name of others, but the primary movement of the speech ("sisters in slavery") is an equation of femininity and oppression that *Mary Barton* makes as well: its notion of female power—whether auxiliary or not—stems from an identical movement into the public realm.

When Miss Ruthwell invokes the epithet of a "bold and forward girl" she will obtain from "the ranks of the middle and upper class," she invokes as well the sexual plot that doubles the political plot of *Mary Barton*, and pinpoints exactly that plot's class dimensions. From the start, Mary's "romance" is her attempt at a movement "forward," out of the lower classes, into comfort and ease, into a world where

> she should ride from church in her carriage, with wedding bells ringing, and take up her astonished father and drive away from the old dim work-a-day court forever, to live in a grand house, where her father should have newspapers, and pamphlets, and pipes, and meat dinners, every day—and all day long if he liked. (p. 121)

Mary first "listens to the voice of the tempter [Harry]" on a "hot summer evening, when, worn out by stitching, and sewing, she had loitered homewards with weary langour," and her desires are entirely to escape her labor, to do "all the elegant nothings appertaining to ladyhood." (The rest of her plans, as the passage above suggests, are for her father, "her dear father, now oppressed with care, and always a disheartened gloomy person"; her vision of wealth is one that will allow him his—presumably Chartist—pamphlets.) Mary's romance is a form of class warfare, and her seduction is itself a staple of working-class political fiction. As Anna Clark has noted, radical political journals often featured stories framed around the violation of decent working-class girls by upper-class bounders, despite all evidence that the real threat of rape and violation came to these women from men of their own class.[15]

Mary's romance, then, is not just her passive status as "love interest," but her plot for social improvement, paralleling once more the political plot, for the rejected Harry Carson becomes not only *her* persecutor but the persecutor of the striking workers. In turn, her race to rescue Jem Wilson will lead her to break free of her "place" in society, and her placement as a passive love object. At that moment, as de Lauretis suggests, the heroine "may resist confinement in that symbolic space by disturbing it" and by resisting the narrative closure she has come to represent.[16] For Mary, who says to Jem's cousin Will, "It seems so flat to be left behind" (p. 244), the plot to save her lover allows her to leave her space by the fireside, much as she imagined the dalliance with Harry would allow her to leave her father's dark home. The heroine's movement *out* of the predictable plot (far from repeating the "minstrel's story" Gill invokes) disrupts narrative closure, as much as does her father's quest for political freedom, or the movement of the characters out of Manchester, into Canada.

In this light, the intersections of the double plot (Harry's pursuit of the "little witch," the "sweet little coquette" whose powerlessness draws him on, even as he "besets" the workers; the doubled secret of Mary's lover and her father's act of murder) account for more than a Freudian unity of daughter's desire and father's denial; they constitute at once a critique of the myth of a separate, domestic, private sphere (and of the woman's static place within it) and an interesting examination of what might seem conventional plotting, of the heroine's role within that plot. The seduction plot is far from a romance in a tidy bower, and that dual quest of Mary and her father (which ends in the political assassination of her lover, and her public statement of her own sexual desire) is at once political and personal, speaking (in both) for the quest for personal expression, for a language for desire—the same quest for a better form of representation that motivates the novel's author, as well.

We might, then, want to reverse the customary critic's praise of *Mary Barton* for its representation of politics to note its attention to the politics of representation, and the way it focuses our attention on the particular difficulty of the woman's struggle—on the struggles of, as Miss Ruthwell puts it, "sisters in slavery." To understand the novel's critique of novelistic and political authority, we must return to the (biographical) conditions of writing, which will in turn set the specific terms of the novelist's revisioning of authority. If the assumption of most criticism has been that Gaskell's achievement was her insight into the silencing of the worker, the assumption here must be that the experience of writing about the powerlessness of the workers led Gaskell to a new understanding of the silencing she experienced as a woman writer. It is with that idea that we can begin our discussion of her coming to authorship.

ii

I am almost frightened at my own action in writing it.

For the neophyte novelist, as for her heroine, a seemingly conventional story masks a complexly motivated movement into the public sphere— and a serious critique of existing patterns of authority. For Gaskell, as well, the move from love (interest) to politics is complicated, serious, and crucial to establishing her own (fictional) authority. Discussions of Gaskell and authority face an initial difficulty, for Elizabeth Gaskell was far from quick to put herself forward as an authority: "I know nothing of Political Economy," she writes in the preface to the novel; "I have tried to write truthfully." This is the plea to which critics have responded: that the novel offers no solutions, no sophistication, only the truth of the heart. But this self-denigration is what Sandra Gilbert and Susan Gubar have called a "cover-story," a story about authorship that in fact allows the woman novelist more authority than she would be granted if she claimed to "know" anything.[17] In Gaskell's disavowal of authorial aggression, we can see her carving out for herself other territory (that of earnestness and truth) and reinserting herself—as a sympathetic authority—into the story, a self-authorization that will have important thematic implications for *Mary Barton* as well.

Elizabeth Gaskell liked to present herself as a misunderstood writer. People were always accusing her of ideas she did not say she held, of moral views she could not endorse. "I must be an improper woman without knowing it,"[18] she once complained, and there is some validity in her complaints, for she took care to appear to be the world's least offending novelist. Although the author of *Mary Barton*, she is neither a "Socialist" nor a "Communist" but a Christian, just as, although she has written a novel that takes on all existing theories of trade and labor, and was herself a reader of Adam Smith, she "know[s] nothing of Political Economy." She was to write disingenuously to a friend, "Is Miss Jewsbury's review shallow? It looked to me very deep, but then I know I'm very easily imposed on in the metaphysical line, and could no more attempt to write such an article than fly."[19] She guarded herself against expressing opinions, especially those that seemed to take on any authority. In a letter to her daughter she suggests what is at stake when those who are not "deep" espouse opinions: "You must have a 'reason for the faith that is in you'—and not suppose you can know enough to form an opinion about measures of state."[20] Before Marianne can "fully make up [her] mind," she should read "a paper in the Quarterly on the subject . . . in (I think) the year 1839," and "I will read with you Mr Cobden's speeches[.] But first I think we should read together Adam Smith on the Wealth of Nations." It is even more important that women not "meddle with politics," for—she goes on—"women are apt to take up a thing without being even able to state their reasons clearly, and yet on that insufficient knowledge they take a more violent and bigoted stand than thoughtful men dare to do." The writer of *this* sentence seems unlikely to "dare" any "stand" at all—or even, quite, to have much of an individual "I" that "dares" to write at all.

This obliteration of a writing self is paradoxically connected to Gaskell's constant awareness of a reading public. For Gaskell, surveillance, like writing, began at home: not only did she live and write in a large family, "too much pressed upon by daily small Lilliputian arrows of peddling cares,"[21] but her literary voice was as much "pressed upon" (and as little her own) as her time. She seems never to have written anything she imagined as for her eyes only. The collected letters begin at the time of her marriage—"Elizabeth Cleghorn Stevenson" left no literary remains when she became Elizabeth Gaskell. A reader following her through these letters (the "unique revelation," as the editors call them, of "the inmost thoughts and feelings," "the intimate and even apparently insignificant experiences [out of which] the stuff of writing takes its birth") will perhaps be surprised to discover that these are not private at all.[22] Rather, she announces somewhat casually to her husband William's sister, Elizabeth, that her husband is in the habit of reading her letters before she mails them. About her last letter, she says, "Willm looked at it, and said it was 'slip-shod'—and seemed to wish me not to send it," though she did. Still, she adds, "I was feeling languid and anxious and tired, & have not been over-well this last week, and moreover the sort of consciousness that Wm may any time and does generally see my letters makes me not write so naturally & heartily as I think I should do."[23] And she goes on, "Don't begin that bad custom, my dear! and don't notice it in your answer." The message of "don't begin that way" suggests not only the difficulty of breaking this marital habit but that the authority William exercised over her letters set a dangerous precedent for their relationship, and for her writing—and it puts an altogether different color to the tale of how he encouraged her to write *Mary Barton*: "Cheer up, Lily," one can hear him urging, "write something natural and hearty"—and, of course, she did.

What "private" writing we have of Gaskell's is equally problematic, and suggests again an anxiety about appearing in public. The diary that she kept in the years before writing *Mary Barton* offers not self-commentary or self-examination but the disappearance of the author into the role of mother in a way that anticipates the narratorial presence of *Mary Barton*. The diary is "dedicated" to "my dear little Marianne," in the trust that "if I should not live to give it to her myself," it will "be reserved for her as a token of her Mother's love, and extreme anxiety in the formation of her little daughter's character."[24] It is written in the hope that if the "little daughter should in time become a mother herself, she may take an interest in the experience of another," and with the wish that "I could give her the slightest idea of the love and the hope that is bound up in her." Behind this writing, motivating it, is not just the hope of a more perfect communication between two who love each other (the hope of a more perfect conversation that we have seen in *Mary Barton*) but Gaskell's fear of dying, as her own mother did, before her children and her husband. She writes her diary to her daughter, whom she imagines in the role of an ideal listener, one with whom she shares, as she says, "the love which passeth every earthly love . . . the dear and tender tie of Mother and

Daughter"—but she is also anticipating another reader, the person who will, "if I should not live to give it [Marianne] myself," reserve this "as a token." Gaskell's fear is of people's reading this after her death to "discover" her; her defense is in appearing only in her role as tender and anxious mother, and in writing only so that Marianne can later discover more about herself and her early character. Little of Gaskell's life other than her children enters the diary (William's absences are noted occasionally; the death of the aunt who raised her is mentioned as an explanation for her silence; her second child appears only as a kind of contrast to the first, with no mention of her pregnancy), and from the first, Gaskell's feelings of responsibility as a mother are subsumed into a kind of *generic* motherhood: "If I should misguide from carelessness or negligence! willfully is not in a mother's heart" (p. 5).

Gaskell's own early literary history suggests a similar blend of modesty and canniness, of the subsuming of self into mother love; it is the canniness that the myth of the grieving mother disguises. Gaskell was in fact fairly bold in initiating her literary career. In 1838, the year she stopped keeping her diary and probably began writing fiction with great seriousness, she wrote to William and Mary Howitt, a husband-and-wife team who wrote often for working-class audiences, expressing her admiration of their work for its "charming descriptions of natural scenery and the thoughts and feelings arising from the happy circumstances of rural life."[25] Her letter is similarly rural and nostalgic, recalling summer mornings in "old solitary manor-houses," "solemnly poetical places." She sent them a description of a childhood visit to Stratford-upon-Avon; the piece pleased them, and appeared almost verbatim in their volume *Visits to Remarkable Places*. She then wrote again, describing the customs of the country where she grew up, and describing the literary projects she had undertaken with her husband, and the sketches they planned "in the manner of Crabbe . . . but in a more seeing-beauty spirit."[26] Not only does Gaskell write what are clearly audition letters, with more formal, literary prose than one sees elsewhere in her correspondence, but these letters suggest an already formed literary ethos. The sketches, she declared, were to echo the sentiment Wordsworth described in "The Old Cumberland Beggar," that "we each of us have a human heart," and her letters stake out as her territory the "poetry of humble life" that is to be "met with on every hand," "even in a town."

The Howitts responded in exactly the tone she must have wanted, encouraging her to "use her pen for the public benefit," and when they launched their working-class weekly, *Howitt's Journal*, in 1847, she contributed three stories.[27] When she completed the first volume of *Mary*

Barton, she sent it to William Howitt, who showed the manuscript to John Forster, then reader for Chapman and Hall, and it was Forster who recommended submission of the manuscript to the press. But her relationship with the Howitts suggests not only her literary preparation and the Wordsworthian politics always implicit in her writing but some of the practicality she brought to publication—and her secret enjoyment of her own "employment" in fiction. "My word!" she wrote to her sister-in-law, "authorship brings them in a pretty penny!"[28] In this blend of economic pragmatism, Wordsworthian humanism, and detailed, nostalgic history, we find many of the ingredients of *Mary Barton*, and much of Gaskell's subsequent literary project.

But there is a gap between the eagerness this history suggests, and Gaskell's general reticence about her own ambition. Her letters contain no mention of the writing of *Mary Barton*, and she seems to have told no one of its publication. Friends recount her "popping" "down under the table to look for something which I am sure wasn't there," when the authorship of the novel was discussed at the breakfast table.[29] She claimed to have resented every attempt to determine the authorship of the work—she even encouraged false reports, writing to Catherine Winkworth[30] and to Edward Chapman that

> I am only just returned from Wales; I find every one here has most convincing proofs that the authorship of Mary Barton should be attributed to a Mrs Wheeler, nee Miss Stone, and authoress of some book called the 'Cotton Lord'.[31]

But we must set against this quite respectable authorial modesty the next sentence of the letter, in which Gaskell continues,

> I am only afraid lest you should also be convinced and transact that part of the business which yet remains unaccomplished with her. I do assure you that I am the author.

Despite the middle-class respectability Gaskell attempts to maintain through her anonymous publication, she is quite willing to claim that "I am the author" when it comes to pocketing "that part of the business" still due her—and she writes several letters to Chapman on the subject of the money he owes her. The Howitts tried to talk her into publishing under her own name, William arguing that "it would be as well for [her works] to be known as the works of a lady, I think they would be more popular,"[32] but Gaskell refused—though she also decided against using a pseudonym. All of this suggests a curious ambivalence about "being known"—and being acknowledged—by readers.[33]

Gaskell eventually decided that it was "better simply to acknowledge the truth, in order to put a stop to all these unpleasant manifestations of curiosity," but she declares she "certainly did not expect that so much curiosity would be manifested; and I can scarcely yet understand how people can reconcile it to their consciences to try and discover what it is evident the writer wishes to conceal."[34] In a similar vein, she remarks that "hitherto the whole affair of publication has been one of extreme annoyance to me, from the impertinent and unjustifiable curiosity of people."[35] But her later comments have more bite than wonderment in them: in December of 1848 she wrote to a friend of her surprise at "the intelligence that 'Mary Barton' was so much read, and that you had guessed (*I cannot imagine how?*) that I had written it."[36] She continues:

> I did write it, but how did you find it out? I *do* want it to be concealed if possible, and I don't think anybody here has the least idea who is the author. . . . I am almost frightened at my own action in writing it.

She then goes on, as in the preface, to state that "I can only say I wanted to represent the subject in the light in which some of the workmen certainly consider to be *true*, not that I dare to say it is the abstract absolute truth." But though she does not "dare" to claim absolute truth for her ideas, she seems to claim something more for the novel: the concern with secrecy has as much to do with her own response to the novel she is "almost frightened at my own action in writing." Concealing the act of publication becomes a safe response, the next best thing to concealing the act of writing, or to not having written at all—not only is she an "improper woman without knowing it," who does "so manage to shock people," but she manages to shock, she suggests, even herself.

The shock is that of criminal behavior: "*no one* in Manchester, (except my husband of course)" knows of the publication or "can do more than suspect it," and the one person who does suspect most strongly "was the person to fix suspicion on me before."[37] Here the language of literary detection becomes the language of criminal detection: in ways that anticipate the criminal nightworld of *Mary Barton*, with its misplaced suspicion, confusing evidence, and dangerous acts of writing, Gaskell wants to absent herself from her own text—much as the criminal races from the scene of the crime, or as Aunt Esther skulks the streets of Manchester in *Mary Barton*, not wanting even to be addressed. Like criminals assuming names, the pseudonymous writer can become "a lady of Manchester" or "Cotton Mather Mills" and escape conviction. There will be no evidence to link her to whatever crime her writing has committed, a crime she spends pages defending herself against.

And yet, this woman who wrote without wanting to be "suspect" took care to address her novel to an audience she was convinced was out there; she also did much, in hastening publication and in writing the preface, to focus attention on the novel's relevance and its controversial subject. She asserts, innocently, in a letter of 1850, that "I don't think I cared at the time of it's [*sic*] publication what reception it met with," that "the reception it met with was a great surprize to me," but then goes on to say that "a good deal of it's [*sic*] success I believe was owing to the time of it's [*sic*] publication,—the great revolutions in Europe had directed people's attention to the social evils, and the strange contrasts which exist in the old nations."[38] But the time of publication was not accidental, and her own preface encourages readers to draw these connections:

> To myself the idea which I have formed of the state of feeling among too many of the factory-people in Manchester, and which I endeavored to represent in this tale (completed above a year ago), has received some confirmation from the events which have so recently occurred among a similar class on the Continent. (p. 38)

When her publisher asked for a preface, she claimed to "hardly know what you mean by an 'explanatory preface,'" and claimed further she wanted only to make clear that her novel was "no catch-penny run up since the events on the Continent have directed public attention to the consideration of the state of affairs between the Employers & their work-people."[39] She attempts to deny the charges of opportunism and sensational press, but the preface in fact encourages an hysteric response: readers who might fear what "recently occurred among a similar class on the Continent," ought to read *this* book, *now*.

The "now" of this book is an essential theme in all of Gaskell's correspondence with Chapman. She writes to him in March of 1848 that she is "naturally a little anxious to know when you are going to press," for "I can not help fancying that the tenor of my tale is such as to excite attention at the present time of struggle on the part of work people to obtain what they esteem their rights";[40] in April that "I hope you will not think me impatient in expressing my natural wish to learn when you are going to press, as I think the present state of public events may be not unfavourable to a tale, founded in some measure on the present relations between Masters and work people";[41] eleven days later, that she fears "from your delay in writing, you have thought it desirable to defer the appearance of my work" and reminds him that from his agreement with Howitt and "from your own statement to me, I believe there was no doubt it would have been published by this time."[42] More than conventional authorial anticipation, the "this time" of her plea carries the weight of "this time" of *Mary Barton*, a novel written consciously for perilous times. But, as she continues, "I am, (above every other consideration,) desirous that it should be *read*; and if you think there would be a better chance of a large circulation by deferring it's [*sic*] appearance, of course I defer to your superior knowledge, only repeating my own belief that the tale would bear directly upon the present circumstances."

After one further, more conciliatory mention of the question ("I would rather leave the decision regarding the time of publication to you; as your experience must lead you to judge better than I can do on the subject,"[43]) Gaskell seems to have gotten her way: the novel appeared in 1848, and although it captured the excitement of "events on the Continent," it was not attacked as an example of the "catch-penny" press. The reception of the novel makes clear that despite her insecurity, that "at present, I have no idea what to say," Elizabeth Gaskell had more than some idea of "what to say." Somewhere between modesty and "the great revolutions in Europe," we find an author intensely concerned with questions of literary authority.

Two of the concerns of publication enter directly into the narrator's voice and the heroine's progress in this novel. The first is the assertion of self, the moment when Gaskell decides it is "better simply to acknowledge the truth," despite the "manifestations of curiosity." Like Miss Ruthwell standing up before her "brothers," both the narrator and the heroine of *Mary Barton* must move to the moment of "simply acknowledging" what she might "wish to conceal." But the other concern, with which I will begin, is the larger critique of authority implicit in Gaskell's exchanges with Chapman, and domesticated in the maternal submission of *My Diary*. The myth of maternal narration in fact allows Elizabeth Gaskell a very different kind of novelistic authority; its inclusion is at the center of many of *Mary Barton*'s transformations of novelistic form. The aim of this novel is not to quiet the grieving mother, but to bring the mother back into the novel with a vengeance.

iii

"I put this and that together, and followed one, and listened to the other."

Mary Barton

"A cry is a child's only language for expressing its wants."

My Diary

At this point I want to return to *Mary Barton* to interrogate further the connections between the politics of discourse, anxiety about authorship, and the faith in maternal power. If the structure of *Mary Barton* has seemed to readers somewhat jumbled, blurring genres and moving between one narratorial tone and another, I want to argue that its mixture actually signals an intense examination of what made for both fictional and political authority in the England of the Chartists. What this examination suggests further is that the heroine's plot and the possibility of a maternal language are at the heart of the novel's critique of authority.

In the strangest scene in *Mary Barton*, the original Mary Barton (the heroine's mother, dead since the novel's second chapter) returns to comfort her grieving daughter. Mary has returned to her father's empty house after Jem's arrest for the murder of her rich lover, and lies dreaming on the floor, delirious, remembering "those days when she hid her face on her mother's pitying, loving bosom, and heard tender words of comfort," "those days when she had felt as if her mother's love was too mighty not to last for ever," "those days when hunger had been to her . . . something to be thought about, and mourned over;—when Jem and she had played together," the days "when her father was a cheery-hearted man," "when mother was alive, and *he* was not a murderer" (p. 286). As Mary re-creates this past—which is pre-narrative, re-creating a moment just before the novel's tense first chapter—there "came a strange forgetfulness of the present, in thoughts of long-past times," more specifically in the thought of a maternal love ("too mighty not to last for ever," in the words of Gaskell's *Diary*) that connects food, paternal love, romantic love, even undoes the death of Harry Carson. Mary falls asleep, and dreams "of the happy times of long ago, and her mother came to her, and kissed her as she lay, and once more the dead were alive in that happy world of dreams" (p. 286). But then, in a truly uncanny scene, the dead come alive, for Mary awakens to hear a voice outside telling her to open the door, a voice with "the accents of her mother's voice; the very south-country pronunciation, that Mary so well remembered; and which she had sometimes tried to imitate when alone, with the fond mimicry of affection." And when Mary goes to the door she sees

> a form, so closely resembling her dead mother, that Mary never doubted the identity, but exclaiming (as if she were a terrified child, secure of safety when near the protecting care of its parent,)—
>
> "Oh, mother! mother! you are come at last!" She threw herself, or rather fell into the trembling arms, of her long lost, unrecognized, Aunt Esther. (p. 287)

It *couldn't*, of course, be Mary's dead mother at the door, but Gaskell moves so successfully between realism and gothic that we would not be surprised if it were; we are completely inside Mary's thoughts here, in some haunted half-world. The reader has not been told that Aunt Esther is coming to see Mary at this point; the suspense that has been built up is maintained until the last moment, as is the close attention to Mary's nervous state and her fear. But the scene—and the confusion and desire it creates in us as well as Mary—also works thematically: the novel argues that what we all want, like Mary, is security, the "safety when near the protecting care of the parent."

The confusion of Mary's aunt with her mother suggests some of what is at work here: Aunt Esther, whose quest for love and riches first inspired Mary's romance with Harry Carson, is the novel's chief outcast, left in the exile reserved for those who abandon their families. But in this scene she is not only the prostitute, a lonely, haunted alcoholic, but an amateur detective, a would-be mother, and a narratorial surrogate—she is there, in large part, because she has already been working as a narrator. It is she who warned Jem that Mary loves Harry Carson; through this warning, Jem came to quarrel with Carson, striking the blow witnessed by the policeman who will later accuse Jem of Carson's murder. Further, it was Esther who found the evidence pointing to John; by giving the paper to Mary she prevents John's discovery and inspires Mary to act to save Jem. She seems both to read and watch over the plot: as the novel's "streetwalker," moving about at the mercy of the weather and the police, she is also herself a conduit for information.[44] She follows Mary and overhears her conversation with Carson; she follows Jem to warn him to protect Mary; she returns to the scene of the crime and hunts for the evidence she turns over to Mary, the evidence that brings her to the dark house, in her double capacity as maternal presence and narrating surveyor.

The relation between narration and knowledge is evident throughout the novel, and Esther is far from the only surveyor: the police, overseers, interfering friends abound in *Mary Barton*, much as they do in Gaskell's correspondence when she accuses friends of fixing suspicion on her and accusing her of authorship. The police, as the most visible representatives of the state, seem to be around only to arrest the poor: they catch Esther when she falls after Barton pushes her and, assuming that she is drunk, trot her off to jail on charges of vagrancy; when Harry Carson swings at Jem, and Jem hits him in return, the policeman who has been observing them since the beginning of their conversation offers to "take [Jem] to the lock-ups for assault." The police do, sympathetically, help Jem and Mary find Esther at the end of the novel, but more typical of their activity is the eager young detective who dresses himself as a worker and traps Jane Wilson into identifying the murder weapon as her son's gun. But these policemen, it is important to note, are also novelists in training: the police feel a

> pleasure in unravelling a mystery, in catching at the gossamer clue which will guide to certainty. . . . Their senses are ever and always on the qui-vive, and they enjoy the collecting and collating evidence, and the life of adventure they experience; a continual unwinding of Jack Sheppard romances, always interesting to the vulgar and uneducated mind, to which the outward signs and tokens of crimes are ever exciting. (p. 273)

Here, the novel seems to make explicit the connection between the detective, the prostitute, and the novelist, the "romancer" always on the "qui-vive," "collecting and collating evidence"—like Esther, both observing and altering the evidence as she finds it. This is the insidious watchfulness Gaskell's early letters suggest, fiction becoming surveillance, narration (and "excitement") linked to criminal acts.[45]

But through describing Esther's experience of "supervision" and her desire for another, more beneficent observation of "signs and tokens," *Mary Barton* leads its readers to a different view of both official and narrative surveillance: one of affection rather than curiosity, one not of the "romancer" but of the narrating "mother." When Esther goes to prison for vagrancy and drunkenness, just at the moment when she wants to be free to save Mary, her experience is one of "shrinking," of "hopelessness," of total surveillance. She becomes doubly a "character," for she "received a good character in the governor's books: she had picked her daily quantity of oakum, had never deserved the extra punishment of the tread-mill, and had been civil and decorous in her language." Gaskell echoes the language of the prison warden to undermine it, criticizing the severity of the prison and commending Esther's superiority to her surroundings. But the shift suggests the degree of Esther's own identification of her "character" with the "civil and decorous" language of the prison, and suggests further that this is the *only* world in which she receives a "good character" in the "books." The nature of this comfort in the world of limitations is suggested in the next sentence, which describes her release, for when she is out of prison, "the door closed behind her with a ponderous clang, and in her desolation she felt *as if shut out of home*—from the only shelter she could meet with, houseless and pennyless as she was, on that dreary day" (emphasis added).

Here again, the mother's absence is felt, for to be shut out of home is the worst fate in this novel: home may be variously cold, dark, or cheerless, but it is home. Even Mary, in the depths of her troubles, "instinctively chose the shortest cut to that home . . . the hiding place of four walls where she might vent her agony, unseen and unnoticed by the keen, unkind world without." Esther's leaving "home" begins the novel: she haunts that old home in scene after scene, noting "in her wild night wanderings . . . the haunts and habits of many a one who little thought of a watcher in the poor forsaken woman," who takes a "double interest" in "the ways and companionships of those with whom she had been acquainted in the days which, when present, she had considered hardly-worked and monotonous, but which now in retrospection seemed so happy and unclouded." It is only her return to those places where she is a "watcher," an exile from home and yet its guardian, that gives her a purpose when she is "turned out" from prison, so that she "did not feel her desolation of freedom as she would otherwise have done."

Esther, like all victims in the novel, has no real "home"—the penniless and homeless need authority to give them identity, because there is no loving "watcher" for them. Freedom here seems to be nothing more than desolation—the desolation of the unloved and unwatched over, the desolation Mary finds at home "where no welcome, no love, no *sympathising tears* awaited her" (emphasis added). What this view of homeless desolation does is create a *need* for both watchful love and for loving watchfulness—and it is Gaskell here who is the prime watcher, her narrative authority offering an identity to these characters she declared were so "real" to her in writing that parting with them was like parting with friends. The novel becomes a kind of haven, a closed-in place where nothing lacks meaning.

But that haven must be recast as a different kind of home, unlike the domestic authority we have traced in Gaskell's letters, or the fictional and political certainties that have enclosed John and Mary Barton. The scene with which we began suggests some of what is at stake in the novel: that by bringing back the dead mother, creating a different kind of fiction (blurring genres and moving between melodrama and psychological realism), by drawing on her own need to believe in persistent "traces" of love, Gaskell suggests a way back to both sympathizing tears and sympathizing fiction.

The dead mother is the key to much of this recasting of authority—and of fiction. The parent previously in this novel has been the angry father; if God is the father, the Bible told John Barton, we must bear what he sends us, and the critique of the cold, indifferent father extends beyond the home into the marketplace. What brings grace for Mary is a mother who will take her back to a time when she was not hungry rather than tell her to bear her hunger more cheerfully now, who might offer a way out of patriarchal authority. Mother love offers a similar model of care to Esther, who says that Mary is like her own child; to Mrs Wilson, who tells the orphaned Mary that she shall be her own "ewe-lamb"; to the dying Alice Wilson, who talks once more to her dead but forgiving mother. Maternal wisdom suggests a way of watching over that protects, nurtures, binds, connects—that restores what has been lost.

That is to say, this "watching over" is a narrative impulse, which in turn will revision authority. Maternal authority, unlike supervision, is an authority that can *name* its charges. Its opposite is embodied in Mr Carson, who, when Wilson goes to his home to ask for a medical order for the dying Davenport, does not "know the name" of this man. Wilson reminds him he "worked in your factory better nor three year." "Very likely," says Carson, "I don't pretend to know the names of those I employ: that I leave to the overlooker" (p. 109). The overlooker—like Carson—does, indeed, manage to overlook: to overlook breaks in machinery like the one that cripples Jane Wilson, or those injuries that even the doctors at the hospital where Barton once stayed know come late in the day when the workers are tired. "Overlooking," barely listening, judging harshly are all forms of missed connections and failed love in the novel—real "overlooking," in the sense that Gaskell means to reinstate here, is the watching out of sympathetic love, the provenance of mothers—or here, of mothers turned novelists. Reinstating the authority of the mother also places Gaskell as (maternal) author at the center of her text, and makes the mother the perfect novelistic authority. If mother love is to redeem the world, who better to write novels than Gaskell herself? Just as Mary assumes her dominant role in the second half of the novel in part by taking on the authority of the *dead* Mary Barton, so the providence behind the fiction becomes female, a different kind of authorship.

At this point, my argument might be seen as overlapping with recent feminist theory, which argues that it is through the mother—and specifically, through the mother's body—that we get the kind of textual disruption I am arguing Gaskell invokes here. For such critics, maternal language, as Mary Jacobus explains it, has the power to disrupt phallogocentric authority: the "discourse of maternity," the "archaic language of the pre-oedipal . . . rhythms, melodies, and bodily movements" "precede[s] and prepare[s] the way for the language of signification."[46] Though the paternal, "symbolic dimension of language works to repress the semiotic . . . the maternal nonetheless persists in oral and instinctual aspects of language which punctuate, evade or disrupt the symbolic order—in prosody, intonation, puns, verbal slips, even silences." Such a criticism, rooted in a psychoanalytic view of language, argues, in Julia Kristeva's words, that language separates itself from the body through the mother's body; "the woman-subject" is a "thorough-fare, a threshold where 'nature' confronts 'culture.'"[47]

One could read the scenes of maternal visitation in *Mary Barton* in such a way, as Mary's mother's "ghost" invokes the *sounds* of memory, speaking the soft dialect Mary recognizes. The scene's disruption of genre, its gothic use of the mother's haunting return, might be seen as disrupting the symbolic order, as does the repetition of the maternal figure in the text. The mother blurs into her darker self, the prostitute Mary almost became, or, most movingly, as in the hallucination Aunt Esther recounts, her own daughter, her mother, and her sister (Mary's mother) walk around and around her bed as she lies in prison. In this Burne-Jones–like duplication of some eternal (familiar) woman, end-lessly repeating herself in Esther's nightmares, endlessly authoring and erasing herself, we see what Kristeva recounts: the mother who "by giving birth . . . enters into contact with her mother; she becomes, she is, her own mother; they are the same continuity differentiating itself"[48]—that is, the mother/daughter who is *both* Mary Bartons, and neither.

But I want to historicize this psychoanalytic move, to ask again what particular power the "semiotic" might have in this novel's political econ-omy—to argue, in fact, that the nightmare/vision of maternal presence has a more powerful (and specifically political) authority. Elizabeth Gaskell imagined a maternal authority that would make of England a home; that would cure the condition of England; that would feed the hungry workers; that would redeem the lost children. More than a maternal, slippery language (the "fond mimicry of affection") Gaskell decribes something like a maternal plot: an alternate structure of power, an alternate family, an alternate England. In the new world, families "will go up as well as down," so that Mary and Jem can bring Mrs Wilson with them to Canada, instead of a child; in the new world, as Mrs Wilson somewhat comically but hopefully announces, "Perhaps in them Indian countries they'll know a well-behaved lad when they see him"; in the new world, Mary will be restored as "a ewe lamb" to a new mother. In this new world, there is more than maternal "continuity differentiating itself"; there is a potentially new order.

We can ask, of course, how far the "authority" of these dead mothers extends. To make only the most obvious point, the end of the novel finds Aunt Esther dead ("she held the locket containing her child's hair still in her hand, and once or twice she kissed it with a long soft kiss"), finds Mary Barton transformed into Mary Wilson, and the voice of her dead mother presumably silenced. Judith Newton has noted that female authority too often takes the form of "influence" instead of "ability"; as she quotes Sarah Ellis's *The Wives of England*, to have influence, "all that has been expected to be enjoyed from the indulgence of selfishness, must then of necessity be left out of our calculations, with all that ministers to the pride of superiority, all that gratifies the love of power, all that *converts the woman into the heroine* (emphasis added)."[49] Only in Mary's efforts to save Jem from hanging do we find female action directly embraced by the text; later, when Mary wants to perform the same redemptive work for Aunt Esther, "vehemently" rising "as if she was going on the search there and then," Jem "fondly restrain[s] her," ending the progress of "the woman into the heroine." But the other conversion, of woman into mother, remains, and maternal activity, as it can be learned and imitated, is at the novel's heart. The scene where Job Legh carries his dead daughter's child from London, wearing a woman's nightcap to try to calm the baby's screams, suggests that it is as mothers that we will love, teach, travel best.

But even if one allows it to be a real power, with a wider sphere than that of "influence," matriarchal authority creates a second problem: what does wielding this power do to those around you? If the problem with the patriarchal power of the masters is that it turns workers into animals to be guided and governed, matriarchal power in the novel seems to make the workers infants. The recipients of maternal wisdom move back, almost beyond language, to what Tennyson described as a state of "no language but a cry." (In *Mary Barton*, once you get the mother back in the world, you can't talk to her.) In Gaskell's mind, all her characters are like "terrified children," only "secure of safety when near the protecting care" of the mother, and they attain moral goodness only when they become "protecting."

On the text's conscious level, that protection is Christ's, the "friend of the orphan," but on its deepest level, it is the care of the mother. The messianic overtones of Mary's "you are come at last!" are echoed in the "they know not what they do" of Mr Carson's final revelation, and its implicit messsage (be like Christ, be like a mother) is brought out in a series of scenes with children. When John Barton leaves home to assassinate Carson, he stops long enough to help a small child; in the scene before Mary's mother's "return," Mary has been stopped in her panicked run by a little Italian boy who utters "in his pretty broken English," the words "Hungry! so hungry!" Mary races past him, only to think better of her impatience, and returns to where "the little hopeless stranger had sunk down . . . in loneliness and starvation, and was raining down tears as he spoke in some foreign tongue, with low cries for the distant 'Mamma mia!'" (p. 284). The most important scene of conversion in the novel, Mr Carson's, is also prepared for by an encounter with a child. After he has left the home of John Barton, still unwilling to forgive the worker who claims not to have known what he was doing, Carson sees a rough young boy run headlong into a beautiful, well-dressed girl and knock her down. The girl's governess pounces on the boy, only to have the angelic young girl forgive him, exclaiming that he didn't know what he was doing; this message haunts Carson till he goes home, takes down the family Bible and reads the Gospels. Then he comes to "the end: the awful End. And there were the haunting words of forgiveness" (p. 440). Only after witnessing the young child's forgiveness toward her enemy on account of his essential ignorance can Carson absorb the message of this explicitly Christian novel, picking up the text he and John Barton share and have both "puzzled over." But for this to happen, for Carson to be moved to compassion for Barton, Barton must become like that child and be forgiven for not knowing what he is doing. For Carson to be Christ-as-mother, Barton's autonomy (his most articulate demands, the wickedness of the masters) must be denied.

The problem with mothering, then, is that it requires children: the more they are like the Italian boy, uttering brokenly, "Hungry! so hungry" the better. People are returned to that world where desire and demand become one; they have a language to ask for only the simplest needs to be fulfilled. The workers themselves become, in the words of one of Barton's visitors before his trip to London, people who have "been clemmed long enough, and [who] donnot see whatten good they'n been doing, if they can't give what we're all crying for sin' the day we were born" (p. 128). However moving this plea is, and it is in some ways the perfect summary of the blighted lives of the workers, it is also reductive, compared to the strongest arguments for dignity Barton makes in the course of the novel. There is a difference, which Gaskell never addresses, between Barton's reasoned arguments for work, for reform, for individual autonomy, and the crying of starving children, to which this statement reduces the Charter—there was more at stake, somehow, before.

However much we might prefer the sympathizing mother to the angry father, and whatever the creation of maternal narratives allowed Gaskell to do, the mother's return does not seem to solve all the problems the novel set out to answer. The difficulty Gaskell faces as she nears the end of her novel is to avoid setting up yet another structure of authority that will silence people like John and Mary Barton as effectively as did the structure she set out to criticize. As John Barton's voice gets swallowed up by the discourse around him, be it Job Legh's or Carson's, so the potential for transforming the language of authority seems to disappear as well. Gaskell appears to have trouble imagining a world without authority, in England at least, and this may be why she moves the novel to Canada for its final chapter. It may also be why she tells us so little of life in Canada, that mythic place where class relationships will no longer exist. If happy marriages could not take place in the world of Manchester but had to occur in the new world, perhaps free, unlegislated space can exist only there as well. And perhaps that space exists only outside the novel; to impose any narration may be to freeze it into something supervised and "overlooked." It may, further, reduce the narrative to one of expertise, of "political economy," rather than "truth." Gaskell's novel does not promise a solution; it promises, rather, a changed heart.

If the move to Canada is not a solution, Gaskell's vision of maternal narrative presence, along with her questioning of narrative authority in general, does present solutions of a different kind. If the world cannot be transformed absolutely, our ways of seeing and describing it can—and as the novel's critique of received languages suggests, to write the story differently may be to write a different story. *Mary Barton* contains within it the story of Gaskell's learning to speak, a rewriting of stories of female heroism and female authorship played out in a world of spectacle and silencing in which Gaskell finds for herself a language "expressing her wants" that is more than just "a cry," and for her heroine, a chance to speak openly, choose her life, and overcome some of the plots that have been written for her.

iv

"You've set up heroine on your own account, Mary Barton"

The question of the displacement of narrative authority returns us to the question with which we began: what does it mean that this novel became *Mary Barton*? What is the relationship between its heroine's triumph and its author's? What, short of another story of a resistant and heroic author, can we make of Mary's testimony; of the elaborate courtroom spectacle of the novel's end; of the novel's careful realism and engaged narration; of the notorious success of Elizabeth Gaskell's debut novel? What transformations does this novel enact?

By the end of the novel our heroine Mary has "set up" on her own account: she has left Manchester, as she always wanted; she has gone to sea, where she always longed to go; she has won herself the husband she loved, she has "testified" in public, she has saved her father and her lover from conviction and certain hanging; she has gone through the crisis of illness and recovery; she has helped bring about some reconciliation between masters and men. She has moved beyond normal spheres of action for a woman in a novel: from private to public space, from silence to speech, from flirtation to love. In a sense, she has won the battle over the novel that might have been called *John Barton*: it has become her story. Further, Gaskell has made the point that a novel about an unimportant woman, a worker, a "girl," can be effectively subtitled, "A Tale of Manchester Life": Mary's life has become representative as well as heroic.

Examining the notion of female heroism means, for Gaskell, both taking on the question of Mary's appearance in the public sphere (her testimony at her lover's trial for the murder her father has committed) and locating her own authorial voice in the "sea" of language the trial specularizes. Gaskell examines Mary's testimony as a part of a scene of linguistic chaos, charting the madness it leads her to, her attempt to retreat again from the public sphere, and the problem for women, especially, of speaking out. These problems parallel her own ambivalence about speaking out as a novelist, being, as her heroine eventually is, "all in print."

By the time of the trial, Mary is a mass of blushes and pallor, sleepless, and, in her own words, "mad." Like Elizabeth Gaskell diving under the table for something that is not there, she is in retreat from her own boldness. After her testimony about her love for Jem she is unable to stand, needing the rails "to steady her, in that heaving, whirling court" (p. 393). In a re-creation of her recent ordeal at sea, where she sailed off in search of the "alibi," she imagines that in the courtroom "they were all at sea, sailing away on billowy waves." But the "sea" here is language, where "it was such pain, such weary pain in her head, to strive to attend to what was being said." The "pain" is both linguistic chaos and her fear of speech, for "every one [was] speaking at once, and no one heeding her father, who was calling on them to be silent, and listen to him." Jem stands "opposite, looking at her, as if to say, am I to die for what you know your—. Then she checked herself, and by a great struggle brought herself round to an instant's sanity. But the round of thought never stood still" (p. 393). Finally, Mary's divided consciousness, the conflict between speech and silence, freedom and modesty, topples her into a sickbed "in the ghastly spectral world of delirium"; to speak, for a woman, is to be "spectral."

What Mary wants to do after her "trial" is exactly what her nemesis, Sally Leadbitter, reminds her she cannot do: "You can't hide it now, Mary, for it's all in print" (p. 426). Gaskell tries to protect Mary here from the vulgarity that Sally represents: by presenting Sally as "almost jealous of the fame that Mary had obtained herself, such miserable notoriety," she tells us that her Mary, never unmaidenly or eager to display herself, shuns that attention, and that Sally remains ignorant of Mary's need to save Jem and her father, the necessity that overcame virginal modesty. But the mere fact of Sally's presence in these scenes reminds us that Mary did put herself forward:

> "Nay! there's no use shunning talking it over. Why! it was in the Guardian,—and the Courier,—and some one told Jane Hodson it was even copied into a London paper. You've set up heroine on your own account, Mary Barton. How did you like standing witness? Arn't them lawyers impudent things? staring at one so. I'll be bound you wished you'd taken my offer, and borrowed my black watered scarf! Now didn't you, Mary? Speak truth!" (p. 426)

Mary, like Gaskell in publishing her novel, like the Chartist Miss Ruthwell speaking for her "sisters in slavery," has encouraged people "staring at one so." It is useless for her to protest she never craved attention at all. She has even, as Sally tells her, turned her appearance into an economic asset for the dressmaking shop where she works: 'You may come back to work if you'll behave yourself, [Miss Simmonds] says. I told you she'd be glad to have you back, after all this piece of business, by way of tempting people to come to her shop. They'd come from Salford to have a peep at you, for six months at least" (p. 427). In Sally's admonition, we hear the ironic return of Gaskell's promise to "speak truth": Mary's speaking has led her into "business" for herself.

Mary Barton, the six-months wonder, is not the pale, retiring heroine readers are used to; she has to be tamed, quieted a little, before the novel ends. Gaskell turns her into a woman who "worships" Jem and "hangs" about her father, into the personification of innocence tending the guilty, who droops appropriately and does little to move the rest of the book. But as Sally tells her, asserting, "I don't pretend to know more than is in every one's mouth," Mary is in the public eye, part of the spectacle. Sally makes the connection with theatre when she tells Mary that Jem has been turned off from the foundry:

> "To be sure! didn't you know it? Decent men were not going to work with a—no! I suppose I mustn't say it, seeing you went to such trouble to get up

an *alibi*; not that I should think much the worse of a spirited young fellow
for falling foul of a rival,—they always do at the theatre. . . ."

"Tell me all about it!" [Mary] gasped out.

"Why you see, they've always swords quite handy at them plays," began
Sally, but Mary, with an impatient shake of her head, interrupted.

"About Jem,—about Jem. I want to know." (p. 427)

For Sally, the trial is a place for "looking out for admirers." "If I've ever
the luck to go witness on a trial, see if I don't pick up a better beau than
the prisoner. I'll aim at a lawyer's clerk, but I'll not take less than a
turnkey." "Cast down as Mary was," Gaskell says, "she could hardly keep
from smiling at the idea, so wildly incongruous with the scene she had
really undergone, of looking out for admirers during a trial for murder."
But it is not so incongruous: Mary has captured an admirer there; she
was, as Sally humorously puts it, "All for that stupid James Wilson."
She may not have dressed up in the borrowed "black watered scarf," but
she dressed in her neatest, most maidenly character, with her hair tucked
back, thinking not to draw attention to herself at the moment when she is
most part of a public spectacle.

This returns us to the question of the nature of the trial in the novel,
and the role of spectacle. As Sally's comments remind us, Mary's appearance at the trial was part of an economic construction. She may not have
been a "piece of business" herself, that phrasing suggesting the prostitution she has escaped, but Gaskell makes clear that the trial itself is run by
and for monied interests. Further, it is *meant* as a kind of show: Carson is
out to set an example, and the trial is a both a "show" of force, and a kind
of entertainment for the audience. Gaskell pays careful attention to the
onlookers at the trial, to those who study the face of the murderer for
"marks of Cain," of Mary for the beauty of the "fatal Helen," of Mr
Carson for the look of "Jupiter." But it is Will Wilson who reminds them
that the entertainment is being paid for. When Will races into the
courtroom at the drama's climax to give Jem his alibi, the only objection
the prosecuting attorney can find to his testimony is to ask who paid him.
In one of the strongest speeches of the novel, Will asks:

"Will you tell the judge and jury how much money you've been paid for
your impudence towards one, who has told God's blessed truth, and who
would scorn to tell a lie, or blackguard any one, for the biggest fee as ever
lawyer got for doing dirty work." (p. 397)

Mary, like Will, is part of the spectacle that releases the trial from the
realm of mystification. Further, in answering the question from the
"monkeyfied" lawyer about whom she loved, and giving the unexpected

answer, she suggests Gaskell's other idea, of values that transcend, ignore, or alter monetary equations: a world outside the capitalist division of wealth-poverty, master-man, public-private. In that moment, she thinks, "she might own her fault; but now she might even own her love." In the space that has been created, she can both avow what she feels and possess some integrity.

Elizabeth Gaskell, the anonymous novelist who ducked under the breakfast table to hide her embarrassment at the mere mention of *Mary Barton*, duplicates Mary's mixed humiliation and pride in her position at the center of the spectacle. Like the courtroom in the novel, the marketplace for literature is a place where economic interests, questions of "character," beauty, political arguments, persuasion all intersect. Again as in the courtroom, various modes of discourse abound: the formal language of the judge, the insolence of the attorney, the heartfelt testimony of a loving mother, the matter-of-fact recitations of the practiced police, all form an arena of choices about language. Gaskell's narrative voice guides a reader through these scenes, with its protestations, like Mary's, of truth—but, again like Mary, Gaskell's position as narrator amid all these choices of viewpoint and language is a mixture of the forward and the hidden.

Gaskell's narrator is certainly present in the text: she is confiding, she apologizes for her characters, she offers to tell her readers what others have told her, at times she even claims to have known her characters. Often she seems to be making concessions to her middle-class readers. She apologizes for what she at least claims to know is inaccurate economic thinking: "I know this is not really the case; and I know what is the truth in such matters: but what I wish to impress is what the workman feels and thinks" (p. 60). But admitting what she shares with her readers also gives her the stronger "I" to convince them of the essential accuracy of her case: "When I hear, as I have heard, of the suffering and privations of the poor . . ." (p.126). Her "I" is present as strongly in passages where a reader aware of the drama of Gaskell's own life may find specific echoes in the text: at one point she refers to the dreams of the near-mad as "that land where alone I may see, while yet I tarry here, the sweet looks of my dead child" (p. 327).

Gaskell uses that "I" to create a "you" out there: you must, she says once, "picture for yourself," for "I cannot tell you."[50] Part of the novel's challenge to representational fiction is to make demands of its readers as well, to "try seeing all around you."

> But [Barton] could not, you cannot, read the lot of those who daily pass you by in the street. How do you know the wild romances of their lives; the

trials, the temptations they are even now enduring, resisting, sinking under? You may be elbowed one instant by the girl desperate in her abandonment, laughing in mad merriment with her outward gesture, while her soul is longing for the rest of the dead, and bringing itself to think of the cold-flowing river as the only mercy of God remaining to her here. You may pass the criminal, meditating crimes at which you will to-morrow shudder with horror as you read them. You may push against one, humble and unnoticed, the last upon earth, who in Heaven will for ever be in the immediate light of God's countenance. Errands of mercy—errands of sin—did you ever think where all the thousands of people you daily meet are bound? (pp. 101–102)

This attempt to bring to light the "wild romance" of lives alien to her readers is linked to Gaskell's need to explain her own life. Her description in the preface of having become "anxious (from circumstances that need not be more fully alluded to) to employ myself in a work of fiction" leads her to think: "How deep might be the romance in the lives of those who elbowed me daily in the busy streets of the town in which I resided" (p. 37). Gaskell has "employed" herself in fiction, put herself on the market, to express this sympathy, "give some utterance to the agony which, from time to time, convulses this dumb people." She is making use of her own unhappiness to reach outward, much as her own experience of loss, the loss of parents and of children, gives her an emotional vocabulary to draw on in the novel, to express the alienation and empty desire of the workers she depicts. We are all, in this world, orphans, she seems to say; the child-bereaved mother has a particularly relevant story to tell.

The model for a reader's activity is different as well. Gaskell demands an audience for her own kind of truth, for a novel that embraces different voices, dialects, kinds of storytelling, and in turn makes different demands of her readers: to be present as a "you" out there, to make a novel "true" by asking a reader to change with it. Moving beyond what some have argued is the "consensus" realism calls for,[51] Gaskell expects of the novel a conversion, and for her readers, a new kind of attention. "The utmost I hoped from Mary Barton," Gaskell wrote in 1850, "has been that it would give a spur to inactive thought, and languid conscience,"[52] and the novel provides a model for that "spur" in its own conclusion.

At the end of the novel, when Mr Carson has heard John Barton's story, has seen what was in front of him all along—has, in essence, finally read the novel we have been reading—the narrator says,

> To those who have large capability of loving and suffering, united with great power of firm endurance, there comes a time in their woe, when they are lifted out of the contemplation of their individual case into a searching

inquiry into the nature of their calamity, and the remedy (if remedy there
be) which may prevent its recurrence to others as well as to themselves.
(p. 459)

What this passage suggests is a progress of suffering and understanding:
first, one must bring to experience "a large capability of loving and
suffering," then be lifted out of the "individual case" into a larger "inquiry," then into "the remedy" for themselves and others. What Carson
has learned—"that the interests of one were the interests of all"—is the
essential lesson of this novel, and of the Wordsworthian spirit with which
Gaskell began: "that we each of us have a human heart," that there is
poetry all around us, that we are bound to each other by "ties of respect
and affection." Those "ties" form the process by which the narrative itself
moves: we have lived with these characters, been to their tea parties,
inside their homes, we know them; more, we have lived with our own
suffering (dead children, lost parents, alienated affection). Like Barton,
we have learned that you cannot, casually, "read the lives of those who
daily pass you by," but the lives of those we have before us can be read,
precisely because they have done more than "pass by." Having read these
lives, like Mr Carson, we cannot turn away.

George Levine has argued that "the real" is itself a convention for
nineteenth-century novelists,[53] each of whom tries to claim that space for
her or his own novel, but the space of this novel seems unique. Gaskell's
incorporation of her husband's footnotes on regional dialect, the details of
prices of foods, the nautical terms, the insights into the policeman's tasks,
all account for the realism that makes *Mary Barton* seem true in a way that
Dickens's and Disraeli's industrial worlds are not. The heart's truth, the
endless quality of Elizabeth Gaskell's own sympathy, the shared suffering
that makes for *Mary Barton*'s particular immediacy are less easy to catego-
rize. Like the attempt to break through the spectacle of the trial, this truth
depends on the articulation of the heart and on informed action, but it
refuses to stop at its own narration. Through both its details and its
attempts to reach out beyond the text it follows the model of Mary's
testimony, of what she urges Jem to do at the end of the novel:

"You will never persuade [Esther] if you fear and doubt. . . . Hope yourself,
and trust to the good that must be in her. Speak to that,—she has it in her
yet,—oh, bring her home, and we will love her so, we'll make her good."
(p. 463)

Mary wants to "speak out": she urges Jem to lose no time, to "find her
out," to investigate, narrate, turn to direct address, to "love her so, we'll

make her good." And so, at its heart, does *Mary Barton*: to find and persuade; to speak and transform.

That enterprise was for Victorian readers—and remains, for us, in many ways—a gendered task. In his letter of praise for the author of *Mary Barton*, whom he detected to be a woman from "the treble of that fine melodious voice," Thomas Carlyle declared that her book deserved "to take its place far above the ordinary garbage of Novels—a book which every intelligent person may read with entertainment; and which it will do every one good to read"—which will make people good. Her book is "a real contribution (about the first real one) towards developing a huge subject, which has lain dumb too long, and really ought to speak for itself."[54] Elizabeth Gaskell, as well, had "lain dumb too long," and wanted to speak for herself; like Carlyle, she knew all too well the dangers of "speaking for" others. In that tension between her "huge subject," presumably the condition of England itself, and the "treble" of her voice, we see the dilemma of the woman novelist trying to speak, to "set up heroine," to "entertain" and "do every one good." Even Carlyle's praise (the only real pleasure Gaskell said she had gotten from publishing *Mary Barton*)[55] repeats the difficulties she found everywhere about her, the difficulties the heroine and the heroine-as-author continue to face.

When *Mary Barton* was published, it provoked everywhere a great fuss; Gaskell was, in Jane Welsh Carlyle's phrase, in danger of being "spoiled" by being made a "lioness."[56] In that classic nineteenth-century confusion of novelist, heroine, and text, she was constantly addressed as Mary Barton. Her next novel was itself in danger of being retitled in the public's imagination, for it was, of course, identified as "by the author of *Mary Barton*." Like the Kristevan mother, the woman writer here gives birth to herself, as author and character, but seems doomed to "continuity differentiating itself." But her novel has already differentiated itself; in its "treble" we hear something perhaps different from what Carlyle heard, some different truth, some different subject. Like Mary Barton, Gaskell had found herself a voice, and then found herself "all in print": "There's no use shunning talking it over," for it is "in the Guardian,—and the Courier,—and . . . even copied into a London paper." Unable to retreat into authorial virginity, to hide forever under a table, the "*author of Mary Barton*"—criminal, prostitute, mother—had for herself a new "subject" for fiction.

2

The Plot of the Beautiful Ignoramus: *Ruth* and the Tradition of the Fallen Woman

Elizabeth Gaskell's second novel, *Ruth*, in many ways duplicates the dialectical social moves of *Mary Barton*: it begins with a public, social problem, one just coming to the attention of middle-class readers; in attempting to turn that "problem" into fiction, Gaskell pushes the limits of available form. In 1850, W. R. Greg's essay on prostitution in the *Westminster Review* raised the problem of women's sexuality and poverty in ways that both revised the Gaskell of *Mary Barton*, which he quotes, and anticipated *Ruth*.[1] If the 1840s saw a renewal of interest in "the great social evil," the 1850s saw a pouring out of writing about the problem: articles, book reviews, Mayhew's essays in the *Morning Chronicle*—all the spurs to a conscience like Gaskell's were there. But as with *Mary Barton*, we can see as well a more immediate impetus for the writing of the novel: in 1849, while visiting prisoners in a Manchester jail, Elizabeth Gaskell met a sixteen-year-old prostitute named Pasley who had been incarcerated for theft, a career she had fallen into after having been seduced by a doctor, abandoned, and sent off in the care of a neglectful female procurer. In a letter she wrote to Dickens in 1850 describing the meeting and asking his advice, Gaskell comments that the girl is "a good reader[,] writer and a beautiful needlewoman."[2] In 1852, she began, with great difficulty, a novel that constructs the story of a daughter of nature, passive, simple, and good, whose beauty marks her for a fall and whose docility is both redemptive and fatal; and in 1853 she published *Ruth*, a novel described in contemporary reviews as having an "unfit subject for fiction,"[3] and burned in respectable households.

Ruth, then, takes its place in a field of debate about women and sin, and it speaks self-consciously about the uses of fiction to transform social wrongs. But *Ruth* is also very much a novel with a literary self-consciousness and a literary rebelliousness that *Mary Barton* lacks. *Ruth* is a novel about becoming a novelist and taking a position within a literary tradition; it is specifically a novel about one woman's attempt to rewrite romanticism, and write the woman's story into the tradition. As its divided origins might suggest, it is itself a divided and contradictory work.

Like *Mary Barton*, *Ruth* has been treated—often dismissed—as a work of moral outrage and moral courage, in which the gentle but angered novelist forces her resistant Victorian audience to face the consequences for one woman of a fall from purity, and allows that heroine to work out her salvation before killing her off.[4] As such, the novel has been treated as either purely conventional in form or as a failure, the limits of its plotting set by the limits of Gaskell's imagination or of Victorian morality itself to "comprehend" the fallen woman's story. Because Gaskell is usually treated as a naive writer, one who came to literature as a great reader but without literary training, critics have only rarely paid attention to the use of literary discourses in the novel.[5] But the specific weight of the allusions and the stories of the novel is Gaskell's examination of the connection between sexual and poetic uses of the female.[6] As in her writing of *Mary Barton*, she is drawn by her need to describe existing social tragedies, but in *Ruth* she reflects on the machinery of literary production; this is a novel about the transformation of women into works of art—and into works of narrative.

Narratives of fallen women were plentiful in the 1840s, and especially so in the journals in which Gaskell began publishing fiction. Novels like Elizabeth Inchbald's *Nature and Art* (1794) and Amelia Opie's *Father and Daughter* (1802) remained in print in inexpensive editions, and both were popular as stage melodramas (*The Maniac Father* was the stage title of the latter). Further, reformist writers like Frances Trollope and Eliza Meteyard, in novels like *Jessie Phillips* and stories like "Lucy Dean; the Noble Needlewoman" and "The Angel of the Unfortunate"—the latter published in *Howitt's Journal*—focused on many of the social issues (substandard wages, faulty education, reforms of bastardy laws) that *Ruth* in part confronts.[7] Other contemporary novels mark the persistence of what Raymond Williams describes as the "romances of the radical melodrama kind in which a poor girl is seduced and abandoned . . . [by] . . . the aristocrat or the officer."[8] But *Ruth* invokes a different literary heritage—and it reads, to quote a contemporary review, not like a novel with a purpose but like a "poem."[9]

The specific literary heritage the novel invokes and criticizes is the Romantic project Gaskell claimed as the inspiration for her earliest attempts at writing, and Pasley's story is the heroine's transformation into what we can only call a Wordsworthian fallen woman, a "tragic poem." The Romantic story at the novel's center—the plot of the fallen woman, of the pliant subject seduced yet once more, this time into posing for the lyric poet—was at the center of key Victorian debates about the connections between art and morality, between beauty and society, specifically the revision of romantic aesthetics carried through by John Ruskin and the Pre-Raphaelite Brotherhood. *Ruth* reflects not only on the Romantic poet and his female "text" but on Gaskell's own cultural moment, and the ways in which patterns of writing—and reading—translate into ways of viewing women, socially and legally, sexually and economically. *Ruth* shows how artistic "ways of seeing" bolster social definitions of women, and at the same time, the ways cultural definitions of women limit the forms fiction about them can take. The novel focuses on forms of perception, taking as its "object" or its text female beauty—in literature, in art, in the market—and in turn taking its place as document, as icon, as commodity, turning that plot (the expression of female sexuality) into a recognizable story (the "fallen woman").

But *Ruth* in many ways turns against its own plot: as Gaskell's contemporaries and subsequent critics have noted, it martyrs its own heroine, sacrificing her to a plot of Christian forgiveness; indeed, it turns on some of its own assumptions, and in its jumpiness, its contradictions, its shifts in discourse, its inability to reach a satisfying ending, suggests some of its author's own dissatisfaction with the form of the novel. It seems to resist its own transformation into a perfect work of art, keeping alive a resistant reader, reminding readers of the possibility of other stories. Coming after the controversies and debates over *Mary Barton*, which brought only pain to its author, and taking on the even more threatening controversies of the "fallen woman" and debates over the decency of both women and novels, *Ruth* reveals some of Gaskell's own anxieties about its subject matter. More, coming as it does in the 1850s, in a time of increasing commodification of fiction and of female virtue, it shows signs of its own cultural moment, demonstrating what Adorno calls the true work of cutural criticism, the work of "social physiognomy."[10]

One way to approach the complexities of a novel like *Ruth* is through the broader social history of which it is a part, the cultural discourse surrounding women in the 1850s, particularly the figure of the prostitute. Like the novel, the cultural debates circled around the observation of the woman. As Judith Walkowitz has noted, while "early social investigators had identified prostitution as the intolerable evil that threatened the sanctity of the family as well as the social order," for later investigators, "prostitution remained a 'social evil,' but one that could be contained by a system of police and medical supervision."[11] To quote W. R. Greg, "The same rule of natural law which justifies the officer in shooting a plague-stricken sufferer who breaks through a cordon sanitaire justifies him in arresting and confining the syphilitic prostitute who, if not arrested, would spread infection all around her."[12] An essay like Greg's moves in two directions at once: on the one hand, he argues against the cultural logic in which public opinion keeps fallen women from "retrac-[ing] their steps," in which, "forgetting our Master's precepts we turn contemptuous aside from the kneeling and weeping Magdalen," in which "the English constitution recognizes parish apprentices, but not prostitutes"; on the other hand, his "recognition" of the prostitute led to her enclosure under surveillance. The period that "wrote" *Ruth* in turn wrote the Contagious Diseases Acts of the 1860s, which viewed the woman's body as the site of all contagion, and turned control of that body (its public inspection, its objectification) into a function of the state. To the extent that *Ruth* shares its language (and concern with sin, nature, and corruption) with the Acts, we can view the texts as contiguous and complicitous, and can "read" *Ruth* back into its cultural setting as a further objectification of the fallen woman. But this can be accomplished only by in turn simplifying not only the textual difficulties the novel poses but questions of literary production and reception. It was her reading of *Ruth* that led Josephine Butler to organize the women's groups that won the repeal of the Contagious Diseases Acts; at the least we can say that the history a text writes is as complicated as the text "history" wrote—and as incapable of yielding a programmatic reading.

Our reading of *Ruth*, then, must begin with its program and with the contradictions that evolve whenever either a social or literary project is undertaken—that is, with Gaskell's avowed social conscience, with the literary forms it could take, and with the tensions between them. Adorno argues that it is the "consistency or inconsistency of the work itself [that] expresses the structure of the existent," and it is precisely the inconsistencies of *Ruth* on which I will concentrate in this chapter. At issue is the status of Gaskell's heroine as the "object" of fiction, and particularly as the "object" of a story Gaskell inherited, the Romantic story of the fallen woman. My immediate concern is with the ways in which Gaskell's martyring of her heroine duplicates the aestheticizing she set out to criticize—her Ruth remains a Romantic subject—but what this suggests is the deeper question of the woman writer's relationship both to her predecessors and to the forms she inherits, a relationship she may not be able to control even when it is a connection she has chosen; the relationship that, as Pierre Macherey has suggested, "is the general problem of all interpretation: how to understand, how to grasp, in the elaboration of a new work, the interference of the old and the new, a debate never resolved, a duplicity which finally gives the work its consistency."[13] That duplicity—and its consistent and constitutive inconsistencies—begins with the Romantic inheritance and the Victorian revisions of the fallen woman.

i

> There are many such whose lives are tragic poems which cannot take formal language.
>
> GASKELL *Letters*

> It is a woman sitting quiet—quite quiet—still as any stone. . . . This, to my mind, is the only imaginative.
>
> RUSKIN, *Modern Painters II*

When Gaskell wrote to Charles Dickens to describe Pasley's fate and ask his assistance, her initial narration suggests the form the story will take: she has seen the girl

> in prison at Mr Wright's request, and she looks quite a young child (she is but 16,) with a wild wistful look in her eyes, as if searching for the kindness she has never known,—and she pines to redeem herself. . . . She is a good reader [,] writer, and a beautiful needlewoman. . . . She is such a pretty sweet looking girl. I am sure she will do well if we can but get her out in a *good* ship.[14]

Gaskell's search is for not only a good "ship" but a good "plot" in which to "get her out," and the plot here is already Wordsworthian: Pasley had been abandoned by her widowed mother, apprenticed to a fashionable dressmaker, and, when the dressmaker's business failed, seduced by a young surgeon with the compliance of the next woman for whom she worked. More, she is "a young child," with a "wild, wistful look in her eyes," a "pretty, sweet looking girl"; she is ready to become a heroine.

What is most Wordsworthian here is Gaskell's own aim. As I argued in my first chapter, Gaskell's own literary apprenticeship was with Wordsworth, her earliest authorial experiments connected with what she called "tragic poems."[15] Her letter to Mary Howitt announcing her intention of pursuing a literary career emphasizes the "beauty and poetry of many of the common things and daily events of life in its humblest aspect," and quotes as support the belief of "The Cumberland Beggar" that "we have all of us a human heart."[16] Talk of Wordsworth would have been all around Gaskell when she began writing *Ruth* in 1852. In the years immediately preceding and following Wordsworth's death in 1850, several major collections of his work had appeared.[17] *The Prelude* was published in 1850, and had led to re-evaluations of his oeuvre. (As early as 1831 Wordsworth's poetry was included in schoolbooks.) While writing *Ruth* Gaskell visited the Lakes, where she said "all the world at the Lakes was full of the 'Prelude', [which] Miss Brontë has promised that Mr Smith (& Elder) shall lend . . . to me" and where she met Wordsworth's wife, who told them "some homely tender details of her early married days."[18]

Wordsworth was then particularly on her mind, and at any period in early Victorian literature one cannot overemphasize Wordsworth's importance as a myth-maker who set the project and validated the language of the novel of the self. But Gaskell's reading of Wordsworth was, I think, enacted through the particular lenses of a Victorian woman trying to write herself into the story; and she turned, in writing *Ruth*, her most Wordsworthian novel, to the specifics of the woman's experience in Wordsworth's poetry.[19]

What Gaskell found in Wordsworth was not women who write but women who are read: women, for Wordsworth, exist to conjure up poetry. If the commitment of "The Cumberland Beggar" and of much of Wordsworth's early poetry is to see experience as it is reflected in the poet's sensibility, the poem literally needs an object—not just to summon up poetic inspiration but to stand as an emotional equivalent for what the poet needs to bring out of himself. The poem's object seems at first to shock the poet into response, then to serve as a receptacle for his reflection on his feelings: as Wordsworth writes when describing poems on "the Naming of Places, as a Transition to the Poems relating to human life," the objects are those most "interesting to a meditative and imaginative mind either from the moral importance of the pictures or from the employment they give to the understanding affected through the imagination and the higher faculties."[20] The object is, for the essentially solitary Wordsworthian poet, a proof of his presence in the world. In a world of dichotomized subjects and objects, the poet needs a mediating figure.

The figure of the woman, particularly a seduced woman, does more than provide a subject for the poem: she represents aesthetic perception itself. This figure is at once empty and overfull of meaning: the poet needs a victimized woman to represent both a blankness he can fill and the excess of his own emotion. Her silence justifies his writing about her, while his poetry fills up the space around her. When "She Dwelt Among the Untrodden Ways" ends, "But she is in her grave, and, oh, / The difference to me!"[21] the "difference" to the poet is precisely what the poem is about; if Wordsworth didn't see her, Lucy would have no story, for she exists outside writing—indeed, almost outside language. The silent but adored heroine justifies the poetic enterprise (marking the difference) at the same time that the speaker holds up her life as itself "poetry." The relationship is symbiotic: neither poet nor subject exists without the other.

Ruth asks about the sexual politics behind the sexual poetics: what is the "difference" when a woman reads and rewrites this story? It is a peculiarly empowering story for male writers; Laura Mulvey has argued in her discussion of "narrative cinema" that

> woman then stands in patriarchal culture as signifier for the male other, bound by a symbolic order in which man can live out his fantasies and obsessions through linguistic command by imposing them on *the silent image of woman still tied to her place* as bearer of meaning, not maker of meaning [emphasis added].[22]

Wordsworth is constantly writing—and constantly interrupting—that story of silence. But what Gaskell focuses on in *Ruth* is the way the male "ordering" transforms those "fantasies and obsessions" not merely through "linguistic command" but through their re-formation into story. The specific story at issue in the novel is that of the abandoned woman, a story Gaskell would have read over and over in Romantic poetry. These poems suggest the pattern I have been examining, where the consciousness of the woman remains unnarrated, existing only to evoke consciousness in others. Like the "difference"-making Lucy, the abandoned women in Wordsworth stand in front of a baffled speaker, and, through their "bearing," generate narratives that, though themselves queasy and unsettled, "make" a poem.

The abandoned-women poems all focus on the difficulty of reading the meaning of the woman: her story is hard to elicit; her appearance is hard to describe; her voice is difficult to hear. In each, the focus is on the simplicity of the heroine, the pastoral setting with which she is in harmony, the "nature" that absorbs her loss, and of which she is also, somehow, an emblem. There are specific plot elements that link them to Gaskell's abandoned heroine: the women have been driven mad by deserting lovers, by lost husbands, by passion turned bitter; they have children who link them to their community; they have been mistreated by dead or neglectful parents. But in each, the difficulty focuses on the nature of the story to be told—or, more basically, the question of what the "event" of the poem is.

All of these poems, to some extent, place the women outside history, outside human society, only "placed" in nature. The identification of the woman with the natural setting, and the attempt to interpret her the way one might a waterfall or a rainbow, as an object of one's own vision, is carried furthest in "The Thorn," where we are given a narrator, but also given a critique of him; in fact, this problem of interpreting the female parallels a critical crux about the poem. The work begins with a long description of an object in nature: "There is a thorn; it looks so old, / In truth you'd find it hard to say, / How it could ever have been young." This object, which is already "hard" to describe, is described in increasingly detailed and pedantic terms by the poem's narrator, who has "measured" as well the pond next to it: "from side to side: / 'Tis three feet long, and two feet wide." Beside this savage, erect thorn is "a fresh and lovely sight," a "hill of moss" that "is like an infant's grave in size." But beside the thorn, the heap of moss, and the pond, we find a woman. Uncharacteristically, her size is not given in the poem, though one might note ironically that size becomes important to her story when, after the desertion of her sweetheart before her wedding day, it becomes clear to the villagers that she is pregnant. But the narrator is forced to stop measuring things, for the poet[23] interrupts him to ask questions about the woman next to the thorn, who sits out there in a red cloak, who may have murdered her infant (some say by drowning it in the pond, some say by hanging it on the tree), and who has buried the infant under the moss, which, surprisingly, is not only the size of "an infant's grave" but may be in fact that very thing.

The woman in the poem describes nothing; she says nothing besides "Oh misery! oh misery! oh woe is me! oh misery!" Her story is told by the pedantic narrator, who has pieced it together from various sources in the village, and whose only meeting with the woman came when he went up the mountain with his telescope one day, hoping to "view the ocean wide and bright," only to be forced by the rain under a jutting crag, where he sees her instead, seated on the ground, crying, "Oh misery! oh misery!" But the woman has been on the mountain so long she has become a part of it; her dead baby's image, according to rumor, has become its own natural fact. The description of her and the itemizing of nature become one; she is unable to tell her story.

The question of who does the describing, the question Gaskell will ask, was key to Wordsworth's own view of the poem. In his notes, Wordsworth comments at great length on the role of the narrator, and of those men, superstitious and "credulous and talkative through indolence," who

> have a reasonable share of imagination, by which word I mean the faculty which produces impressive effects out of simple elements; but they are utterly destitute of fancy, the power by which pleasure and surprise are excited by sudden varieties of situation and by accumulated imagery.[24]

Jack Stillinger notes that most critics have discounted Wordsworth's statement of intention, "preferring to read the poem as a study in social morality, with the main focus on the plight of Martha Ray," the abandoned woman, but he argues that Wordsworth intended the poem to focus on the impossibility of proving the narrator's perspective.[25] For the purposes of "The Thorn," it makes no difference if, as another critic wrote, the "central 'event' has no existence outside of the narrator's imagination," and the woman is just a superstition, or if there is indeed a madwoman in the mountains.[26] The point of the poem is to watch the narrator's "association" of ideas, the "working of his imagination."

But here one might question the assumption of previous critics that the object on which the narrator's imagination works is unimportant. He asserts he expected to find a "jutting crag" but "instead" found "a woman seated on the ground"; one could say that he found exactly what he expected, the scarlet woman he had imagined earlier, who takes the place of the "wide and bright" view of the ocean he wanted to encompass with his telescope. And one could argue that the Romantic poet always has his telescope trained on a scarlet woman; because he cannot "size" her up the way he can a natural fact, he reads her story into natural facts, denying her the chance to tell her own story, but proving, as the interrupting poet does in this poem, the superiority of his blend of "imagination" and "fancy," "the power by which pleasure and surprise are excited by sudden varieties of situation and by accumulated imagery." Poetic power here comes from "seeing" women, but only from seeing their faces and turning away before they cry out, so their cry never becomes more than a repetition of a few words that may, in this poem, be the moaning of wind or the creaking of branches produced by "the faculty which produces impressive effects out of simple elements," the mark of inferior poetic gifts. Here, as so often, Wordsworth seems to approach a critique of his own perspective as pedantic, slightly hysterical narrator: the figure of the observer is made ironic in the poem, but the poem's dismissal of its object (is it thorn or woman?) walks away from responsibility.

Gaskell's Ruth descends from a series of these abandoned, silent women—even her name is taken not only from Wordsworth's abandoned Ruth but from a similar poem in Crabbe's *Tales of the Hall* (1819), in which a "tall and fair, and comely to behold, / Gentle and simple" Ruth is wooed, impregnated, and then abandoned when her lover is seized by a press-gang. The larger question for our view of Gaskell's "inheritance," however, is not just the conventionality of these stories of abandoned women but the story of female silencing. And this was a Victorian, as well as Romantic, literary problem, as a range of poems from Patmore's *The Angel in the House* to Morris's "Defense of Guenevere" suggests: the voice of that madwoman heard in Oenone's passion; in Mariana's "I am aweary, aweary"; in Porphyria's silence; that lost (last) woman's face framed by the jealous Duke, framed again by Andrea del Sarto's hands.[27]

The Wordsworthian story of the beautiful, lost woman, then, constitutes what Macherey would call a "fable"—for Victorian culture, for Gaskell in her revisionary fiction. It is the narrative form the ideological "programme" of the text will take, but it is in turn shaped by the "climate" that surrounds the text—in this case, the transformations of Victorian aestheticism. These habits of perception set the model for Victorian thinking about images: in 1850, the year that Wordsworth died and that Gaskell's "girl" sailed to Australia on a "good ship," the Pre-Raphaelite Brotherhood began publishing its journal *The Germ*. The volume opens with a poem about a "beloved lady" in which the spirit of a woman, who is "very fair," "sits aloof, and high," and the speaker announces,

> Altho' her beauty has such power,
> Her soul is like the simple flower
> Trembling beneath a shower.[28]

Dante Gabriel Rossetti's "Hand and Soul," the artistic manifesto he published in the same issue of *The Germ*,[29] again focuses on the positioning of the female (uninterpretable) icon. In Rossetti's fable, Chiaro, a Pisan painter, has fallen into a decline after the flush of his first fame. As he despairs, a beautiful woman, "clad to the hands and feet with a green and gray raiment," visits him in his room, and "it seemed that the first thoughts he had ever known were given him as at first from her eyes, and he knew her hair to be the golden veil through which he beheld his dreams." The woman, as she announces herself to him, is "an image, Chiaro, of thy soul within thee," but Rossetti presents the process of imagining the soul as sexual possession, a spiritualized version of *Ruth's* seduction story. Here, the woman "cast[s] her hair over him," and Chiaro weeps "into her hair which covered his face"; the encounter has the intensity of morbid eroticism, of possession and bondage, where the man is instructed to "take now thine Art unto thee, and paint me thus, as I am, to know me: weak, as I am."

Chiaro's possession of his Art leaves him exhausted, and as he sleeps off the intensity of his effort, "the beautiful woman came to him, and sat at his head, gazing, and quieted his sleep with her voice." In that singing, which sings him to his death, one hears the voice of not only Wordsworth's mad musical women but the Belle Dame sans Merci, the "Virgin of the Rocks" in Pater's *Renaissance*, the Victorian Angel whom Alexander Welsh has suggested is the angel of death.[30] To succumb to the feminine, here, is to be fatally absorbed: the world of art, the world of the female soul, is a world of alienation. But the real alienation at work is not of the male artist, who does at least create, but of the idealized female "soul," frozen into a portrait that serves as a mediating form between the dead painter and the modern reader, between Rossetti's *soi-disant* alienated self and the public he loved to scorn, an alienation suggested in the scenes of misinterpretation that follow the painter's death and the display of the portrait. In this particular "dream of fair women" there is no art without the female, but there is no real female either; this is men looking at the paintings of other men, paintings that exist only to embody their own souls.

If this obsession with nameless women in green gowns were peculiar to Dante Gabriel Rossetti, whose sexual preferences were at the least self-advertised, if not entirely self-mythologized, they would not concern us here. But the image of the nameless, sweet, freshly dressed girl is at the heart of *Ruth*, and at the heart of that most Wordsworthian of Victorian art critics from whom Gaskell learned aesthetics: John Ruskin.[31] Throughout *Modern Painters II*, the Bible of the Pre-Raphaelites in the 1850s, we see repeated instances where objectifying the quiet woman stands as a mark of male aesthetic creation. Repeatedly, Ruskin resolves the problem of what to do with art through scenes of women, as if their blankness made them more easily vessels of truth, but at the same time he suggests the threat of female beauty itself. Tintoretto's "Annunciation" and his "Massacre of the Innocents" can be summed up by their use of female icons. In the former, the "wild thought" of the artist is balanced by the "pure vision" of the "exceeding loveliness" of the meek, seated virgin, desolate amid the ruined city. And in "Massacre," among the "hopeless, frenzied, furious abandonment of body and soul" of the other victims, one woman, again "sitting quiet,—quite quiet—still as any stone, . . . look[ing] down steadfastly on her dead child," represents "the only imaginative; that is, the only true, real, heartfelt representation of the being and actuality of the subject of existence."[32] The stillness of women is the critic's place of faith for the "truth" of art. Like Chiaro's soul, with its threat of death, decay, and dissolution, female beauty must be mastered, described, looked at from all sides; truth *must* be read into it, so that one is not absorbed by it. Only the man watching the deceptive beauty can see the truth in it, and only by watching his own observations can he create an audience for his truth.[33]

All this leaves Gaskell, as a reader of Ruskin and a fellow inheritor of the Romantic tradition of "seeing" as "poetry, prophecy, and religion all in one," with the problem of what happens when women begin to see. Women, in the tradition I have been sketching, exist not to observe but to be observed; as such, they are "poem," "image," "type," and their emblematic status is transformed into narrative only through the (male) artist's imagination. For Rossetti and the Pre-Raphaelites, a woman's only story is her beauty made into narrative, that is, when she is seen by a man; for Ruskin, a woman's story, as it appears in art, is only an object through which narrator and reader negotiate an aesthetic understanding. Beauty, in both cases, is made moral. The thought that a woman's beauty might be as much a physical, as a moral, fact, that it might have an experience of its own, not aestheticized, is not imaginable in either system. Gaskell, on the other hand, refuses to ignore the possibility that a woman's beauty is a fact not in an abstract moral or aesthetic situation but in a very real context in a socially determined world.

ii

> Then he saw the young girl whom he had noticed at first for her innocent beauty, and the second time for the idea he had gained respecting her situation.

Gaskell begins her critique of the Wordsworthian story with the nexus of meaning that forms around the beautiful woman. Ruth's beauty is what makes her an object of interest in the novel; it is what causes her to have any story at all, and her own love of natural beauty and confusion of beauty with truth lead to her fall. In her revisions of the Wordsworthian fable, Gaskell asks again what it means that we are reading a woman's story of her own beauty: in the construction of Ruth's "fall," and in her movement inside that story, she makes us aware of the specific limitations of that story *as* story. The attempt to tell that story differently will create its own problems of representation in the novel.

What *Ruth* must do is to make readers uncomfortable with the story of the abandoned woman they are accustomed to reading. It must present that story as a "text" to be interpreted—that is, the novel must remind its readers of interpretation, for Ruth's "story" is the story of conflicting, powerful interpretations placed on her. The problem of interpreted beauty, which reappears throughout the novel, focuses our attention on this activity of reading. From the beginning, beauty is present in a variety of ways: Ruth's own beauty, natural beauty (her analogue), art (created beauty), and the "production" of beauty, the dressmaking Ruth works at in the novel's opening chapters. These images of constructed, supervised, and interpreted beauty overlap and interact throughout the novel, finally—through our discomfort at the end of the work—presenting us with a version in which beauty is both shaped by and distorted by our perceptions and expectations and which, particularly in a marketplace society, has proven disastrous for women.

The opening scenes of the novel set the essential contrast between Romantic images of beauty and dressmaking, the alienated labor in which Ruth is engaged, but unlike the Wordsworthian ballad, they begin in history, in the constructed history of architecture, the building, destruction, and remodeling of the town's streets. The opening chapter fixes the village in time and Ruth herself in the captivity of her workplace, moving slowly from the historical to the individual to suggest her relationship to nature and to created beauty, from the town's customs to the dressmaker's shop.

> The traditions of those bygone times, even to the smallest social particular, enable one to understand more clearly the circumstances which contributed to the formations of character. The daily life into which people are born, and into which they are absorbed before they are well aware, forms chains which only one in a hundred has moral strength enough to despise, and to break when the right time comes—when an inward necessity for independent individual actions arises, which is superior to outward conventionalities. Therefore, it is well to know what were the chains of daily domestic habit, which were the natural leading-strings of our forefathers before they learnt to go alone.[34]

By reminding her readers that they should see her characters in their historical moment, Gaskell is already suggesting that one cannot escape one's own moment in reading: if Ruth is to be known in the small assize town "of picturesque grandeur" "in one of the eastern counties," and the history of that town to be traced through the particular history of its streets, a reader is moved toward a relativism of perception or, at the least, an awareness of her own position as a reader in 1853. The passage both holds up the possibility of individual action "which is superior to outward conventionalities" and makes such action possible for "only one in a hundred"; that is, the novel will study heroic action but will make clear why heroism cannot always occur, since we are tied to the "leading-strings" of "the chains of daily habit."

What distinguishes Ruth from the "chain," from the other women workers—what marks her for "individual actions"—is her love of natural beauty. The women have all been kept late at their work, and are "stitching away as if for very life," and even when allowed a rest, they remain dehumanized by their work: one woman falls asleep as soon as the break is declared; some, Gaskell says, eat "with as measured and incessant a motion of the jaws (and almost as stupidly placid an expression of countenance), as you may see in cows ruminating in the first meadow you happen to pass" (p. 4). Ruth, the new girl, races to stand by the window, "pressed against it as a bird presses against the bars of its cage." Nature, then, is the escape from labor. For Ruth it is connected to memory, for she was in the habit of running out, and "when I was once out, I could hardly find in my heart to come in, even to mother, sitting by the fire;—even to mother," a poignant memory for the newly orphaned girl. The landscape she observes in this scene is Ruskinian not only in its summoning of memory and its release from alienated labor but in the intensity of its glory and connection to the changing vista of the town itself:

> Old stables had been added to, and altered into a dismal street of mean-looking houses, back to back with the ancient mansions. And over all these changes from grandeur to squalor, bent down the purple heavens with their unchanging splendour! . . . Ruth's eyes filled with tears, and she stood quite still, dreaming of the days that were gone. (p. 5)

The model of vision here is of emotional identification with the object perceived not only for its own "splendour" but for its connection to past scenes one has viewed, people one has loved, a "purple heaven," suggestively religious, which transcends the earthly "changes from grandeur to squalor." The beauty exists, in Romantic terms, because it is "half created." Ruth is already being posed for the reader as a perfect observer, one whose own history is caught up in what she sees, and who sees with the keener eyes of love.

But the object, in Gaskell's eyes, is the appropriate object of vision because it is organic. Jenny, Ruth's friend, is "glad that the orphan apprentice . . . should find so much to give her pleasure in such a common occurrence as a frosty night," but for Gaskell, the beauty of a frosty night is not common at all. Ruth, like the simple-hearted Wordsworthian heroines, feels a particular affinity—an appropriate affinity—for a nature that, she believes, never did betray a heart that loves her. The ideal of man-made beauty (one that will speak to that heart) is equally organic. After Ruth leaves the window to go back to her sewing, she faces a wall, but even there,

> on these panels were painted—were thrown with the careless, triumphant hand of a master—the most lovely wreaths of flowers, profuse and luxuriant beyond description, and so real-looking, that you could almost fancy you smelt their fragrance, and heard the south wind go softly rustling in and out among the crimson roses—the branches of purple and white lilac— the floating golden-tressed laburnum boughs. Besides these, there were stately white lilies, sacred to the Virgin—hollyhocks, fraxinella, monk's hood, pansies, primroses; every flower which blooms profusely in charming old-fashioned country gardens was there, depicted among its graceful foliage, but not in the wild disorder in which I have enumerated them. At the bottom of the panel lay a holly-branch, whose stiff straightness was ornamented by a twining drapery of English ivy, and mistletoe and winter aconite; while down either side hung pendant garlands of spring and summer flowers; and, crowning all, came gorgeous summer with the sweet musk-roses, and the rich-coloured flowers of June and July. (pp. 6–7)

Here again, the reader is given a model of the relationship between observer and object: the panels have an organic unity, taking in, as they do, the winter's "English ivy and mistletoe, and winter aconite," and "garlands of spring and summer flowers," all the seasons and all that makes up what readers are to recognize as "old fashioned country gardens." Further, the work, though appearing to be natural "wreaths of flowers . . . thrown with the careless, triumphant hand of a master," has its own order—not the "wild disorder" with which the novelist "enumerated" them. The panels have the conviction of truth, conjuring up not only the real flowers but the gardens in which they appear: "so real-looking, that you could almost fancy you smelt their fragrance, and heard the south wind go softly rustling in and out among the crimson roses." The perfect work of art creates in the viewer the impression of the complete environment, but only, Gaskell makes clear, if the viewer brings the right perspective to it: this "master," "Monnoyer, or whoever the dead-and-gone artist might be," gives pleasure to the "heavy heart of a young girl," only because she has in her own imagination "visions of other sister-flowers that grew, and blossomed, and withered away in her early home." That vision of growth, fruition, and decay, suggesting Ruth's own story and, more generally, the progress of a three-volume novel itself, links the work of art to seasonal cycles, human memory, human love, and death—again, a view of art not severed from natural growth.

But Ruth's view of art, her simplicity, her identification with others, all that makes her the perfect romantic heroine, is what marks her for her fall—and here we find Gaskell's most explicit critique of the Romantic poet's story about the untrained female sensibility at one with natural beauty. What Ruth's love of beauty excludes is any understanding of power; even her idea about her own beauty is entirely naive. She says without vanity that she knows she is pretty because people have told her so: the sight of "her own loveliness" gives her

> a sense of satisfaction for an instant, as the sight of any other beautiful object would have done, but she never *thought of associating it with herself*. She knew that she was beautiful; but that seemed abstract, and removed from herself. Her existence was in feeling, and thinking, and loving [emphasis added]. (p. 74)

All of this is dangerous for her. Wordsworthian daughters of nature can have an existence in "feeling, and thinking, and loving," but not seamstresses in urban societies; while Ruth discounts her loveliness as "abstract," her fate as a "beautiful object" in her society is severely limited.

Ruth's disassociated beauty marks her out for her seducer, Mr Bellingham, whom she meets only because she is more beautiful than the other seamstresses. Mrs Mason needs to take some of her girls to a ball to mend torn dresses for the society women; she says she is looking for the hardest workers, but when Ruth protests, after being selected, that others have worked harder than she, we realize that Mrs Mason really wants the most presentable. Ruth, who constantly underestimates the value of her beauty, declares that she doesn't even have anything to wear, but her very appearance is an advertisement for Mrs Mason's wares: she is "such a credit to the house, with her waving outline of figure, her striking face, with dark eyebrows and dark lashes, combined with auburn hair and a fair complexion" (p. 11). And indeed, once at the ball, Ruth's appearance draws attention. She is mending the gown of one of the women when she is noticed by the woman's partner. The woman herself is "very pretty, with long dark ringlets and sparkling black eyes"; she is also strikingly rude, for she speaks "sweetly and prettily" to her "young and elegant" gentleman partner, but when she addresses Ruth "her voice became cold and authoritative." Mr Bellingham's attention

> had been thereby drawn to consider the kneeling figure, that, habited in black up to the throat, with the noble head bent down to the occupation in which she was engaged, formed such a contrast to the flippant, bright, artificial girl, who sat to be served with an air as haughty as a queen on her throne. (p. 15)

He is drawn to her because she serves; because she is serious; but largely because she is so beautiful. He can look down on her, knowing his power over her—she is there to work—but it is the "nobility" of the head and the "rich auburn hair of the girl in black" that he looks back to see. What she sees, of course, is a world of "bright, happy people—as much without any semblance of care or woe as if they belong to another race of beings," but she immediately imagines for him an empathy we know he lacks. She wonders, "had [these people] ever to deny themselves a wish, much less a want?". But she fancies that "Mr Bellingham looked as if he could understand the feelings of those removed from him by circumstance and station," and what she loves in him is the compassion for others he in fact displays only to attract her further.

Where Ruth's trouble begins, then, is in the sexualizing of her natural empathy, and her utter inability to understand the desire to exercise power over "a thing of beauty." Ruth's way of "feeling, and thinking, and loving," leaves her incapable of perceiving Bellingham's duplicity; he, unlike her, "did not in general analyse the nature of his feelings, but simply enjoyed them with the delight which youth takes in experiencing new and strong emotion." His pleasure is a demoralized sensuality, a pure aestheticism she cannot imagine. For Bellingham, she is an object that produces sensations, whose allure is not just beauty but her ability to offer that beauty, something

> bewitching in the union of the grace and loveliness of womanhood with the *naiveté*, simplicity, and innocence of an intelligent child. There was a spell in the shyness, which made her avoid and shun all admiring approaches to acquaintance. It would be an exquisite delight to attract and tame her wildness, just as he had often allured and tamed the timid fawns in his mother's park. (p. 33)

That Ruth cannot see his almost abstract desire is largely a product of the "*naiveté*, simplicity, and innocence of an intelligent child" that he notes in her—specifically, an "innocent child" whose mother is dead and whose surrogate mother, Mrs Mason, has "her ideas of justice, too; but they were not divinely beautiful and true ideas; they were something more resembling a grocer's, or tea-dealer's ideas of equal right" (p. 19). Ruth cannot imagine this exchange-value variety of "equal right," but the gaps in her education (precisely her "beautiful and true ideas") keep her from seeing the ways in which she is a "dealer's" commodity for Bellingham, and the ways in which he has set out to purchase—or "attract and tame"—her.

This gap in Ruth's knowledge shapes her understanding of what has happened to her—and, in turn, determines the way the *novel* can deal with what is, after all, its central "event": her seduction and her impregnation. It is a problem, specifically, of representation, of what Macherey calls the "elaboration of a new work": if Gaskell's project in *Ruth* is to turn the outlines of the story (the fallen woman's fall) into a specific history, this is its most narratable moment. But to the degree that the novel has as its other goal the internalization of this story ("how I fell"), it cannot tell the story at all, because Ruth cannot know that she is fallen. This makes for a corresponding literary gap in the novel: one idea—and it is an explicitly literary one—must absorb another, one literary language give way to another. The novel can, and does, move outside its heroine, to the social construction placed on that fall, but it cannot make us read that "difference" explicitly—in part, of course, because of the limits of Victorian narrative, but in part, as well, because of the limitations (or more accurately, contradictions) within the (inherited) fallen-woman story. How, that is to say, can Ruth be innocent, and still be fallen? How can we narrate what she cannot know? What could be the sin of, to echo Bellingham's name for her, a "beautiful ignoramus"?

Her sin is, we soon realize, social: after she has been seduced by Bellingham, Ruth has no name for what has happened to her, no idea of how she is seen. The novel narrates the seduction, in fact, explicitly by depicting Ruth's incomprehension, saying,

> She was too young when her mother had died to have received any cautions or words of advice respecting *the* subject of a woman's life—if, indeed, wise parents ever directly speak of what, in its depth and power, cannot be put into words—which is a brooding spirit with no definite form or shape that men should know it, but which is there, and present before we have recognized and realized its existence. Ruth was innocent and snow-pure. She had heard of falling in love, but did not know the signs and symptoms thereof; nor, indeed, had she troubled her head much about them. (p. 44)

The Victorian confusion of desire with destruction, and the unrepresentability of both are evident even in this passage, where it is unclear whether

that which "in its depth and power, cannot be put into words" is love or
sex. By its very unmentionability, sexuality becomes dangerous to
women. If it cannot, even by "wise parents," be put into words, how can
young women be taught about it? How can Ruth be blamed for not
knowing better? If Ruth cannot "fall in love," how can she "fall"?

The real "sin" may be Ruth's ignorance of the *social* name for what she
does, as Gaskell suggests, when, after having fled the assize town with
Bellingham and moved on to a Welsh town, she is hit in the face by a
young boy. The boy's nurse rebukes him for hitting "a lady who is so
kind," but he says, "She's not a lady! . . . She's a bad, naughty girl—
mamma said so, she did; and she shan't kiss our baby" (p. 71). For Ruth,
this is entirely "a new idea"—that she is a "naughty girl"—and for a
reader, too, who has been so completely inside Ruth's imagination, it is
impossible to imagine our heroine kept from kissing a baby and hit with
"a great blow on the face." The violence makes us uncertain of these
questions of morality and appearance.

That the fall is the problematic moment in the text, the moment when
Gaskell's inherited languages come into conflict, becomes clear when we
consider the range of explanations offered for it. Initially Gaskell's discussion of Ruth's sexual experience criticizes only her ignorance: she has
been doing what was wrong, but she doesn't know what her actions
meant. Ruth was living in a prelapsarian world where her appearance was
not an object of speculation and interpretation. Further, because she is
unaware of her own appearance—the importance, in a world of seducers
and aesthetes, of her beauty—she is unable to judge accurately the people
who cross her path. She is indeed a beautiful ignormaus, so shamed at
being called a whore that she is afraid to tell Bellingham, for she believes
"he would be as much grieved as she was at what had taken place that
morning; she fancied she should sink in his opinion if she told him how
others regarded her; besides, it seemed ungenerous to dilate upon the
suffering of which he was the cause" (p. 73). Ruth's more generous nature
is, of course, equally the ideal of Victorian femininity: that docility and
ignorance that are her great charm for Bellingham, and that mark her, in
the beginning, as the ideal passive heroine into whose face any meaning
can be read, make her easy to seduce and abandon. Gaskell here, as
George Watt has noted, makes her fallen woman out of the same cloth as
the perfect heroine, showing where that model of feminine passivity
leads—that is, to a fall.[35]

But what Watt does not note is the aestheticization of that femininity
and that fall. Gaskell's defense of Ruth's fall throws us back on the model
of aesthetic appreciation, and the novel points us toward scenes where

Ruth's blankness and her beauty make her a plaything for Bellingham, who can transform her into a work of art, as he does in one scene where he places flowers in her hair. She sits "quite still while he arranged her coronet, looking up in his face with loving eyes, with a peaceful composure . . . [knowing] he was pleased from his manner, which had the joyousness of a child playing with a new toy, and she did not think twice of his occupation." But this scene comes immediately after Ruth was hit by the young boy and her discovery that she has been "condemned alike by youth and age." She cannot "put into words the sense she was just beginning to entertain of the estimation in which she was henceforward to be held"; she has become aware of the world's opinion, and yet, she can only sit still, loving her seducer, as he plays with his new toy. He tries to force her to look at her own beauty, abstract as it is to her, but her pleasure comes from giving him pleasure, from being his toy.

> Her beauty was all that Mr Bellingham cared for, and it was supreme. It was all he recognized of her, and he was proud of it. She stood in her white dress against the trees which grew around; her face was flushed into a brilliancy of color which resembled that of a rose in June; the great heavy white flowers drooped on either side of her beautiful head, and if her brown hair was a little disordered, the very disorder only seemed to add a grace. She pleased him more by looking so lovely than by all her tender endeavours to fall in with his varying humour. (pp. 74–75).

This is aesthetic prostitution portrayed here: the sensations are both sexual and visual, allowing him to watch his own pleasure in watching. Ruth's beauty is owned and paraded by Bellingham; it gains value by being his alone. To discuss her sexuality in this way is to put aesthetic perception itself into question. The same trafficking in women one saw in Rossetti's work can be seen here: from woman as a piece of art to woman as sexual "piece" is a short step, and Gaskell draws the analogy carefully by making the description of Ruth here so like that of the panels she admired earlier. Surrounded by white flowers, her face itself is like "a rose in June," the "disorder only seem[ing] to add a grace." But unlike Ruth, who saw the flowers on the wall sympathetically, thinking of her dead mother, the progress of the seasons, the human bond beneath the beauty, Bellingham cares only for the beauty itself, and his own pride in it. Ruth's "tender endeavours," in the novel's terms, are precisely what make her graceful and lovely. While for Bellingham, they are pleasant embellishments to his toy, for Gaskell, they are part of that "thinking, and feeling, and loving" that are Ruth's true beauty, and that make her a perfect observer of nature.

The fluidity of Ruth's movement from observed to observer in the natural world begins to make her—and her fall—seem natural fact; seem almost to have no history. She is, as we have seen, completely at home in nature, a nature in which "there was no change or alteration . . . that had not its own peculiar beauty" in her eyes. Like the "common frost" that she observed at the beginning of the novel, "even rain was a pleasure to her." Bellingham, whose attitude toward nature would mark him as a villain even if his sexual violence did not, is impatient with this:

> "Really, Ruth," he exclaimed one day, when they had been imprisoned by rain a whole morning, "one would think you had never seen a shower of rain before; it quite wearies me to see you sitting there watching this detestable weather with such a placid countenance; and for the last two hours you have said nothing more amusing or interesting than—'Oh, how beautiful!' or, 'There's another cloud coming across Moel Wynn.'" (pp. 65–66)

Ruth's sympathy toward all natural beauty and her feeling of oneness with it contribute to her fall, for Bellingham takes her on lovely walks on her free Sundays, and she cannot imagine anything wrong with these natural pleasures. But Gaskell uses this discussion of Ruth's feeling of safety among natural beauty to interesting effect here, for if Ruth is, indeed, the daughter of nature, and the way to her heart is through natural pleasures, what then *is* the sin in her fall into sexuality? When Bellingham wants her to go with him to a meadow, "at first she declined, but then, suddenly wondering and questioning herself why she refused a thing which was, as far as reason and knowledge (*her* knowledge) went, so innocent . . . so tempting and pleasant" (p. 40). Ruth's "knowledge" is insufficient; she is only fifteen when she meets Bellingham and she has had no one to tell her right from wrong—but Gaskell's critique goes further.

Ruth's innocence, when it fits so absolutely with natural right and natural beauty, *is* perfect: she is a fallen woman only when she meets with (artificial) social limitations, walking into a wall of social judgments that hit her with the force of that small boy's fist. Gaskell does try to argue that her initial hesitation is right, but the force of her integration of Ruth with nature argues the opposite. In another early scene, Ruth thinks,

> "How strange it is . . . that I should feel as if this charming afternoon's walk were . . . not right. Why can it be? I am not defrauding Mrs Mason of any of her time; that I know would be wrong; I am left to go where I like on Sundays; I have been to church, so it can't be because I have missed doing my duty. If I had gone on this walk with Jenny, I wonder whether I should have felt as I do now. There must be something wrong in me, myself, to feel

so guilty when I have done nothing which is not right; and yet I can thank
God for the happiness I have had in this charming spring walk, which dear
mamma used to say was a sign when pleasures were innocent and good for
us." (p. 41)

These pleasures are, of course, not socially considered "innocent and
good for us"—in fact, Ruth is being seduced, she will have an illegitimate
son, the rest of her life will be spent, as she realizes in that Welsh town,
fallen in the "estimation of the world." But in another way, Ruth's
innocence is valid: there is nothing obviously "wrong" with Ruth except
her own "guilt"—there is nothing, perhaps, wrong in the eyes of nature.
Ruth, as a natural heroine, cannot "fall," except into confusion and guilt;
as a socialized being and, in the terms of the rest of the novel, as a
Christian heroine, she is already fallen. For that "other" novel that begins
after her abandonment, the novel of sin and redemption, she must fall so
as to be redeemed; her sexual sin is only an acting out of the sin of all
men, which she is fortunate to realize in time to go on to lead a more
perfect life. But in the world of the natural novel we have been reading,
Gaskell cannot make Ruth's sexual pleasure—or, for that matter, her
desire—into a sin. Ruth's "loving" heart makes her innocent as well as a
victim; the purity of her fall creates doubts about the distinctions that so
troubled Ruskin, between purely aesthetic and aesthetically pure pleasure.

Critics, even contemporaries of Gaskell, have seen this as a flaw in the
novel: she carefully creates Ruth's innocence but spends the rest of the
novel insisting on her guilt in order to work out her repentance.[36] One
way of explaining this is that Ruth's "sin" is like so many others in the
novel, a slipping off from perfection, and Gaskell, as a Christian working
for social reform, has to produce the most sympathetic sinner she can.
But this explanation argues a certain naiveté and lack of skill out of
keeping with the careful plotting and construction of the novel in other
regards. Another explanation, and a more convincing one, would follow
through the language of value and exchange that Gaskell examines
throughout the work, to argue that Ruth's guilt grows out of her awareness that her seduction by Bellingham was a violation of her integrity, a
purchasing of her beauty and her sexuality made possible by her status as
a dressmaker. Ruth's emotional vulnerability has led her to love anyone
who sympathizes with her, and natural sexuality draws her to love
Bellingham for his physical attractions, but this is not the more perfect,
spiritual and intellectual love that would lead her to greater growth and

enlightenment. Thus, although Ruth's love for Bellingham is not an absolute evil, in the way conventional Victorian morality would dictate, it is imperfect and must be transcended for her to become a true heroine.

There is much that is right in both these answers, much to help readers out of the dilemma we must fall into when we find the two parts of this novel in conflict. But it is possible that this conflict is deliberate; Gaskell meant the reader to feel jarred, so as to return our attention to our own *role* as reader, conditioned as we are by the various stories of women's lives we have read, and our expectations for the heroine's role as object rather than author of her own being. Our attention has been so focused on Ruth's receptivity and passivity that we, too, have become unaware of society's forces moving in on her; the jolt reminds us of the socialized existence of the romantic heroine, in a way that Wordsworth, with his focus on madwomen *after* the betrayal, cannot. The story behind the story, what we get in *Ruth*, shows up that gap in the Wordsworthian story. Here, we experience that shift through the movement to the other plot, through the play of our expectations as empathetic readers and our generic expectations as post-Romantic readers. What happens when Ruth discovers her own sin and is taken into the household of Mr Benson, the dissenting minister, is that she falls into another plot, one that requires a different way of reading.[37] We, as cunning readers, have been aware that she is being seduced; she was not. We realize that her sympathetic love of nature has drawn her into false, "natural," pleasures; she does not. She cannot, essentially, read herself mythically; she lacks our irony, for she cannot see herself as a "heroine."

Ruth suggests that it is precisely the myth of nature's daughter that has led Ruth to fall, and that this is not a myth we are in the habit of questioning. Ruth's perfect receptivity has made her a sexual victim, and while society demands that she be the "beautiful ignoramus," it is clearly not the right thing to be. Ruth can have no such knowledge. To reveal that myth requires revealing the deception of narration; to show the way in which Ruth's "story" has been made requires the alignment of her "making" as a woman with the "making" of the text. We need to be made self-conscious about both, to accept neither as "natural." The story behind labor—the moment Ruskin discusses when he considers the creation of the artist in his essay "Pre-Raphaelitism," Rossetti's fable of the "soul" behind his "hand"—has not, previously, been female; in *Ruth*, Gaskell uses the connections between the social creation of a woman and artistic creation to deconstruct the Romantic myth, and at the same time suggest the relativity of social as well as literary conventions. What had previously seemed mere convention—woman equals soul, man appropriates soul for his art—here is made literal, and we see Ruth appropriated, taken up in turn by one story after another.

iii

The second half of the novel reverses its earlier project: having presented Ruth as unaware of her own status as object, it now looks directly at those looking at her; having given us the story of her betrayal, it now turns its gaze on the attempt precisely to make it into "story." It moves from crises of individual (character) interpretation to its own examination of forms; from thematics to structure; from its "fable," to use Macherey's term, to attention to its own "figuration." *Ruth* makes us aware of the "labor" behind the writing and our own expectations in reading, by showing us so many people watching Ruth and attempting to tell the story behind her sad beauty, again locating the tension of interpretation around the woman's stillness. This technique is made explicit in a novel like *To the Lighthouse*, which recounts ruminations of others on Mrs Ramsay's beauty:

> But was it nothing but looks, people said? What was there behind it—her beauty and splendour? Had he blown his brains out, they asked, had he died the week before they were married—some other, earlier lover, of whom rumours reached one? Or was there nothing? nothing but an incomparable beauty which she lived behind, and could do nothing to disturb?[38]

In this novel, these "rumours," the questions we overhear, we know to be untrue, because we have the (inside) story ourselves. Because we know Ruth's secret, we can criticize the stories people tell. And we have plenty of opportunity, for Ruth is under observation through the rest of the novel, and, as with Mrs Ramsay, no one can believe there is "nothing but an incomparable beauty." What we see in *Ruth* is the use (social, and in turn literary) to which that beauty is put.

People in the town where Ruth goes to live with the minister and his family are intrigued by her beauty and her silence from the beginning—but they explain it according to their own lights. Mr Bradshaw, the wealthy industrialist, notices Ruth's "quiet manner, subdued by an internal consciousness of a deeper cause for sorrow than he was aware of, [which] he interpreted into a very proper and becoming awe of him." Like everything else in his world, she appears to him only to reflect back his superiority. His daughter Jemima, with a romantic and passionate soul, sees Ruth as looking "so pale and awed because she was left a solitary parent; but Ruth came to the presence of God, as one who had gone astray." When Ruth goes to work for the Bradshaw family, she is under constant surveillance to see if she makes a fit governess; Jemima's suitor, Mr Farquhar, tired of Jemima's moods and considering falling in love with Ruth, observes her at work; Jemima, consumed with jealousy, sets herself up to watch Ruth, though the tension of watching "makes her soul weary"; under that surveillance her beauty turns in Jemima's mind to "your sickly, hypocritical face," which is only "innocent seeming."

This observation, though elicited by Ruth's aesthetic appeal, serves clear social purposes: the Bradshaws need to know if Ruth is a suitable companion; Jemima fears losing her own lover; Mr Farquhar seeks an appropriate wife. Ruth's whole presence in the town depends on an "innocent seeming," and on the deception by which she is passed off by Mr Benson and his sister as their widowed cousin, and her son as a legitimate, if fatherless, boy. Yet when Ruth's "sin" is revealed, the town quickly forgets her "seeming," treating her as the pariah they expect an unmarried mother to be, not as the virtuous, quiet woman who has lived among them all those years. And here the effect of leaving Ruth's soul pure become clearer: the novel plays off the expectations for a fallen woman's state to suggest what happens if Ruth does not meet them. To the people of the town, the worst of Ruth's sins is that she has lived among them as one of them, that they would not recognize her as fallen.

The character through whom this interpretive crisis is most fully worked out is Jemima, who is going through her own ritual of desire and independence when Ruth comes to the town. Jemima is attempting to free herself from her father's world of utilitarian, economic values; for her, Ruth represents beauty, sadness, romantic love, all that will help her escape from her father's house. From the first, Jemima understands clearly that she is, to her father, a kind of property. In her father's desire that she marry Mr Farquhar—whom she in fact loves—she feels that "Mr Farquhar was cold and calculating in all he did, and that she was to be transferred by the former [her father] and accepted by the latter, as a sort of stock-in-trade" (p. 228). For Jemima, their relations are merely manueverings negotiated by her father: "She felt as if she would rather be bought openly, like an Oriental daughter, where no one is degraded in their own eyes by being parties to such a contract." Jemima refuses to "hang on [Farquhar's] arm" as she once did, and she refuses to accept her father's view of the world, in which, he says, "once allow a margin of uncertainty, or where feelings, instead of maxims, were to be the guide, and all hope of there ever being any good men of business was ended."

The language here is that of the "dealers," reminiscent of the rhetoric Bellingham uses when he finds Ruth at Eccleston, and thinks, "What a stately step she has! How majestic and graceful all her attitudes were! She thinks she has baffled me now. We will try something more, and bid a higher price" (p. 302). Ruth's beauty still leads him to equate her with any object he can buy, just as his mother left Ruth money after Bellingham deserted her, as if her virginity were something he had acquired without paying the bill.

But the question of "price" is really one of interpretation, of how to move between seeing and valuing, and specifically, how to evaluate once the stable, female object seems to shift, to resist your valuation. Putting a price on everything, of course, saves one from having to decide the value of individual souls and individual actions; whether one has a financial account book or something like Mr Bradshaw's "maxims" that save him from having to judge his fellow man charitably, one lives in a world that one always knows how to interpret. But for Gaskell, morality is never absolutely fixed. The good characters in *Ruth* live in state of moral doubt and debate; only the evil characters, Bradshaw and Bellingham, live in a world where their actions are always right, because they have already set a moral code and no longer need to make judgments. What Jemima faces when she first learns of Ruth's past is a dissolution of what she has always believed to be a recognizable morality. What she must learn is what Gaskell wants her readers to believe: that anyone can sin; that sin is not an absolute; that knowledge itself may be circumstantial.

Jemima's shock arises from the recognition that she has "come in contact with any one who had committed open sin," that sin made "open," most literally, by the reality of Ruth's child.

> She had never shaped her conviction into words and sentences, but still it was *there*, that all the respectable, all the family and religious circumstances of her life, would hedge her in, and guard her from ever encountering the great shock of coming face to face with Vice. Without being pharisaical in her estimation of herself, she had all a Pharisee's dread of publicans and sinners, and all a child's cowardliness—that cowardliness which prompts it to shut its eyes against the object of terror, rather than acknowledge its existence with brave faith. (p. 323)

It is the horror of realizing that she could sin, that there isn't what her father saw, a "clear line of partition, which separated mankind into two great groups, to one of which, by the grace of God, he and his belonged; while the other was composed of those whom it was his duty to try and reform, and bring the whole force of his morality to bear upon, with lectures, admonitions, and exhortations" (p. 323–24). "Who was to be trusted," Jemima asks herself, "if Ruth—calm, modest, delicate, dignified Ruth—had a memory blackened by sin?" "Who was true? Who was not? Who was good and pure? Who was not? The very foundations of Jemima's belief in her mind were shaken. Could it be false? Could there be two Ruth Hiltons?" (p. 324–326)

There aren't, of course, two Ruth Hiltons, despite the deception about her name, her marital status, her child's legitimacy. The novel wants to shake "the very foundations," to teach readers to imagine the unity of a character who can do contradictory things, to imagine seeing and being seen at one moment. Further, Jemima's question pushes at the limits of at least middle-class (that is, circulating-library) Victorian morality. Her ability to imagine Ruth's suffering is a model in the text: What if, she is able to ask herself, Ruth had made a tragic mistake when young and had truly worked through her own repentance? What if she, Jemima, equally passionate, were capable of sin? What if, then, conventional notions of sin and blame were, if not wrong, at the least not all of morality? What Jemima says, after her father's denunciation of Ruth, stands not so much as the novel's testimony, as the way it wants us to read:

> I have been thinking a great deal about poor Ruth. . . . You know I could not help it when everybody was talking about it—and it made me think of myself, and what I am. With a father and mother, and home and careful friends, I am not likely to be tempted like Ruth; but oh! . . . if you knew all I have been thinking and feeling this last year, you would see how I have yielded to every temptation that was able to come to me. (p. 365)

This understanding of Jemima's—that moral categories have this kind of fluidity, and that "temptations" are socially determined—undermines further any romanticization of Ruth's fate, and undermines especially any absolute judgments on her. This moment in the text is the challenge the Romantic poet resists: the identification made concrete, turned to "what if I *were* a fallen woman?"

The question for *this* novel, though, remains: what is it that Gaskell has made of Ruth's beauty? *Ruth* itself, as fiction, has taken the experience of the woman Gaskell met in the prison, embroidered it and added to it, made it into an aesthetic object. It is the novel's conclusion that most highlights this concern, presenting Gaskell's final wrestling with the problem of representation—of the reading of Ruth's redemption, and of the "useful" fiction she has attempted to tell by making that fallen woman's story into art. *Ruth* ends with a particularly vicious twist. After her humiliation at Mr Bradshaw's house, her difficult and brave return into the life of the community, and her son's painful and only partial adjustment to the news of his illegitimacy, Ruth becomes a competent, much needed and much loved nurse in the town. Her gentleness, the empathy and softness that have marked her all along, comes to have genuine usefulness, and when typhoid strikes the village, Ruth is transformed into a kind of saint, praised on all sides, her sin entirely forgotten in the good she is doing. Once again, she becomes a kind of icon—here, of virtue personified. Her son overhears a conversation in which one man remarks, "They say she has been a great sinner, and that this is her penance." Another replies:

> "Such a one as her has never been a great sinner; nor does she do her work as a penance, but for the love of God, and of the blessed Jesus. She will be in the light of God's countenance when you and I will be standing afar off. I tell you, man, when my poor wench died, as no one would come near, her head lay at that hour on this woman's sweet breast. I could fell you," the old man went on, lifting his shaking arm, "for calling that woman a great sinner. The blessing of them who were ready to perish is upon her."
> (p. 429)

Leonard, finally, is proud to say, "Sir, I am her son!" and Ruth's beatification seems complete. When she returns to her home after the epidemic ends, "even Mr Benson's anxious eye could see no change in her looks, but that she seemed a little paler. The eyes were as full of spiritual light, the gently parted lips as rosy, and the smile, if more rare, yet as sweet as ever." Ruth's spiritual and physical beauty have merged absolutely.

But after this apotheosis, the novel seems to shift genres again, suggesting yet once more the difficulty of presenting a human heroine, one who acts or moves apart from an allegorical figuring. Not content to rest with the praise of the village, Gaskell insists on martyring Ruth completely, by having her volunteer to nurse her seducer, Bellingham, and having her succeed in curing him only to die herself. One can see this as the final pressure to force Ruth's redemption in the eyes of her audience, but even contemporary readers objected to her martyrdom: Charlotte Brontë, on being given a sketch of the novel, wrote to Gaskell, pleading:

> Yet—hear my protest! Why should she die? Why are we to shut up the book weeping? My heart fails me already at the thought of the pang it will have to undergo. And yet you must follow the impulse of your own inspiration. If *that* commands the slaying of the victim no bystander has a right to put out his hand to stay the sacrificial knife, but I hold you a stern priestess in these matters.[39]

Barrett Browning wrote as well, again stressing the novelist's responsibility for "her" heroine:

> I have just finished 'Ruth'. . . . I am grateful to you as a woman for having treated such a subject—Was it quite impossible but that your Ruth should *die*? I had that thought of regret in closing the book—Oh, I must confess to it—Pardon me for the tears' sake![40]

Both women, writing to Gaskell, single out her own severity in slaying "her" Ruth, and feel some guilt ("my heart fails me"; "I must confess to it") at not being able to accept the clearly Christian, typological ending of the novel in which the heroine moves toward "the light" and leaves a message of love behind. Ruth's death follows the model Mr Benson has laid out as the best man can hope for in life, to try "more than ever I did in my life to act as my blessed Lord would have done," but readers' discomfort with this ending—and it is largely because of the ending that the book has remained unpopular—suggests its failure to convince. We resent Ruth's sacrifice to a Christian myth of martyrdom, in part because it seems too clearly a continuation of her earlier passivity in the face of seduction, and in part because it seems a plot in conflict with the novel we have been reading: it does not satisfy us emotionally or generically. But perhaps it was not meant to. If, as Garrett Stewart has suggested, death in the Victorian novel marks "something like the intersection between (and at the same time final divergence of) sociology and psychology in their mutual plotting of identity within community,"[41] Ruth's end, singing a "childish ditty" her mother taught her, sounding like nothing so much as the Lady of Shalott, reminds us of the "plotting of identity" not only "within community" but within plotting.[42]

Ruth's death, then, may be an attempt to murder fiction itself, to reveal the tension between the pleasures of "invention" and the viciousness of plot. The central "fiction" of the novel, of course, is that this novel *can* transform the world, but Gaskell's sense of despair and anger at the slowness of social change (a sense heightened no doubt by the mixed response to *Mary Barton*) can be sensed throughout the work, and may be acted out in her "sacrificial" slaughter of her heroine. But our concern with the novel's examination of the relation of the woman to the work of art might lead us to see in that sacrifice an attention to the silencing of woman into art—the very "perfection" of the work of art is a deception, the need to unify at the cost of that fluidity the novel praised earlier. Miss Benson, after discovering her love of inventing lies, describes it as a kind of violent plotting, of "mak[ing] the incidents dovetail." "It is so pleasant to invent," she says, and "after all, if we are to tell a lie, we may as well do it thoroughly, or else it's of no use." "I am afraid," she goes on, "I enjoy not being fettered by truth." The notion of a useful, "thorough" lie may take us back to the novelist in prison, Gaskell justifying her "use" of fiction as a necessary falsehood beside the suffering she saw, but the evident fictionality of the end (Pasley, after all, sailed cheerfully off to Australia, neither a mad mother nor a "thorn") is both a useful "lie" and a suggestion of the failure of even this novel to step outside the fallen woman's plot.

Gaskell meant to write a novel that was not like other narratives of fallen women; she might have called out, as Mr Benson does in *Ruth*, "Oh! for a seraph's tongue, and a seraph's powers of representation" for her task of revealing the mythology of aestheticized female suffering while depicting that suffering herself. But, as Mr Benson notes, "There was no seraph at hand." There rarely is in a postlapsarian world, and Gaskell, like her heroine, lives in a world of interpretation, social and literary convention, flawed powers of "representation." If the end of the novel does not escape the post-Romantic dilemma of making the woman stand for—represent—more than her own story, it does include its heroine's ironic comments on her own imperfection, and her resistance to meanings imposed on her. Unlike a Wordsworthian heroine, Ruth gets to talk back to those who mystify her. Unlike Chiaro's soul, Ruth is never just "truth"; she remains a real and suffering heroine, the specifics of whose struggle to find "circumstances in which she might work out her self-redemption" move us. She speaks of her own inability to objectify her life, see herself from the outside, in a moving passage at the end, when she realizes that, despite her new status in Eccleston,

> She herself did not feel changed. . . . She and the distant hills that she saw from her chamber window, seemed the only things which were the same as when she first came to Eccleston. (p. 392)

These moments of reflection call up again the novel's beginning, its opening meditations on change: here, the heroine herself tries to posit a stable self, a "she" outside of the change of history, a "she and the distant hills" that are not different from what they once were. But while the novel (especially in its loyalty to Ruth's gentleness) at moments seems to yearn for such stability—both of self and of perception—it is finally committed to a world of shifting, active, changeful response, more like what Ruth herself saw when studying the clouds for hours on end. *Ruth* calls out for a more active, inventive observation; finally, it hopes not for a stable object, but a questioning subject. Like its heroine, like Gaskell, the novel believes in pilgrimages.

iv

If the novel is as much a pilgrimage of author as of heroine, what story does it offer us of Gaskell's efforts, as a woman writer, to "half perceive and half create"? What is the relationship between the moralizing of the novel, which has stopped so many readers cold, and its author's struggle to write it? The connection, oddly enough, is martyrdom: if Ruth's transformation into an object lesson is at the heart of readers' distrust of the novel, a view of herself as—to quote a letter—"St Sebastian shot through with arrows" is at the heart of Gaskell's authorial self-conception. When Ruth unwrites the more optimistic version of her story, choosing her martyrdom against the plot's other possibilities, she may be echoing Gaskell's own dislike of the Victorian reading audience that had rejected *Mary Barton*, and would in turn reject this novel.

It is easy enough now to miss what was most radical in Gaskell's vision: she did write a book that was burned and denounced, a novel she was not even willing to let her own daughters read unsupervised. It was, as she remarked often in her letters, an "unfit subject for fiction," and she was considered an "improper" woman for writing it. Many readers wrote to her that they were sadly disappointed in the author of *Mary Barton*, and those few letters she received announcing their approval of the novel she cherished—and answered immediately and gratefully.[43] "Saint Sebastian" after the novel was published, Gaskell said she "knew it before," and knew the dislike of the book "must be endured with as much quiet *seeming* . . . as I can."[44] When she writes in the novel of the words that "have come to many in their time of need, and awed them in the presence of the extremest suffering that the hushed world has ever heard of," she means the passion play, but she also means to invoke *Ruth* itself. The martyred fallen woman dies to provide this kind of lesson, to move readers out of themselves. But then the woman novelist, using the model of "quiet,—quite quiet" womanhood that Ruskin invoked, becomes the one to transform her audiences.

Something more seems to me to be happening in the relationship of the novelist to her audience. The martyring of the heroine may be, as I have suggested, a slap in the face of her readers, shocking readers out of complacency, to remind them of the excessively plotted lives women lead—the ways they are made into characters from the moment they are born—but it also has a harshness to it that suggests Gaskell's deeper hostility to Victorian mores and to the demands of polite readers—to the way, in a sense, novelists are made. She asserted in letters that *Ruth* was not "*written* yet," that she didn't know "*when* or *if*" she would finish it; more, "I hate publishing because of the talk people make"[45]—and people did "make" the talk she dreaded about this novel. Critics have suggested, with the conclusion of this novel as with *Mary Barton*, that Gaskell remained to the end a middle-class Victorian wife, unable entirely to overcome her moral training, unable to imagine her heroine "a heroine" apart from absolute martyrdom, absolute abnegation of self. But this self-abnegation, given Gaskell's identification with her heroine, involves real hubris as well. Narrator and heroine here become Christ-like: the female destiny, to the extent that Ruth has embodied it, consists in taking on all suffering in order to redeem the world. And the crucifying crowd here is both Ruth's community and Gaskell's readers, who would not be satisfied with anything less than death.

This movement from writing the heroine's story to writing the novelist's story recurs in Gaskell, and returns us again to the difficulty with which she wrote *Ruth*, but does it mark this text as unique? One wants to resist the impulse to read all novels as telling the story of their own writing, and yet this remains an important question for *Ruth* because the problem it raises is about the *male* writer's relationship to the female subject. The novel must, successfully to resolve the problem it states so clearly, avoid re-creating the terms of the problem. If Gaskell is escaping a male mythology of writing only to create her own, that is in part only to suggest that the Romantic model of artistic creation and artistic suffering was almost impossible to escape. In *Cranford*, Gaskell will begin to deconstruct the model of narrative authority she inherits, but for *Ruth*, it remains intact.

But we might return here to Pierre Macherey's distinction between the "ideological project" of a text, and its "figuration"—"the specificity of the writing of the page"—and within the figuration between the "reservoir of images" that "seems to establish a closed and self-sufficient totality," and the "formal unity [of the narrative] corresponding to the content which it has discovered, which directs and organises it" (pp. 175, 187). This unity is that of the "fable"—in the case of a Verne novel that of the adventure story, which must be organized around a journey. But the fable does not always correspond to the initial project, and we may find "discord" between the levels of "representation" and "figuration." In this reading, it is not that the form "betrays" the content, that is, displays the hidden ideological agenda of the novel. To do this, to display the "contradiction in ideology," is not possible; rather, Macherey claims, we see "ideology put into contradiction."

It is not enough to say that Jules Verne is a bourgeois of the early Third Republic with all that this implies. . . . We know that a writer never reflects mechanically or rigorously the ideology which he represents, even if his sole intention is to represent it: perhaps because no ideology is sufficiently consistent to survive the test of figuration. And otherwise, his work would not be read. The writer always reveals or writes from a certain *position* (which is not simply a subjective viewpoint) in relation to this ideological climate: he constructs a specific image of ideology which is not exactly identical with ideology as it is given, whether it betrays it, whether it puts it in question, or whether it modifies it. (p. 195)

What novelists can do is register the "limits" of their historical situation, and the situation of the text, which signals those limits by its own limitations. "The work exists only because it is not exactly what it could have been," and it arises from the realization "of *the impossibility of the work's filling the ideological frame for which it should have been made.*" This, in Macherey's memorable phrase, is "why the questioning of the fiction is accomplished by the fiction itself" (p. 222). And that, he concludes, is why we must "read it against the grain of its intended reading" (p. 230).

This distinction between project and figuration is useful in reading *Ruth*, and one can adapt Macherey's terms of the "fable" and the "representation" to play out this "against-the-grain" reading we have already engaged in. Gaskell, like Verne, is using another text for her fable: that, in her case, of the fallen woman, a fable primarily inscribed by Wordsworth. But her figuration of the fable, intended to carry out her project of deconstructing the mythology of the Romantic story, cannot successfully break from the terms she means to criticize. One might use the narratological terms of "story" and "discourse" here as well; the story Gaskell has abstracted from the tradition of the fallen woman she intends to use ironically, but since so much of the discourse is lifted from that story, there is not enough distance between the two for the project to succeed.

But one can see the confusion of narrative attitudes coming out of this tension: the narrator of the organic novel comes with the story—she is a version of the Wordsworthian narrator, intent on revealing the "tragic poem" in the humble life. The typological version of Ruth's story—in which her beauty *does* reveal her essential goodness, and her passivity leads her to martyrdom—is the "thematic" that eventually takes over the novel, revealing the limitations of the text but beginning its own version of the story. The difficulties of using the Christ story to present a new story suggest the tensions of the ideology Gaskell means to criticize but somehow reactivates. But in the third narrative voice, with its attention to representation itself and its awareness of the market, is the "questioning of the fiction accomplished by the fiction itself." That voice is the voice of literature commenting on its own production, and it sounds different from the voice of the literature on which it comments. In that discord, the novel realizes its limits but also makes them clear to the reader. The voice of the laboring novelist, like the gaps of the narrative, confirms the text as "symptom," rather than opening the text to what Macherey elsewhere calls the "normative fallacy" in which "the work should be other than it is." But that voice doesn't always speak clearly; a novel like *Ruth* can comment only through what it leaves out. The voice that speaks of representation and exchange is the voice of absence, the voice that does not intervene to make the end of the novel coherent, the voice that does not resolve the serious questions within the work about lying and fiction, the voice that leaves contradictory perspectives in contradiction.

In part, we can use Macherey's terms to discuss the *literary* contradictions of the novel, but they return us as well to the cultural contradictions that gave it birth: the concern over the fallen woman, and a need to "place" her in Victorian society. Macherey's description of the "impossibility of the work's filling the ideological frame for which it should have been made" recalls what Adorno suggested of the work of art: "The consistency or inconsistency of the work itself expresses the structure of the existent." *Ruth* "consists" of its "inconsistencies"—the same inconsistencies that mark Greg's account of the "fallen woman" who needs to be "recognized" and "contained"; that mark the gap between the Wordsworthian and the Christian plots; that mark the position of the woman writer before a male tradition. One might be tempted to argue that Gaskell "calls up" an older story to cover up the gaps her culture encounters in its story of the fallen woman, but the fictional plot and the cultural account at once overlap and contradict each other; Gaskell puts both into question, in her attempt to create her *own* fiction of (for) the fallen woman.

Macherey does not raise the question of the female author attempting to find her own voice—a voice of resistance to a stunningly masculine tradition—and most feminist critics who have done so have not taken on the social novel nor really described what happens to male voices inscribed within the female text. To begin to find your voice by commenting on the tropes and icons of others is at once the way of a literary apprentice, and the way of a woman intent on creating her own individual voice for herself by consciously rejecting what is offered her. Gaskell's sense of unease as she did so may account for some of the uncertainty of tone in the novel, but her indirect and somewhat ironic plea for the "tongue of the seraph" suggests she knew all too well what she was up against, and was not unhappy with the challenge. This questioning of inherited languages marks her movement from reader to writer—from daughter to self-created author. She remained a passionate reader of Wordsworth and Ruskin her whole life, but her relationship to male authority shifted: *Ruth* marks the moment of that shift. In this way, the heroine's story and the novelist's story do come together. Neither escapes entirely the plottedness of the narrative already written before she comes to it, but Ruth as character and *Ruth* as literary production suggest new alternatives and new ways of reading (and writing) the old tale.

II

MY SCHEHEREZADE:
THE WOMAN NOVELIST'S
HOUSEHOLD WORDS

3

Affairs of the Alphabet: The Novel, the Train, and the Woman Writer in *Cranford*

At first glance, *Cranford* might seem out of place here: it has no romance; no heroine's progress—in fact, it has no heroine. But what this novel without a heroine offers instead is the novelist as heroine, and her most original experiments with narrative and social observation. Furthermore, while I will be substituting two slightly different narratives for the one I have been tracing, both will have to do with authorship and seduction: the first, of Elizabeth Gaskell's literary flirtation with Charles Dickens; the second, of the evolution of the narrator, Mary Smith, into a different kind of storyteller. That means that though my primary focus here will be forms of storytelling (the inscription of storytelling in class, gender, and history) and Gaskell's own evolution as a professional novelist, I intend through these concerns to draw on the opening section of this book (and its concern with prostitution, narration, and romance) to suggest some of what is at stake for the woman historian of a dying rural life. Although my first goal will be to delineate the differences *Cranford* inscribes, what insures the place of this novel in the progression I am tracing is the romance of the marketplace, and the woman writer's relationship to her own shifting authorial presentation.

Cranford has enjoyed a special place in the hearts of Gaskell's readers, and its continuing nostalgic popularity[1] and the resistance that its charms have inspired among more ironic critics have perhaps blinded us to what a truly peculiar novel it is. For many reasons (literary, historical, and biographical) it holds a unique place in Gaskell's literary production: it is stories that became a novel; it is entirely rural, domestic, and private; it is almost entirely a story about women and a story self-consciously, conspicuously narrated by a woman. It was begun in 1851, after the success of *Mary Barton*, at the request of Charles Dickens, the "conductor" of *Household Words* and of so much literary activity in the 1850s; in form and content it reflects some of the central changes in Victorian publication that mark that decade, everywhere from railways to publishing houses. More, it reflects Gaskell's own growing sense of her "career" as a writer, of what it meant to be "in print." If the problems of society it poses seem initially small in contrast to the works that border it—*Mary Barton*, *Ruth*, and *North and South*—it makes that smallness its literary province as well. *Cranford* asks clearly what the voice of the woman writer can be; how a woman can speak in this new environment; what female narrative, dispossessed and displaced, can look like.

Cranford rewrites marginality to form its own kind of experiment with narrative: like more famous Victorian examples of self-conscious narration, it comments on its own status as text, but it does so by indirection, a narrative viewpoint it names as peculiarly female. Although following French feminist theories of "writing like a woman" (*l 'écriture feminine*) might lead us to look for a universally female language in *Cranford*, one in which, as Luce Irigaray declares, "a woman's desire would not be expected to speak the same language as man's, . . . [but] would undoubtedly have a different alphabet, a different language,"[2] we might ask instead how it was possible for one woman to reshape the forms of Victorian fiction, to write as a woman within a specific historical, economic, literary structure. Hélène Cixous argues that woman "must write her self . . . must put herself into the text—as into the world and into history—by her own movement";[3] here, my question is, what was the world (and the world of the text) into which Gaskell could "put herself," and by what "movement"? As elsewhere in her fiction, Gaskell begins by placing herself in an inherited literary tradition, but here it is one of parody and subversion, a tradition she can use to rewrite the novel;[4] where the concerns of *Mary Barton* and *Ruth* were with female plots, here it is the woman (writer)'s language that is at stake.

This chapter will move between stylistics and politics, to ask what the particular language of *Cranford* means, for if *Cranford* is a novel about women's languages, it asks these questions within a specific world. As every critic has noted, *Cranford* moves between the world of the "Amazons," the small, old-world village of spinsters and widows, and the new world of Drumble, the industrial city to the north, populated by men of business, and connected to Cranford only by trains and affection. *Cranford* itself narrates only the world of the women, and its aim is to create for readers the experience of reading a world about to disappear, and of learning the language of that world. But to achieve this, *Cranford* must teach us a lost language, and must in turn revise some of the languages of literature.

Cranford's own revisions are of some interest. The first version of *Cranford* Gaskell wrote was an essay entitled "The Last Generation in England," which was published in *Sartain's Union Magazine* in July 1849, and was announced as "by the author of 'Mary Barton'"; "communicated for Sartain's Magazine by Mary Howitt." The essay begins with Gaskell's regret that Robert Southey did not live to write, as he promised, a "history of English domestic life"; what Gaskell wants to do is "put upon record some of the details of country town life, either observed by myself, or handed down to me by older relations," because "even in small towns, scarcely removed from villages, the phases of society are rapidly changing; and much will appear strange, which yet occurred only in the generation immediately preceding ours."[5] This quality of transition (revisions again) is central to the novel Gaskell went on to write. *Cranford* is most often praised for its own quality of loving nostalgia, but what it in fact registers is panic about change; it is being written in the face of its own demolition, in the face of the social changes that novels like *Mary Barton* and *Ruth* address more directly.

Change in this novel is the world of the railways, and the railways mark not only a change in the ways of life but a change in ways of publication as well. In the 1850s, novels became more plentiful precisely because they were being read on the move; as the trains revolutionized movement, so Smith's railway publications revolutionized literature.[6] But these mobile readers in turn closed down possibilities in fiction: as the circulating libraries grew in power, so possibilities for new forms of fiction decreased, and publishers increasingly preferred their authors to duplicate past successes rather than start off for new territory. These spatial and motional metaphors shared by trains and novelists suggest the peculiar joining of both and their shared presence in *Cranford*.

In November of 1848, W. H. Smith opened the first Smith bookstall at Euston station;[7] a fortnight later another contract was made, and "others followed in quick succession." In the next decade, Smith turned to lending libraries, and, in turn, to issuing popular editions of more portable novels in yellow covers—the first "yellow book," ironically, was *Cranford*. Indeed, *Cranford*'s publishing history suggests the interconnections of trains, novels, and a changing world of Victorian fiction: it is the republication of *Cranford* that prompts Gaskell's most professional letters to Chapman,[8] inquiring after numbers and costs; *Cranford* was the first of her novels to be reprinted in a "cheap edition"; only over *Cranford* does she inquire about her right of "copyright" over her own text; and most important, it is *Cranford* that taught her the demands of serial publication and the difficulty of writing for (and defying) Charles Dickens. As the train seemed to readers like Ruskin to suggest the transformation of traveler into "parcel,"[9] so the "parceled" text of *Cranford* led Gaskell to question her own relationship to fictional form(ation). *Cranford*—like Gaskell herself—moves away from this: as the "place" of the novel is set apart from these things, so the time of the text seems to be. We may have to commute to the world of this novel, but it seems a world of more fully realized people, of unparceled subjectivity, of life *not* lived in parts.

At the same time that *Cranford* seems to participate in the latest techniques in fiction, it conjures up a different (older) kind of storyteller: the anecdotal, intimate, immediate storyteller of village life. Gaskell was herself an inveterate storyteller, fond of ghost stories and lengthy letters, and both these forms enter *Cranford*, in memoirs and letters that are almost interpolated tales in the novel. The text of *Cranford* seems at times an anthology of storytelling techniques, but it also takes its storytellers at one remove: the narrator becomes a kind of anthropologist, an ethnographer visiting an alien culture and watching it "make meaning." Critics have assumed, simplistically, that Gaskell was only describing from *within* the village life she missed, but the other terms with which we might describe her project are those of Clifford Geertz. Gaskell is writing what he calls a "thick description," one that "tr[ies] to rescue the 'said' of [social] discourse from its perishing occasions and fix it in perusable terms."[10] Geertz's description of "perishing" occasions and "perusable" ethnography anticipates much of what I will discuss in Gaskell:

> What the ethnographer is faced with . . . is a multiplicity of complex conceptual structures, many of them superimposed upon or knotted into one another, which are at once strange, irregular, and inexplicit, and which he [*sic*] must contrive somehow first to grasp and then to render. . . . Doing ethnography is like trying to read (in the sense of "construct a reading of") a manuscript—foreign, faded, full of ellipses, incoherences, suspicious emendations, and tendentious commentaries, but written not in conventionalized graphs of sound but in transient examples of shaped behavior. (p. 10)

That manuscript—"foreign, faded, full of ellipses"—is much like *Cranford*, and the novel constantly plays with "transient examples" and "knotted" stories. Its narrator is equally hard to read. At times she is very much the removed ethnographer, "trying to read (in the sense of 'construct a reading of')"; at other times, she seems the daughter of Cranford, not only telling stories she has heard others tell but describing the people she has known telling them. The attempts to tell the story of "Cranford" (the story of its stories) make *Cranford* a divided and deeply self-conscious novel, aware of itself as a document in ways critics have not really noticed.

This literary (self-)awareness is the real project of *Cranford*, but it is one specifically filtered by questions of gendered stories. The novel is most fully read as a woman writer's experiment with narrative, an extended commentary on the ways women are taught to read cultural signs, and a serious critique of the role of literature in shaping female readers. Literature is both a subject and an agent in this novel, but it is the particular literature women read; in *Cranford*, even the genres are gendered. The "multiplicity of structures," as Geertz calls them, are in *Cranford* a variety of texts, ranging from such domestic forms as instruction books, fashion guides, and letter writing to high literature in the form of poetry, epic, and encyclopedias. The literary awareness of *Cranford*—and the lack of awareness on the part of its "subjects"—is formed within a historical structure, but a structure precisely mediated by texts. In this world, books have created their readers; the languages characters have acquired limit their ability to express themselves or to move with changing times. Gaskell highlights this inversion not only to discuss the role of "literature" in shaping ideology but to examine her own fictional authority.

We can observe Gaskell's concern with "authority" by our attention to the "voice" of *Cranford*: significantly, the chief difference between "The Last Generation of England" and *Cranford* is in its narrator. The speaker in the essay registers no distance from "the author of *Mary Barton*": she begins,

> I must however say before going on, that although I choose to disguise my own identity, and to conceal the name of the town to which I refer, every circumstance and occurrence which I shall relate is strictly and truthfully told without exaggeration.

The narrator of *Cranford*, by contrast, is very much her own character, and the "story" of *Cranford*, to the extent that there is one, is in fact of her growth into her own voice. The novel's experiments with textuality—its layering of family letters, literary allusions, poetry, and failed bank notes—are paralleled by the evolution of the narrator: the increased definition of her voice and the active role she takes in the novel. She moves from anonymous reporter to amused reader and finally to manip-

ulator and fairy godmother, the perfect narrative "role" made concrete by
her actions. As the novel concludes, we realize that by telling the story of
the Amazons, "Mary Smith"—who had not looked at all like a character—has resolved her own choice of world and affiliations: to learn how
to narrate their story, which means renouncing narrative absolutism and
detached authority, is to understand and be able to conclude her own
story. Her transformation, like the lives of the Amazons in Cranford,
takes place in the marketed world of men but suggests finally a world of
female storytelling. Gaskell's attention to different kinds of reading suggests her growing awareness of the differences between female and male
writing, and of the uses of marginality in the market of fiction.

By the end of *Cranford*, we know what an Amazonian work would
look like. The idyll of *Cranford*, as place and text, is made possible by
female writing, both of and in the novel. But it is hard to read this as the
seamless "writing herself into the text" Cixous imagined; the writer's
movement into her text ("as into the world and into history") is a difficult
movement. The novel itself draws attention to the difficulties of this
idyll; as we investigate the specifics of Gaskell's attempts to write—and to
publish—her account, we realize the obstacles the (female) ethnographer/
novelist faces, as well as the triumph her movement represents. The
novelist, like the ethnographer, is part of history and part of her own
"story"; the attempt to tell her story at once encloses and discloses the
larger story, much as the story of authorship within *Cranford* makes
Cranford possible. And it is with a story of authors that *Cranford* begins.

i

> She had rather he had knocked her down, if he had only been
> reading a higher style of literature.

Our discussion of *Cranford* must begin with the novel's own beginning,
and with the story of its publication—both of which turn us to the figure
of Charles Dickens. *Cranford* was one of the first works Gaskell wrote
particularly for Dickens; several of the earlier stories he published had
probably been written before *Mary Barton*, and even the stories she
composed for *Household Words* seem revisions of her earlier works.
Cranford not only creates its own fictional world, it signals a new, more
confident narrative persona for Gaskell—and a new relationship with
Dickens. At that time, Dickens's journal had a readership and a kind of

glamour no other journal had; it remained for Gaskell to explore what it meant to be one of "his" writers.

The first number of *Cranford*, which is worth examining in some detail, in fact provides such an exploration. "Our Society at Cranford," in addition to introducing us to the genteel "Amazons," offers an extended meditation on women and their relationship to male texts—and to male models of textual relations. The comic struggles of Miss Jenkyns, the daughter of the rector and the owner of a number of manuscripts of sermons and a library of divinity, the maiden matriarch of the village of "Amazons," to command her own style and to decide "all questions of literature and politics" without troubling herself with "unnecessary reasons or arguments," become a gloss on the struggle of the woman writer to decide for herself without "reasons or arguments"—the struggle that will, in fact, mark Gaskell's own vexed relationship with Dickens in these years.

Significantly, the first number of *Cranford* (which Gaskell initially imagined as a short story, prompting her to kill off her favorite characters[11]) begins with a fight about authorship—specifically, a fight about Dickens. Isolated from the industrial town of Drumble to the north, the "Amazons" who "possess" Cranford have imputed moral superiority to their isolation, as they have turned their practical liability (single, older women, no longer wealthy or important in a masculine, modern, money-minded world) into its own kind of advantage. Into this aggressively female world, with its small rooms, "small slights," and "trivial ceremonies" comes Captain Brown, a brusque military man associated with the "obnoxious railroad." At a Cranford soirée he offers to read out loud from the latest number of *Pickwick*, which he considers a "capital thing" and "famously good." Miss Jenkyns says, "I must say, I don't think they are by any means equal to Dr Johnson," and the fight is on. She continues:

> "Still, perhaps, the author is young. Let him persevere, and who knows what he may become if he will take the great Doctor for his model."

It is, as Captain Brown remarks immediately, "quite a different sort of thing" that Dickens does; this becomes clear as soon as each reads an excerpt from the favored author. When Captain Brown reads the account of Sam Weller's "swarry" at Bath, the listeners "laugh heartily," the textual soirée enhancing their own party. But Miss Jenkyns resists Dickens: after sitting in "patient gravity" while the Captain reads, she turns to the narrator to ask "with mild dignity" that she be brought *Rasselas* "out of the bookroom," and begins to "read one of the conversa-

tions between Rasselas and Imlac, in a high-pitched majestic voice."
After concluding, she says, sounding Johnsonian herself, "I imagine I am
now justified in my preference of Dr Johnson as a writer of fiction," and
gives the argument "a finishing blow or two" by adding, "I consider it
vulgar, and below the dignity of literature, to publish in numbers."
Captain Brown asks quietly, "How was the *Rambler* published, ma'am?"
but Miss Jenkyns goes on.

> "Dr Johnson's style is a model for young beginners. My father recom-
> mended it to me when I began to write letters,—I have formed my own
> style upon it; I recommend it to your favourite."

And here Captain Brown goes too far, saying, "I should be very sorry for
him to exchange his style for any such pompous writing."

Miss Jenkyns's argument is at the heart of *Cranford*: "I have formed
my own style upon it." In a short passage, Gaskell has moved from
reader's response ("laughed heartily") to the economy of publication
("publishing in numbers") to a critique of the way texts shape their
readers. What Miss Jenkyns presents as mere "style," what looks like
"pomposity," is for her a connection as personal and immediate as any
literary affinity can be, and Captain Brown's criticism is indeed a "personal affront." But her "style" has in turn formed *her*:

> Epistolary writing, she and her friends considered as her *forte*. Many a
> copy of many a letter have I seen written and corrected on the slate, before
> she 'seized the half-hour just previous to post-time to assure' her friends of
> this or of that; and Dr Johnson was, as she said, her model in these
> compositions. She drew herself up with dignity and only replied to Captain
> Brown's last remark by saying, with marked emphasis on every syllable, 'I
> prefer Dr Johnson to Mr Boz.'
>   It is said—I won't vouch for the fact—that Captain Brown was heard to
> say *sotto voce*, 'D--n Dr Johnson!'

Captain Brown's retreat to epithet suggests the failure of his "favourite,"
but as the novel makes clear, the style of *her* favorite has betrayed
Deborah Jenkyns. The language in which her father taught her to write
her letters is one that the text never hesitates to mock gently. We are given
a sample of Miss Jenkyns's letter describing a visit from a lord to the
Browns, in which "Johnson" becomes a butcher, and which uses a prose
so Johnsonian as to approach (and to raise as a central question in the
novel) literary parody:

> Mrs Johnson, our civil butcher's wife, informs me that Miss Jessie pur-
> chased a leg of lamb; but, besides this, I can hear of no preparation

whatever to give a suitable reception to so distinguished a visitor. Perhaps they entertained him with "the feast of reason and the flow of soul," and to us, who are acquainted with Captain Brown's sad want of relish for "the pure wells of English undefiled," it may be matter for congratulation, that he has had the opportunity of improving his taste by holding converse with an elegant and refined member of the British aristocracy. But from some mundane failings who is altogether free? (p. 52)

The language, though rich, suggests no pleasure; nor does it allow for specific emotion. One might deduce Miss Jenkyns's personal pique in her rhetorical question, "From some mundane failings who is altogether free?" but the prose makes it impossible for her to describe her anger, and, further, evades its own responsibility—that of the "pure wells of English undefiled"—for her pain.[12]

All of Miss Jenkyns's aspirations for her life, everything her father led her to expect the world to provide, grew out of that prose style. She had meant, she once told her sister Matty, "to marry an archdeacon, and write his charges"; after her mother's death, she vowed "that if she had a hundred offers, she never would marry and leave my father." And she was, Miss Matty tells the narrator, "such a daughter to my father, as I think there never was before, or since. His eyes failed him, and she read book after book, and wrote, and copied, and was always at his service in any parish business. She could do many more things than my poor mother could; she even once wrote a letter to the bishop for my father. But he missed my mother sorely; the whole parish noticed it." And, as Miss Matty notes, when their brother Peter returned, "Deborah used to smile . . . and say she was quite put in a corner. Not but what my father always wanted her when there was letter-writing, or reading, to be done, or anything to be settled." A letter-writing daughter is not a wife, not a son, not even her own writer.

If this discussion focuses our attention on the ways women, in particular, read male writers, we must go on to consider the relationship of these texts to the woman writer, and here the presence of Dickens in the text highlights these concerns for Gaskell herself, suggesting the ways Gaskell too was not (or not yet, at least) her own writer, was "put in a corner." When Dickens published *Cranford* in *Household Words* he forced Gaskell to change the reference: to take his name out and to substitute Thomas Hood's.[13] Not only does the substitution sacrifice the connection between new literary style and new economic patterns in reducing the topicality of the reference but we lose the particularity of representative male writers battling it out. If Gaskell is suggesting the difficulty of a woman's taking her place in that arena, Dickens has demonstrated her

particular powerlessness in this instance. She was able to restore him to
the chapters when *Cranford* was published in book form, but she
resented fiercely his editorial imposition on the initial publication, and
there is evidence to suggest she tried to withdraw *Cranford* from
Household Words at the last minute, after learning of the proposed
change. The editorial involvement Dickens prided himself on often felt
like interference to Gaskell, and in most cases, as here, she has been
proven right. His insertion of Thomas Hood where she had included the
works of the Inimitable does not carry nearly the authority or the humor
she had intended.

Gaskell's fight with Dickens in fact focuses on questions of publicity:
on who will have control over his "name," who will be "the author."
Many of her quarrels with him through the years were over advertise-
ments of her own work. He wrote once to Wills that they were to
advertise *North and South* with an advertisement like that for *Hard
Times*, and warns that "B[radbury] and E[vans] must do what they think
necessary in the advertising way, but if they bill the walls, they must be
very careful only to have the plain, good, sensible bills used in the case of
'Hard Times,' that we had at the office. She . . . altogether refuses (and
no wonder) to be associated with a hideous placard all askew, invented in
Whitefriars for 'Hard Times.'"[14] Gaskell's modesty—and her distrust of
the flashiness she saw everywhere (hideous and all askew!) in Dickens—
provides reason enough for the differences over "bills," but even more to
the point here, it seems to me, is the question of who is to control
Dickens's name. Despite his professions of modesty, Dickens's name was
everywhere in the journal (and in its publicity)—and his was, of course,
the *only* name. All contributions to *Household Words* were anonymous—but Dickens's name ("conductor of Household Words") ran at the
top of every leaf; his imprint was everywhere; his voice was pervasive; and
indeed, his initial vision of the journal (as a shadow that would go inside
the homes of others, would—in *Dombey*'s phrase—"take the house-tops
off, . . . and show. . . .") suggests his desire precisely to intrude, silently,
but potently.

His approaches to Gaskell suggest a mixture of deference, innuendo,
and power that is somewhat disturbing, and that accentuates the issues of
modesty and revelation that might seem to have been the exclusive
province of the woman writer. His initial request that Gaskell contribute
to *Household Words*, in addition to stressing the anonymity of contribution ("no writer's name will be used, neither my own nor any other; every
paper shall be published without any signature"[15]) states that he "should
set a value on your help which your modesty can hardly imagine," but his

own habitual anxiety about modesty was that he might disappear behind it. And that meant that his name, while always suppressed and always there to be seen, was to be used *only* by him. As he wrote to Gaskell after changing her text for *Cranford*,

> Any recollection of me from your pen cannot (as I think you know) be otherwise than truly gratifying to me; but with my name on every page of Household Words, there would be—or at least I should feel—an impropriety in so mentioning myself. I was particular, in changing the author, to make it "Hood's *Poems*" in the most important place—I mean where the captain is killed—and I hope and trust that the substitution will not be any serious drawback to the paper in any eyes but yours. I would do anything rather than cause you a minute's vexation arising out of what has given me so much pleasure, and I sincerely beseech you to think better of it, and not to fancy that any shade has been thrown on your charming writing, by— The unfortunate but innocent.[16]

I quote this letter at such length to suggest some of how difficult it is to refute this address—its "reasons and arguments," to return to *Cranford*'s phrase. Dickens seems to argue without irony that it is precisely his "name on every page" that makes it impossible to "mention myself"— and to forget that it was another author mentioning him. He retains, of course, the right to rename himself at the end of the passage ("unfortunate but innocent" of what, precisely?) and to pose *his* pleasure against *her* vexation—his pleasure as reader, that is, must take precedence over hers as writer. One can imagine only too well Dickens's response to similar editorial interference with his "charming writing"—though the gendered implications of "charm" are such that the phrase could only rarely have been applied to him. Still, if it had been under such circumstances, one can assume that his response would have been much like Gaskell's characteristic response to *his* blandishments: that they were merely flattery, mere "soft sawdor." It is all very well for him to write, as he did,

> As to future work, I do assure you that you cannot write too much for Household Words, and have never yet written half enough. I receive you, ever, (if Mr Gaskell will allow me to say so) with open arms.[17]

Her "reception" seems, to me at least, to have been more mixed; his arms may have been open, but his pages were, in essential ways, closed to her.

The Dickensian "style," for literary daughters inside *and* outside the text, seems one that is not open to them—or at the least, makes problematic their assumption of any voice. The story of the novel's publication suggests the inability of women to realize their intentions in the market:

throughout these early chapters, Gaskell seems to be reflecting on the writer as a literary daughter, still struggling with the language her father gave her for—specifically—domestic (private, "charming") writing. Like Gaskell, Deborah Jenkyns cannot use the appropriate words. What is so absurd about her prose is simply that it is in the wrong place; if she were an archdeacon and writing up charges, if she were, as her sister imagines, writing advice books, the Johnsonian sentences she can toss off so easily would seem neither pompous nor inappropriate. Women have no room for the grand style in their writing, for they never write anything grand. Literary daughters are not given the language they need; rather, they are given languages, often dead languages, that mediate their experience for them. How could Miss Jenkyns write her story as *Rasselas*?—how could Gaskell hope to be Dickens, the "conductor"?

Miss Jenkyns's use of her inheritance, of Johnson, seems overdetermined in just these ways, and is marked by both gender and history. She has relied on the "higher style of literature" because it seems to remove her from her own life—from "elegant economy," from solitude, from the deaths and tragedies of her family. The Johnsonian voice is an attempt at the timeless, in the same way that Boz seems to be entirely of the moment. And this is to suggest the other question at stake in Gaskell's battle with Dickens: they are battling not only over name and publicity but over the relationship of literature to a changing world. Dickens is in *Cranford* not only as editor of *Household Words*, or as the humorous Boz, but as a representative of modern life.

Cranford (both the novel and its characters) connects Dickens with haste and urgency; Captain Brown walks through the streets so engrossed in his newest number of *Pickwick* that he all but runs into Miss Jenkyns. And in the climactic scene of the chapter, Captain Brown himself is run over by that most Dickensian of modern machines, the railroad that had run down Mr Carker in *Dombey and Son* a few years before Gaskell wrote *Cranford*. While "a-reading some new book as he was deep in," the Captain looked up to see a little girl cross a track, and "he darted on the line and cotched it up, and his foot slipped, and the train came over him in no time." The man who gives Miss Jenkyns the news seems to have something Dickensian in his prose, as well—the sentence has more connected phrases and more urgency than the usual Gaskell sentence. Not only is Brown destroyed by a symbol of the new world racing in on the Cranford that had "petitioned" against the railroads but his presentation as a reader of *Pickwick* makes Dickens himself seem the murdering engine. Much as the novel has seemed to generate its entire plot out of literary battles, here narrative revenge is enacted by a novel, as much as by the "novel[ty]" the train represents in Cranford.

That novelty is one suggested by a range of railway articles in *Household Words* during the period of *Cranford's* publication, among them "Railway Waifs and Strays" (28 December 1850), "Railway Strikes"—by Dickens himself (11 January 1851), "Indian Railroads and British Commerce" (15 March 1851), and "Cheap Excursion Trains" (5 July 1851).[18] The variety of issues suggested here—from colonialism to labor, commerce to tourism—suggests again the ways fiction participated in wider social transformations; *Household Words*, a journal that believed implicitly in progress, also attempts to make the world smaller for its readers. Like *Cranford*, it sees itself as poised on the brink of a changing world—in *Cranford*, a letter misses a character because there is no overland route to India for the post to travel on; the novel reaches a happy conclusion precisely because of "Indian railroads." Texts, like the readers we began with, are hurtling at new speeds; novels, letters, journals are suddenly on the road.

And so are characters, as we see in one of the stranger "train" articles in *Household Words*, one that also returns us unexpectedly to the question of Dickens's editorial modesty. "Railway Waifs and Strays," which appeared in the same number of the journal as Gaskell's story "The Heart of John Middleton," reports on lost items found on the train. But among the travelers described as losing belongings is Sairey Gamp—a fictional character, of course, from a novel by none other than Charles Dickens. Mrs Gamp appears "personified by a cotton umbrella with a tremendous horn-head"; she does not speak, she has no further story, but there she is, and she can be there to do little but remind readers of Dickens's role as author—and to play, somehow, with exactly those boundaries of realism and reality that Gaskell seemed to be teasing at with her reference to Boz. If Dickens objected to the inclusion of his creation in this essay by Wills and Hill, his objection has not survived; Mrs Gamp was allowed to appear, where Sam Weller was not.

There is something in the fluidity of Sairey's appearance here, however, that in fact seems very close to the textual fluidity *Cranford* achieves, something that suggests where Gaskell's almost inadvertent collaboration was to lead her. We see this in a passage that begins by blaming Dickens for Captain Brown's death, goes on to absorb (and rewrite) a Dickensian text into its own, and suggests the peculiar uses of parody and textual revision that will be the achievement of *Cranford* and its feminized text.

When the narrator returns to visit Miss Jenkyns on her deathbed, what she witnesses is in fact a textual encounter.

> "If Flora were not here to read to me, I hardly know how I should get through the day. Did you ever read the *Rambler*? It's a wonderful book— wonderful! and the most improving reading for Flora"—(which I dare say it would have been, if she could have read half the words without spelling, and could have understood the meaning of a third)—"better than that strange old book, with the queer name, poor Captain Brown was killed for reading—that book by Mr Boz, you know—'Old Poz;' when I was a girl— but that's a long time ago—I acted Lucy in 'Old Poz.'"—She babbled on long enough for Flora to get a good long spell at the *Christmas Carol*, which Miss Matty had left on the table. (p. 62)

Reading, even the *Rambler*, is the only consolation left for Miss Jenkyns, and a reader by now recognizes its private implications. The public value, all Miss Jenkyns can discuss, is still open to question, for how improving can it be for a younger world that cannot read "half the words without spelling" or "underst[and] the meaning of a third"? But for Miss Jenkyns, the book of her youth has become young again with her in her second childhood, "better than that strange old book, with the queer name." Here, her vision of literature exacts its own vengeance—only in Miss Jenkyns's mind was Captain Brown "killed for reading" *Pickwick*—but "Dickens" allows Miss Jenkyns to recapture her youth in another way; in her unexpectedly imaginative pun on "Boz" and "Poz" a happier, more frivolous Deborah is regained, acting "Lucy" in Maria Edgeworth's play "Old Poz." Dickens, though, has the last word: as Miss Jenkyns babbles on, young Flora gets in "a good long spell" at the *Christmas Carol*, clearly what she would prefer to be reading at the moment—and no doubt as improving as the barely understood, unpronounceable *Rambler*.

Gaskell's point of departure might be seen in this account of Miss Jenkyns's last scene: the rereading of Johnson through a character's reading of Dickens; the layering of texts and awareness of readers; a deliberately multi-vocal writing and reading in which we briefly can imagine the scene as it would be written by several authors.[19] This feeling of a layered text is implicit in the contrast between Dickens and Johnson, a contrast that, I have suggested, collapses in on itself in so many ways, as we learn that the writers are the same in that which they exclude. Gaskell's criticism of Johnson could itself have been inspired by the Johnson Dickens gives us in *Pickwick*: Garrett Stewart has quoted William Wimsatt on Johnson's "'smile behind the ponderosity, a ripple beneath the grave style,'" but has remarked further, "when Dickens gets hold of Johnsonian words, the smile breaks into laughter, the ripple becomes a complete ironic upheaval."[20] If what Gaskell learned from *Pickwick* was that "ironic upheaval," she could in turn both reveal and further displace Dickens himself. As we so often feel with Dickens, the process of reading and writing go on dialectically: through the parade of voices in the opening of *Cranford*, we can see a rare showiness in Gaskell's narrative, an awareness that she is at once taking her place among the male writers, and using that power to register her difference.

The Dickensian train that hurtles through what Gaskell thought would be the end of *Cranford*, murdering Captain Brown and then, somehow, redeeming the vision of Miss Jenkyns, seems to me a way of beginning to talk about the experiment of *Cranford*'s prose. By absorbing and rewriting Dickens, by including and dismissing the train and all the historical forces it represents, Gaskell begins to stake out the territory of technology, history, and narrative for the woman writer; she begins to ask how the woman writer will reread all of literature, and what force she will capture and reabsorb to make real her own literary and social vision. That revisioning is the province of *Cranford*.

ii

Forward, forward let us range,
Let the great world spin forever down the ringing grooves of change.
TENNYSON, "Locksley Hall"

As for the use of globes, I had never been able to find it out myself, so perhaps I was not a good judge of Miss Matty's capability of instructing in this branch of education; but it struck me that equators and tropics, and such mystical circles, were very imaginary lines indeed to her, and that she looked upon the signs of the Zodiac as so many remnants of the Black Art.

I suggested in the previous section that the train that ran down Carker in *Dombey and Son* resurfaces in *Cranford*, like a messenger from another novel, and—perhaps—from another social world, carrying with it the economic critique (and troubled sexuality) of the earlier novel. The train in *Cranford* most likely comes from Drumble, "the industrial center to the North," linked in Gaskell's autobiographical imaginings to Manchester, the industrial city she married into. But that train, with all its obvious phallic associations, can also be seen as arriving from France—whence, after all, Carker has returned when he meets his death-by-train. In that sense, the train represents modernity, industry, the power Cranford attempts to exclude, the forces of history—revolution and imperialism—that in *Cranford* are personified by the threat of things "French."

The presence of things French in *Cranford* matters so much precisely because of the energy it might otherwise seem—that critics have fiercely insisted—the novel exerts to *exclude* them. *Cranford* seems to turn its back on the "modern" world—and I am insisting here, to the contrary, that it also persistently reinscribes history and the modern—in the text. Cranford, as a village, takes its meaning from its transitory nature; it is on its way toward disappearance, about to be run down by the train that will, in the phrase Wolfgang Schivelbusch uses to sum up the nineteenth-century attitude toward the changes of the railway, "annihilate time and space."[21]

It should not, then, surprise us that history is present—both in its explicit inclusion and in the traces of its exclusion—in the novel. History (in the sense of events, change, and narrative) is the unconscious of this text, but it surfaces in anecdotes, in memory, and in the narrative interruptions that dot the text. In this novel, "history" is male; it is colonial; it is French; it is to be feared.

It also requires a different kind of narrative, and in this section I will discuss the difference the novel itself posits between men's and women's realms, and the two ways of *reading* that these worlds demand. If men in the novel live in history, women live largely in silence. Despite the constant "chatter" that makes up *Cranford*, we can hardly hear the woman's story, and to read for it, we must read what Gaskell calls the "effort at concealment"; we must notice when it is busily *not* being told. The "men's story," similarly, is hardly told, but that is because it is too obvious to need (bear) repetition: it is the story of history, and it is written by Napoleon, by revolutions, by market crashes. But these crashes are only echoes in *Cranford*, and our efforts at reading the "history" of "history" in the text similarly commits us to reading what the novel often wants to conceal. The masculine history of the text asks us to read what it mentions casually; the feminine story asks us to read what it studiously avoids. The question for our purposes here is both how do these two "texts" come together to form *Cranford*, and how does the novel imagine the role of literature (as it has been made a self-conscious object in the opening chapters) in mediating between the two novels *Cranford* could be?

History, in the phrase of Siegfried Kracauer, is the "last things before the last,"[22] and that would seem to be the "moment" of *Cranford*. If this is the "last generation in England," last in the sense of one-before-us, it is also the last of its kind, and perhaps the last "English" generation—as it seems at times, in the vast expanse of globe the novel hints at conjuring. The fear of the-end-of-England is teased at in the novel, specifically in the fear of Napoleonic invasion that remains into the 1840s. One of Miss Jenkyns's letters—one of the few in "pretty intelligible English," as the narrator recounts—centers on her fear of Boney's troops; a real fear, as Miss Matty in turn recounts, for "I know I used to wake up in the night many a time, and think I heard the tramp of the French entering Cranford" (p. 91).

The French enter—or at least, their entrance is feared—again in the novel, when a series of events (petty thefts, unaccounted-for vagrants, foreigners) convince the Amazons that "men in dark clothes [were] going round the town, no doubt in search of some unwatched house or some unfastened door" (p. 138). The insularity of Cranford insists "it must have been a stranger or strangers who brought this disgrace upon the town, and occasioned as many precautions as if we were living among the Red Indians or the French." Mrs Forrester, whose father served under General Burgoyne in the American war, and whose husband had fought the French in Spain, draws the latter comparison most strongly:

> She indeed inclined to the idea that, in some way, the French were connected with the small thefts, which were ascertained facts, and the burglaries and highway robberies, which were rumors. She had been deeply impressed with the idea of French spies, at some time in her life; and the notion could never be fairly eradicated, but sprang up again from time to time. And now her theory was this: the Cranford people respected themselves too much, and were too grateful to the aristocracy who were so kind as to live near the town, ever to disgrace their bringing up by being dishonest or immoral; therefore, we must believe that the robbers were strangers—if strangers, why not foreigners?—if foreigners, who so likely as the French? Signor Brunoni spoke broken English like a Frenchman and, though he wore a turban like a Turk, Mrs Forrester had seen a print of Madame de Staël with a turban on, and another of Mr Denon in just such a dress as that in which the conjuror had made his appearance; showing clearly that the French, as well as the Turks, wore turbans: there could be no doubt Signor Brunoni was a Frenchman—a French spy, come to discover the weak and undefended places of England. (p. 139)

This description touches on so many of the central concerns of Cranford—unusual dress and broken English are sure signs of social disorder in the village—that it suggests the "weak and undefended places" are *so* fragile that a turban and an accent could disrupt all that is "English," but it also suggests the way history enters—and is interpreted—for the inhabitants. Events are recounted by anecdote; past events are filtered by family affection (Mrs Forrester's father and husband *are* historians, for her); history in fact *happens* only to people who somehow step outside their community, for "Cranford people," who "respected themselves too much, and were too grateful to the aristocracy who were so kind as to live near the town, ever to disgrace their bringing up by being dishonest or immoral," also could not make history. Their history consists in not doing anything but being grateful, respectful, and "living near"—continuing the connections of the past.

The French, on the other hand, represent the possibility of revolution, the threat of change and invasion that must lie somewhere beyond Gaskell's gently mocking choice of the "Amazons" as her heroines. Paris, as one character puts it, is the "wicked" city "where they are always having revolutions" (p. 81). Miss Matty remarks that Mr Holbrook ought not to visit there, for "I don't believe frogs will agree with him; he used to have to be very careful what he ate" (p. 78); after he becomes ill, his cousin remarks that Paris will have "much to answer for, if it's killed my cousin Thomas," and indeed it seems to have done so. France, whether exporting frogs or trains or emperors, is deadly to the inhabitants of Cranford. The Cranford shopkeeper must learn not to tell his clients clothes come from Paris, for his customers are "too patriotic and John Bullish to wear what the Mounseers wore" (pp. 105–106); even one's fashion-identity is at risk from foreignness, and the ideal (Cranfordian) fashioned-self is one that never changes. Miss Barker, who used to keep a shop, is the finest-dressed lady in Cranford, for she is (five or six years after giving up shop) "wearing out all the bonnets and caps, and outrageous ribbons, which had once formed her stock in trade" (p. 106). "In any other place than Cranford her dress might have been considered *passée*," but the point of dress in Cranford is not to reveal history; fashion is not historical because it has its own history—one of personal history or of individual connections ("once formed") or of the individual meaning within the community but never of the "wicked" revolutionary traces of, say, France.

Given the exclusion, then, of visible counters in the game (events, invasions, fashion) how is one to even locate an *histoire* in *Cranford*? The history of Cranford (and it is clearly a woman's story) is one without clearly readable events; it is one read, in one of Gaskell's lightest phrases, in the "effort of concealment," in the avoidance of certain topics, the ordering of unusual caps, the repetition of odd phrases.

Characteristically, and significantly, Gaskell places the woman's version of history within a romance, but in *Cranford*, this is a romance that cannot narrate itself, a romance of missed opportunities and unspoken affection. Practically speaking, the narrative immerses us in the detail; we are forced to read the way Gaskell argues women read. The text does not argue that women have an inherently (naturally) closer relationship to the "detail" or to silence; rather, that they have been unable to write (or to live) out loud. Hence, what *Cranford* presents is a story that is itself almost absent, and that commits us to the most particularized kind of reading.

In two chapters, "A Love Affair of Long Ago" and "A Visit to an Old Bachelor," which appeared together in *Household Words* as "A Love Affair at Cranford," Miss Matty's old lover, Mr Holbrook, returns after a long absence. As in the first chapter, which set its terms through reading "high literature," the story here is mediated—by reportage, by literary allusion, by speculation. The primary narrative mode is indirection, and information—events themselves—registered by absence. The narrator learns from Miss Pole, cousin to Mr Holbrook, that Miss Matty may once have loved him, and may have turned down his proposal of marriage because he "would not have been enough of a gentleman for the rector and Miss Jenkyns." "They were not to marry him," our narrator says "impatiently," but she subsequently meets Mr Holbrook when out with Miss Matty, and becomes convinced that Miss Matty had, in fact, been in love with him long ago, and never recovered from turning down his "offer." But because Miss Matty did not tell Mary about the "love affair," Mary is never free to mention it herself, or even to ask about it. Not only does Miss Matty's "affection" stay a secret but narrative knowledge is secret; Mary Smith is a closet narrator, and the role of literature is to present secrets as somehow intact in their secrecy. We, too, must believe that we cannot pry or ask too much.

These passages, in a way, ask us to "read like a woman," carrying through *Ruth*'s intuition that men and women encounter different books when they sit down to read. The novel's best "reader" is Mr Holbrook, who is depicted almost exclusively through "literary" conversations, but whose reading is marked within the text as masculine. For him, again as *Ruth* suggests, life is immersed within literature, and reading is itself an activity; Miss Pole says that "he read aloud more beautifully and with more feeling than any one she had ever heard, except the late rector" (p. 69). When the narrator first sees him, she sees a "tall, thin, Don Quixote–looking old man." He invites Miss Pole, Miss Matty, and Mary to spend a day at his house, where he has "six-and-twenty cows, named after the different letters of the alphabet." While he and the narrator walk around his garden, he surprises her "by repeating apt and beautiful quotations from the poets, ranging easily from Shakespeare and George Herbert to those of our own day," "as naturally as if he were thinking aloud" (p. 73). His sitting room is filled with books "of all kinds,—poetry, and wild weird tales prevailing," and his deepest passion is for Tennyson, in whom he sees a nature made more real, visible to him for the first time.

In fact, the closest we come to a scene of romance in the novel is when Miss Matty, Miss Pole, and the narrator sit in his sitting room and he reads Tennyson out loud—but not the poems of nature ("what colour are ash-buds in March," he has impatiently asked Mary Smith, who he feels does not know the depths of Tennyson's descriptions) but "Locksley Hall," which depicts a marriage ruined by familial interference and female weakness. But the poem, too, seems to miss its audience: Miss Pole encourages him to read, because she has reached a difficult part in her crocheting and wants to count stitches; Miss Matty falls asleep, only to awaken and declare, with singular inappropriateness, that it is a "pretty book" and like a poem of Dr Johnson's her sister used to read—a poem that it can resemble only in its soporific quality. The violent passion of the narrator of "Locksley Hall" seems to be out of place in *Cranford* as the pessimism of "The Vanity of Human Wishes," and in any event, both *expressions* of pain are inaccessible to the women—certainly to Miss Matty, baffled by high literary language as she is, and to Miss Pole, caught up in the domesticity of missed stitches, to whom this is all just "beautiful reading."

But the conclusion of this romance has a quiet violence of tragic loss, one completely unlike the ferocity of a Napoleonic invasion or a Tennyson narrator, but one that is felt deeply in the daily rhythms of Cranford. For days after her visit to Holbrook's farm, Miss Matty sits by the window in her best cap, "in order to see, without being seen, down into the street." She never speaks "of any former and more intimate acquaintance with Mr Holbrook." The narrator speculates that "she had probably met with so little sympathy in her early love, that she had shut it up close in her heart; and it was only by a sort of watching, which I could hardly avoid since Miss Pole's confidence, that I saw how faithful her poor heart had been in its sorrow and its silence." He comes once to visit her, before he leaves for Paris, and gives her only Tennyson, "the poems . . . you admired so much the other evening," his assumption of her pleasure as painful as his assumption of her complicity in rejecting him.

The alternative to his blindness—a blindness in which Tennyson and "Locksley Hall" seem implicated as well—is the kind of delicate narration ("a sort of watching") *Cranford* depends on so much, and that works to such effect. Miss Matty's maid writes to tell Mary Smith that Miss Matty is "very low and sadly off her food"; Mary comes back to visit, only to discover that Miss Matty has been "into this moping way" since Miss Pole's visit on Tuesday; Miss Pole tells Mary that she had told Miss Matty "a fortnight or more ago" that Mr Holbrook has been ill since his journey to Paris, and has not long to live. Finally, the narrative moves back to Miss Matty herself, but even then the narrator does not confront Miss Matty with what she—and we—believe to be the truth: "I did not say anything. I felt almost guilty of having spied too curiously into that tender heart, and I was not going to speak of its secrets,—hidden, Miss Matty believed, from all the world." Miss Matty does recount how her sister had nursed her "through a long, long illness, of which I had never heard before, but which I now dated in my own mind as following the dismissal of the suit of Mr Holbrook." But despite the narrator's conclusion, nothing is said directly; rather, the two women "talked softly and quietly of old times, through the long November evening." The next day, they learn of Mr Holbrook's death, and since Miss Matty *says* nothing to Miss Pole, "I have no doubt Miss Pole thought Miss Matty received the news calmly," though "she was trembling so nervously . . . she could not speak."

And Miss Matty never does speak: "she has never alluded to Mr Holbrook again, although the book he gave her lies with her Bible on the little table by her bedside."

> She did not think I heard her when she asked the little milliner of Cranford to make her caps something like the Honourable Mrs Jamieson's, or that I noticed the reply—
>
> "But she wears widows' caps, ma'am?"
>
> "Oh! I only meant something in that style; not widows' of course, but rather like Mrs Jamieson's."
>
> This effort of concealment was the beginning of the tremulous motion of head and hands which I have seen ever since in Miss Matty. (p. 81)

"This effort of concealment" is respected by the narrator, though she never misses a chance to overhear what she can, but that, in a sense, is the text's "effort": only by studying the concealment can we see the story at all.

Cranford argues, then, that while men read, attentively, in the book of nature and in Tennyson's poetry, moving from their understanding of one to the other and back, what women read is the feelings of others: that the narrator's attention to Miss Matty parallels Mr Holbrook's careful study of "ash-buds." This seems a dangerous argument, leaving to women the domestic, to men the natural and literary worlds as texts. But Gaskell distinguishes carefully between the naive response of Miss Matty and the more mixed responses of the narrator, who both listens to "Locksley Hall" and watches Miss Matty. Mr Holbrook cannot do both—the reader of *Cranford*, like Mary Smith, can. And, in fact, we are forced to, by Gaskell's own movement between allusions to Tennyson and "concealed feelings." What Miss Matty's inattention to "Locksley Hall" reveals is not that women don't read, can't read, needn't read poetry, but that the gaps in her ability to question her experience—the simplicity that led her to believe her sister's claims to gentility and to higher knowledge—are *mirrored* exactly in the picture Tennyson gives of his heroine's simplicity and in his inability to give the woman in the poem a voice, mirrored in a way we must acknowledge before we can imagine how literature could give Miss Matty a voice for her secret life. The rantings of Tennyson's hero are uninterrupted by his "gentle cousin's" side of the story; Gaskell suggests that that story can be told, at least at this moment in the sheltered Amazonian world of Cranford, only through the history of the "concealment," writing what wasn't said. Those silenced might be given a voice in a different kind of fiction, one that gave space to that silence, attention to what they cannot say.

But, one might still ask, is that concealment a history, and what is its relation to the overt (eventful) history of France, "where they are always having revolutions"? Moving as Miss Matty's history is, it is hardly earthshaking, and hardly seems to exist in time; romance, we might be tempted to say, exists outside history. But that question returns us again to the problem of history in Cranford. History in this novel, as in the village, seems to be textualized; events rendered anecdotal; truth conveyed not only in stories but *as* story. So, when Peter Jenkyns begins to tell his stories of his travels in India, the women "liked him the better, indeed, for being what they called 'so very Oriental'" (p. 211)—history here is filtered by literary structures, and he becomes part of an Oriental tale, conventionalized, inserted at once into literary and colonial history.

Thus *Cranford* seems to want both things: to point out the different *realms* in which men and women "make" history, and the way all history/ histories are written into culture, through texts and textual understandings. Just as the train reaches us through its literary predecessors, and Miss Matty's story through the echoes of "Locksley Hall," at once registering its differences from its predecessors and rewriting its predecessors, so *Cranford*'s attention to its own telling rewrites the history of stories. Its veerings from one form to another, its wavering from male to female history, its movements from nostalgia to contemporaneity ("Do you ever see cows dressed in grey flannel in London?") form their own commentary on fiction and conventional understanding. Its patchwork qualities of narration, to which I will turn next, suggest that Gaskell's persistent question (How is a story to be told?) turns here on questions of technology, memory, and gender, and on history itself as a *memoir* of styles.

iii

I conceive that words are like money, not the worse for being common, but that it is the stamp of custom alone that gives them circulation or value.

HAZLITT, "On Familiar Style"

If, in the progress of *Cranford*, what looked to be history becomes another story of (about) texts, at the same time the "text" of Cranford, both as village and as novella to be published—by Dickens, in *Household Words*, in the early 1850s—seems increasingly to be written *by* history. To pose the problem of Cranford in/as history, in this particular way, returns us again to the problem(s) of its initial publication, but even more to its somewhat queasy status as itself a document, as not quite a novel, as near (with its Amazons and its chatty narrator) fable, as a history of what doesn't exist, as a memoir of what we all think (want to believe?) once existed. The nostalgia that has marked the response of readers over the years, a nostalgia that quite misses the point of Gaskell's humor and sadness, is not only for the facts of *Cranford*—an odd locution in itself— but for the facticity of its form, its status as field report, its mediated position as speaking for what doesn't exist, from what Lennard Davis has called the "known unknown"[23] places of fiction. As Susan Stewart has remarked of nostalgia in literature:

By the narrative process of a nostalgic reconstruction the present is denied and the past takes on an authenticity of being, an authenticity which, ironically, it can achieve only through nostalgia. . . . The realization of re-union imagined by the nostalgic is a narrative utopia that works only by virtue of its partiality, its lack of fixity and closure: nostalgia is the desire for desire.[24]

In *Cranford*, that desire for closure is repeatedly thematized not only by the ways in which the novel defeats novelistic expectations (it doesn't, as should be clear by now, have a plot, and can barely be said to have characters) but by the way its form "imagines" the "re-union" of which Stewart speaks. In *Cranford*, re-union is marked by its "partiality, its lack of fixity and closure," by its quality of collection, museum piece, anthology, its encyclopedia of readers and reading experiences.

The literary form most evident as collection in *Cranford* is the letter, and two chapters are given over to the narrator's nights spent reading and burning family letters with Miss Matty. Letters stand as an exemplum (a microcosm?) of the kind of text I am arguing *Cranford* becomes, one created by a variety of readers and readerly responses described within the text, one that demands a variety of forms and languages. To quote Stewart again,

> Hence we can see the many narratives that dream of the inanimate-made-animate as symptomatic of all narrative's desire to invent a realizable world, a world which "works." In this sense, every narrative is a miniature and every book a microcosm, for such forms always seek to finalize, bring closure, a totality or model. (xi–xii)

In *Cranford*'s invention (its experiment with the "realizable world") it at once flirts with totality and rejects it; in the letters that make up one of its microcosmic narratives, we see again both its commitment to the fragmentary, and its desire for something more "final," both its nostalgia and its movement toward something new.

The letters illuminate Miss Matty's family history at the same time that they suggest varieties of relationships to writing, ranging from the rector's impetuous letters to his young fiancée to his later formal letters to his idealized wife; from that wife's first letters requesting an elaborate trousseau to her joyful letters as a young mother; from Miss Jenkyns's "instructive" letters about theological disputes to her anxious letter about fears of a Napoleonic invasion; from the "show letters" that Peter Jenkyns, the long-absent son, writes when at school to his tear-spattered letter begging that his mother forgive him his bad behavior. From these fragments of letters—we get very few long excerpts—a whole family history becomes clear.

These letters are being read so they can be destroyed; Miss Matty feels it "a necessity" that they not be allowed to "fall into the hands of strangers," for they contain too much of her life within them. The letters are burned, one after another, and the women "watch each blaze up, die out, and rise away, in faint, white, ghostly semblance." But as the women continue, the letters seem increasingly a "ghostly semblance," even before burning. They already seem at one remove: they have been labeled by Miss Deborah, with "dockets" like

> "Letter of pious congratulation and exhortation from my venerable grandfather to my beloved mother, on occasion of my own birth. Also some practical remarks on the desirability of keeping warm the extremities of infants, from my excellent grandmother." (pp. 86–87)

This letter is the sisters' grandfather's "severe and forcible picture of the responsibilities of mothers, and a warning against the evils that were in the world, and lay in ghastly wait for the little baby of two days old." The grandfather has forbidden his wife to write, "she being indisposed with a sprained ankle, which (he said) quite incapacitated her from holding a pen." But she has, in fact, added a letter to "'my dear, dearest Molly,'" begging her, when she left the room, whatever she did to go *up* stairs before going *down*: and telling her to wrap her baby's feet up in flannel, and keep it warm by the fire, although it was summer, for babies were so tender." This play about writing adds that "ghostly semblance"—a kind of doubling—to the original letter *and* its comment, but so, too, do the emotions and present knowledge of the readers double the texts: in Mrs Jenkyns's first letter after Deborah's birth, she writes that "it was 'the prettiest little baby that ever was seen. Dear mother, I wish you could see her! Without any parshality, I do think she will grow up a regular bewty!' I thought of Miss Jenkyns, grey, withered, and wrinkled; and I wondered if her mother had known her in the courts of heaven; and then I knew that she had, and that they stood there in angelic guise" (p. 87).

As earlier, when Miss Jenkyns's letter about the visit the lord paid to Captain Brown offered little useful information to the absent narrator, so here the dichotomy between formal, correct, abstract correspondence and casually spelled, carelessly written but deeply felt and detailed letters is resolved in favor of the latter, more often female, text. Though Miss Jenkyns's mother can barely spell, this is a model letter, unlike the letter her father sends to her in which she (his "Molly") is "idealized" into "Maria" in a classical poem—this letter is tagged by Mrs Jenkyns, "'Hebrew verses sent me by my honoured husband. I thowt to have had a letter about killing the pig, but must wait.'" Her "letters back" to him—filled with news of how Deborah sewed her seam very neatly and how Miss Matty promised to be a great beauty—must, Gaskell says, have been "more satisfactory to an absent husband and father than his could ever have been to her." Further, they have held their power of affectionate transformation: after Miss Matty hears her mother's hope that "little

Matty might not be vain even if she were a bewty," she "soon afterwards adjust[s] her cap and draw[s] herself up." Her mother's praise of her "bewty" gives her back some dignity.

But the letters also offer a model of failed communication, of "partial" understandings destroyed by time and distance, both of which letters seemed to promise to overcome. When Peter, after playing a hoax on his family, is beaten by his father and decides to run off, letters do not reach him, messages of love and sorrow do not bring him home. We see the letter his mother has written to him, hoping to catch him at the house of a schoolfellow, a letter no one but the writer had ever seen before; its simple pleading might move us, but it never had the chance to move its intended recipient. Similarly, the captain of the ship Peter joined in Liverpool "summoned the father and mother to Liverpool instantly, if they wished to see their boy; and by some of the wild chances of life, the captain's letter had been detained somewhere, somehow." Though the family sets off to see him, "Oh! my dear, they were too late—the ship was gone!" And as his mother is dying, she breaks down and cries, and would "give us message after message for Peter—(his ship had gone to the Mediterranean, or somewhere down there, and then he was ordered off to India, and there was no overland route then)." The mails come to represent the gaps in communication; even when Peter sends a shawl to his mother, it arrives a day too late, and without having seen it, she is buried in it.

The letter, then, takes on the qualities of time (the ambivalence of absence and presence) we have seen elsewhere in *Cranford*'s uneasy history; as Susan Stewart comments on Michel Butor's account in *Inventory*, "Butor goes on to say that in reading dialogue and in reading letters embedded in the text, we are aware of 'going the same speed as' the characters of the novel. . . . In the simultaneity of print, with its rather remarkable capacity for storing information, we find an increasingly complex set of time systems" (p. 9). Letters promise us the time of the "characters" within the "novel"—which is to say, they promise us a more historical sense of the "time" (la durée) of the text. We can tell ourselves we are reading *just as* Mary Smith and Miss Matty are.

But in fact, *Cranford* reminds us equally carefully that we *cannot* share that history. Take, for example, the pleasure Miss Matty experiences in reading her sister's letters, which she holds up as a model (quite equal to Mrs Chapone and Mrs Carter!) and which "she would not let be carelessly passed over with any quiet reading, and skipping, to myself." Her pleasure is emphatically not shared by the narrator, for the letters are, of course, quite "sesquipedalian" and cross-written, and the narrator writes,

"How I wanted facts instead of reflections, before those letters were concluded! They lasted us two nights; and I won't deny that I made use of the time to think of many other things, and yet I was always at my post at the end of each sentence" (p. 90). But Miss Matty's pleasure is both absurd (unshared) and deeply moving (and hence, shared); our reading depends on her response. It hurts her to burn these, for "she said all the others had been only interesting to those who loved the writers; and that it seemed as if it would have hurt her to allow them to fall into the hands of strangers, who had not known her dear mother, and how good she was, although she did not always spell quite in the modern fashion; but Deborah's letters were so very superior! Any one might profit by reading them." In *Cranford*, letters are clearly not for the "profit" of Miss Deborah's instruction but for those who "love" the writers. The novel marks itself carefully as the one place where strangers can learn to know your dear mother and to understand her spelling, and where "superior" letters are of considerably less interest. But the novel also refuses to mock Miss Matty's love for her "superior" sister; even if Matty, in reading, transforms "Herod, Tetrarch of Idumea" into "Herod Petrarch of Etruria," she "was just as well pleased as if she had been right," and in this novel, it doesn't really matter, for the joke is as much on Herod, or Petrarch, or even on us, as on her.

The history constituted by letters, then, works only partially as documentary. The letters matter in their material state (tear-stained, sea-stained, docketed, and tied) and they matter for their relation to their readers. Much as we piece together their stories, so their readers *create* them; as Miss Matty says to Mary as she goes to tell the story of Peter's humiliation and flight, "Put out the candle, my dear; I can talk better in the dark." If this is history, it is domestic, quiet, shadowy; it gives a new depth to the term "familiar letter," the letter that (like the text of *Cranford*, in its fabulist history) establishes a different relationship with the reader, that values gaps and silences, misspellings and awkward phrasings, that brings back the dead parent, the lost beauty, the "parshality" of a mother. This seems, in *Cranford*, to be the woman's letter; Mary describes her father's letter as "just a man's letter; I mean it was very dull, and gave no information beyond that he was well, that they had had a good deal of rain, that trade was very stagnant, and there were many disagreeable rumours afloat" (p. 172). She says of herself later, ironically, "But I was right. I think that must be an hereditary quality, for my father says he is scarcely ever wrong" (p. 204); as we have seen, in the "family letter" that *Cranford* becomes, being "right" matters less than what Mary says of letters she reads:

There was in them a vivid and intense sense of the present time, which seemed so strong and full, as if it could never pass away, and as if the warm, living hearts that so expressed themselves could never die, and be as nothing to the sunny earth. I should have felt less melancholy, I believe, if the letters had been more so. (p. 85)

That sense of "present time," read at the moment when it is already passed, is both what is "melancholy," and what is "living" in the letters; it is exactly that delicacy, poised between nostalgia and realism, *Cranford* achieves.

This mediatory power of letters suggests something further about reading in *Cranford*. It is Mary Smith, as she sits and reads the letters out loud before their burning, and who "vibrated all my life between Drumble and Cranford," who will mediate (just as, I will suggest in the next section, her entire narration does) between the Cranfordians, living and dead, and their non-Cranfordian readers; the letters suggest not only the ambivalence of the realism of *Cranford* but the dialectical relation of texts and readers. The novel needs, then, to place its readers carefully in time and space. The realism of *Cranford* extends to the bodies of its readers; *Cranford* attends to the physical presence of its readers and to the "places" (known or unknown) from which they read. In *Cranford*, when someone sits down to read, we know whether she is reading out loud or silently, in the dark or the light, alone or in a group. Just as the "texts" are embodied—letters have tearstains; descriptions of natural objects in poems are held up immediately against the natural world—in *Cranford*, readers and listeners even fall asleep. If the slightly perplexing generic history we have been giving the novel (novella? fable? report from the field?) seemed to complicate the gentle structure of *Cranford*, no less so does its portrait of possible readers, from the overinvolved Captain Brown, and his readerly train, to Miss Pole counting her stitches to the rhythms of "Locksley Hall," to Miss Matty, left to doze peacefully through her poem. Reading becomes as individual an act as writing in *Cranford*—and as determining; to read is at once to be read by and to rewrite a text.

To say, then, that *Cranford* is a novel about reading is hardly to present a theoretical argument. It is to say something quite precise about readers—and authors—in the 1850s, and particularly to say something about the way *women* read. One of the most humorous episodes of textual explanation provides a telling description of mediated experience in general, and women's relation to reading in particular. When a magic show comes to Cranford, one of the Amazons shows a reluctance to accept it as magic; instead, she goes immediately to an encyclopedia to "nouns beginning with C," in order that she "might prime herself with scientific explanation for the tricks of the following evening." "Tricks" seems to be one area where encyclopedias would prove useless as explanatory tools: surely what baffles the eye would baffle encyclopedists and "science." But what Miss Pole finds—before she has seen the conjuror, of course—explains everything to her:

> "Ah! I see; I comprehend perfectly. A represents the ball. Put A between B and D—no! between C and F, and turn the second joint of the third finger of your left hand over wrist of your right H. Very clear indeed! My dear Mrs Forrester, conjuring and witchcraft is a mere affair of the alphabet. Do let me read you this one passage?"
>
> Mrs Forrester implored Miss Pole to spare her, saying, from a child upwards, she never could understand being read aloud to. (p. 132)

The account of Miss Pole is amusing, and understandable—a fear of being trapped or taken in by experience leading one to read up on something, to master the "mere affair of the alphabet." But it does not, in fact, help her at all. Though she reads aloud throughout the magic show "the separate 'receipts' for the most common of his tricks," she doesn't succeed in convincing anyone that "anybody could do them with just a little practice—and that she would, herself, undertake to do all he did, with two hours given to study the Encyclopedia and make her third finger flexible" (p. 135). Further, of course, she misses a wonderful show; she is "more engrossed with her receipts and diagrams than with his tricks." This is the fear of a literary model linked to Johnson and the Dictionary, to a male-centered, alphabetized, totally explanatory, closed text: we will become engrossed with form ("receipts and diagrams") and not only miss the fun but lose the chance to see for ourselves. Like Miss Jenkyns, we will be able to "reflect" but not communicate.

The joke in *Cranford* is on the witchcraft of writing—what we might now call mystification. "Very clear indeed! . . . Conjuring and witchcraft is a mere affair of the alphabet." Turning to encyclopedias—or fashion guides, or books of baronetcy—to explain the world is futile. One might laugh at Cranford itself for its rigid following of codes like fashion books or guides to manners, for of course all its guidebooks are out-of-date— remember Miss Betty, the former shopkeeper, and the best-dressed lady in Cranford, busily "wearing out all the bonnets and caps, and outrageous ribbons" that had formed her stock in trade five or six years ago. But *all* such codes begin to seem arbitrary. They are codes only because they are agreed on; no one in Cranford is out-of-date, because all the out-of-date fashions are accepted as *à la mode*. And if these systems of textual information are arbitrary, like Mr Holbrook's cows named "A through Z," then agreement about literature, as well, begins to seem a question of communities. If the systems that the Amazons follow so religiously seem absurd to us, then so, too, must the codes of the outside world. Signs and sign systems work because they are shared (because they create a readable world), but when they become rigid, like those of Cranford, they begin to close in upon experience in more threatening ways.

As I have suggested, this argument is not restricted to an abstract literary realm; it is one deliberately connected to social and economic codes that were very much on Gaskell's mind in the early 1850s. The rigidity of "sign systems" in *Cranford* returns us to the social code at the heart of the novel, the one that defines both Cranford and the Amazonians: the code that designates the single women "superfluous." To have given Miss Matty and Miss Jenkyns their own novel is to have begun to break those codes,[25] but *Cranford* goes further; it links their restricted lives precisely *to* literary (novelistic) conventions. When one thinks of Deborah Jenkyns with her useless literary skills, reduced to writing Johnsonian epistles on what the butcher sold Miss Brown, one locates some of Gaskell's resentment at the codification of experience: Miss Jenkyns has indeed been cut off by society from leading a fuller life, for she should have been an archdeacon herself. But when one sees further the ways in which her own experience of that language has shaped Miss Jenkyns's expectations for her own life, one includes all literary systems in the indictment. If Miss Jenkyns's aspirations for her life did grow out of that prose style, and what her father told her it would do, then isn't "style" responsible for her limitations? Thinking of her letters, and "how I wanted facts instead of reflections, before those letters were concluded!" one senses the ways literary signs—mere affairs of alphabet—shape the individual perception, mediate experience for us, limit the ways we read and hence write our own lives. Miss Pole's account of "A represents the ball. Put A between B and D—no! between C and F" is very funny, but has nothing to do with the magic she sees; Miss Jenkyns's "sesquipedalian" and cross-written letters have little to do with the changing pattern of her life. The gap between experience and writing seems immeasurable here; even the description of the fingers doing magic begins to seem like a description of the fingers forming characters of the alphabet, only signs, separate from any signifying power or significance. At this point, we may protest, like Mrs Forrester, that we "never could understand being read aloud to."

iv

Mary Carmichael, I thought, still hovering at a little distance above
the page, will have her work cut out for her merely as an observer.

VIRGINIA WOOLF, *A Room of One's Own*

How, though, is the woman writer to counter the literary experience of
always, only "being read aloud to"? These concerns with mediation of
experience, the voice of instruction, and the relationship of reader to text
lead Gaskell to a new awareness of narration itself. And narrative experimentation was the order of the day. At the same time that Gaskell was
publishing *Cranford* in *Household Words*, Dickens was publishing *Bleak
House*, which engages many of the same questions of who is to *tell* the
reader the story, and who thus tells the reader how to read—questions
that inform such other novels of the period as *Villette* and *The Tenant of
Wildfell Hall* as well. But Gaskell's concern with the voice of instruction,
and with the voice of "authority," has another, perhaps more immediate
Dickensian analogy: with *The Pickwick Papers*, the work she invoked in
her opening chapter.

Cranford can be read as a female version of *Pickwick*: in its spirit of
"benevolence," its focus on social gatherings and "swarrys," and its preoc-
cupations with "bachelorhood," it seems a comment on the earlier work.
Like *Pickwick*, it becomes increasingly dark as it draws to its close, and the
bankruptcy of Miss Matty, though not induced by a breach of promise suit,
draws on that same sense of the protagonist's integrity in the face of a world
of bankers and lawyers. But while *The Pickwick Papers*, as Dickens
scholars have noted, seems to "star" Dickens himself, making the image of
his own language the hero of the text,[26] for Gaskell, the question of who
focuses the text—and of on whom the text focuses—is answered very
differently. Where *Pickwick* takes to the road, of course, the Amazons stay
at home; where the narrative voice of *Pickwick* aims for the impersonal and
the universal, the narrative voice of *Cranford* is increasingly more personal.
Cranford is a kind of narrator's progress. The model it proposes is of
narrative involvement, an involvement Gaskell saw as fundamental for
women confronting essentially male traditions of reading and writing.

Cranford seems so much a "female" text, with its gaps, silences, and
indirections, all that we have came to call *écriture feminine*, that it is all
the more remarkable that it does not, strictly speaking, have a heroine:
Miss Matty represents some kind of moral center for the novel, which
closes with her, and with the idea that we are all somehow better for

having known her. The "story" is largely hers, but the real story is (in keeping with the mediated textuality we have been tracing in *Cranford*) in the narrator's changing perceptions of her—indeed, of her changing understanding of all the "Amazons." And yet, we could not call *Cranford* Mary Smith's "story"; little happens to her—she does not die or get married, her situation does not change.[27] In fact, her real "story"—her daily life with her father—takes place outside *Cranford* novel and Cranford village; we are reading her holiday self. But as *Cranford* concludes, we see the narrator increasingly involved in the plot of the novel, and in its happy conclusion. As she assumes narrative responsibility—telling readers more about herself, admitting her own doubts about that everyday life with her father in Drumble, becoming increasingly ironic and identified with the Cranfordian imagination—so she begins to act in the narrative: writing the letter to Miss Matty's brother, against all the male, practical discouragement she can imagine; coming up with the plan for Miss Matty's financial independence in running the tea shop; becoming more her own person, more her own heroine.

This corresponds, partly, to Gaskell's own conflicting needs in creating a narrator for Cranford: Gaskell needed a narrator who could do several things at once. Because she is telling a story of people already outdated, she needs a narrator who can move from one world to another, without the implied superiority of an omniscient narrator. She needs a narrator detached enough not to take Cranford's "elegant economies" too seriously, but enough of an insider to translate such customs for the uninitiate. Her narrator must understand the business, masculine world of Drumble but have a sense of what Cranford holds that that bustling town lacks. But clearly, no narrator except an omniscient one can move between these worlds—past and present, masculine and feminine, town and village—without tension, and so Gaskell must create a narrator who feels the differences but can mediate between them for a reader.

Mary Smith, *Cranford*'s narrator, lives with her father in Drumble but spends part of every year in Cranford, where, we are told, her father once lived. Indeed, near the end of the novel, she says, with a reluctance that reminds us both of Gaskell's coyness of authorship and of the introduction to "The Last Generation in England,"

> I must say a word or two here about myself. I have spoken of my father's old friendship for the Jenkyns family; indeed, I am not sure if there was not some distant relationship. (p. 170)

From the first, Mary seems slightly allied with the ladies against her father, but her ironic gaze, loving as it is, is too penetrating of the women's foolishness for us not to hear her father's genial contempt for them. It is a contempt she will mock later, when she quotes her father on the subject of one of Miss Jenkyns's investments: "the only unwise step that clever woman had ever taken, to his knowledge (the only time she ever acted against his advice, I knew)" (p. 172). But for the most part, the narrator's loyalties work in the way that the novel seems to be dividing up the world: men control the financial, industrial world, and, in some unexplained but significant way, keep the world going for the women who live in an exclusively domestic world of marrying and gossiping, making calls, burying the dead. The realm of female action—and of female comment—seems closely contained.

That narrative division begins to break down at the moment that the economic system does, and Gaskell must create a bank failure—a failure of "notes"—to create the space for this narrative transformation. As abruptly as Miss Matty's world is shattered, with the loss of her savings in the failure of the bank, so suddenly do the divisions that allow women not to think about "finances" and keep men safely out of the quotidian Cranford life fall apart. But the bank's failure and Miss Matty's way of meeting it accentuate Gaskell's focus on the single woman: through Miss Matty's unexpected strengths and a new contradiction of Mary's father, the strongest male authority of the novel, comes a possible reversal of power. Here, more explicitly than elsewhere in the novel, Gaskell links authority—power and authorship—with the "market," and suggests storytelling that is not commodified, that is more a "Cranford" than a "Drumble" narration.

Miss Matty's fate is what middle-class Victorians must most have feared: she is left with no income but with social obligations; she is embarrassed in front of her friends; she must give up her family home. She faces this disaster in unexpected ways, however. When she meets a man with a note from her bank, knowing herself a shareholder, she chooses to ignore the strong rumor of the bank's instability, and stands behind her obligation, redeeming the note herself. She chooses, in the smallest as in the largest instance, not to profit from the misfortunes of others, but more essentially, she chooses to hold herself responsible to others. When she opens a shop, she refuses to sell green tea without warning customers of its hazards. Further, she is always giving out more than just measures to customers, unable entirely to reconcile herself to market thinking. Mary's father disapproves of most of Miss Matty's "scruples," calling them "great nonsense" and wondering "how trades-people were to get on if there was to be a continual consulting of each other's interests, which would put a stop to all competition directly." But as Mary notes, by consulting Mr Johnson who already sells tea, Miss Matty manages to improve her business, for he sends her customers. While Mary's father says, "Such simplicity might be very well in Cranford, but would never do in the world," Mary adds, "I fancy the world must be very bad, for with all my father's suspicion of every one with whom he has dealings, and in spite of all his many precautions, he lost upwards of a thousand pounds by roguery only last year" (p. 201). By imagining or imputing roguery, Gaskell suggests, Mr Smith (surely Adam Smith) has called it into being.[28]

Miss Matty's movement, the single woman flying in the face of male opposition, is the narrator's movement to freedom as well: the moment when Mary sends a letter off to Peter, the absent brother, ignoring her father's imagined mockery, is her moment of seizing power in the narrative, and the terms she employs sound like those used by Gaskell herself.[29] The letter straddles the world of male factuality and female intuition; the description Mary gives of her prose might almost be one Gaskell would offer for her novel. She writes the unknown Aga Jenkyns "a letter which should affect him if he were Peter, and yet seem a mere statement of dry facts if he were a stranger."[30] The letter, like Miss Matty's life, is an act of faith, based on the coincidence of the traveling magician's foreign wife having met a kind man in India named Jenkyns, and on Mary Smith's involvement in the letter reading and burning of the earlier chapters. Like the description of the prose itself, Gaskell's description of the mailing of the letter and its eventual journey conjures up much of the act of novel-writing as well:

> At last I got the address, spelt by sound; and very queer it looked! I dropped it in the post on my way home; and then for a minute I stood looking at the wooden pane with the gaping split which divided me from the letter, but a moment ago in my hand. It was gone from me like life— never to be recalled. It would get tossed about on the sea, and stained with sea-waves perhaps; and be carried among palm-trees, and scented with all tropical fragrance;—the little piece of paper, but an hour ago so familiar and common-place, had set out on its race to strange wild countries beyond the Ganges! But I could not afford to lose much time on this speculation. (pp. 182–183)

For a moment, the narrator stands firmly in the female world of Cranford, where it is entirely possible to imagine absent brothers returning, but she is also invoking a traditionally male topos: the sea voyage, the fragrance of the tropics, the "strange wild countries" that none of the

Amazons will ever see. And, for a moment, she reimagines both writing and voyaging in female terms: the letter is gone from her "like life—never to be recalled," and writing is at once death, life "gone from me," but also birth. A new "life" goes out of the writer, takes form, is *given* form.

She seems, as a writer, to have momentarily taken on the post of the Johnsonian narrator she invoked at the beginning, while subtly mocking his point of view by reminding herself—and us—that in the busy world of Cranford, "I could not afford to lose much time on this," and so recalls herself from wandering "beyond the Ganges." She tells of Miss Jenkyns, who, when Peter was heard to be in India, "learnt some piece of poetry off by heart, and used to say, at all the Cranford parties, how Peter was 'surveying mankind from China to Peru,' which everybody had thought very grand, and rather appropriate, because India was between China and Peru, if you took care to turn the globe to the left instead of to the right." Mary Smith, who gathers the information about Peter, hunts out his address and transcribes it as best she can, who acts secretly and yet firmly to secure his return, is moving with an almost Johnsonian authority; it is the same authority that shapes the telling of the story, and her increasing insistence that she knows how best to tell it, and why.

But the final vision of the writer Gaskell suggests is hardly of the Johnsonian figure surveying in detachment a steady, fixed world "from China to Peru." The writing woman, sending off a badly spelled letter to a long-lost brother, is detached from nothing; rather, she writes out of feeling and involvement, to connect rather than survey mankind, and without specifying to a reader which way to "turn the globe," for here the "globe" is the constantly moving community of women. *Cranford* ends not with its narrator's description of herself or her fate but with its vision of Miss Matty: that we are all better for having been near her. By ending with the social unit, the whole of Cranford society going in, arm in arm and at peace, to see Signor Brunoni's magic show, Mary Smith suggests that her narrative has meaning only in that community. Perhaps, in writing the history of *Cranford* in so deliberately non-epic terms, with little ironies, delicate perceptions, and subtle appreciations, Gaskell has taken on the Johnsonian challenge in a new and unique way.

But she has not repeated the Dickensian experiment. Although one does not want to re-create criticism of *Cranford* that stresses its "delicacy" and its "fragrance," one must note that in its model of "concealed" narration, it strikes a very different tone from the omniscience of the narrative sun that bursts through *Pickwick*. One cannot imagine *Cranford* ending in this fashion:

It is the fate of most men who mingle with the world, and attain even the prime of life, to make many real friends, and lose them in the course of nature. It is the fate of all authors or chroniclers to create imaginary friends, and lose them in the course of art. Nor is this the full extent of their misfortunes; for they are required to furnish an account of them besides.[31]

There can be no such summary ("account") of the situation of narration in *Cranford*, for the story of Cranford is so much involved with the story of its telling. At no point would Mary Smith be able to locate herself enough outside either the novel or the town of Cranford to comment on it as "chronicler." And yet, she bears a more "authorial" relation to the novel than does, say, Esther Summerson, who cannot comment at all on her position vis-à-vis the "novel-as-a-whole"—only on what Esther calls "my portion of these pages." Gaskell is trying for something between the disappearing author of "The Vanity of Human Wishes" and the self-promoting author of *The Pickwick Papers*; something between the voice-over narration of *Bleak House* and the entirely privatized voice of Esther's narrative.

That position of intentional mediation, between literary figures and literary voices, is what Mary Smith's narration re-creates, and it is as much an experiment in narrative as is *Bleak House*, though it has not been treated as such, perhaps because in its "concealment" and "femininity" it presents itself as so much less radical. To recognize it, we must be the kind of reader Mary Smith learns to be, reading through omissions and small, ironic comments. But through its pattern of oppositions and its insistence on its integrity as a guide to an alien way of life, *Cranford* stakes out its own territory in what it describes as a world of continual change, and Gaskell stakes out her own literary authority.

In her own oscillation between city and village, bustling present and dying past, Gaskell, like Mary Smith, is the perfect guide to Amazonian life. She has written a guidebook for what, to most of her contemporaries, was not worth visiting and not worth describing, and she has done it in Cranfordian terms rather than the terms of Drumble or the terms of "Dictionary" Johnson. Her narrative takes on the tone of Miss Matty's fading letters or unnarrated love story; by the end of the *Cranford*, we too know how to read from such small signs, and how to complete the unfinished stories. The guide to Cranford could not be done in the language of "The Vanity of Human Wishes" or a Pickwickian report; it is the success of *Cranford* as a novel to teach us to read its own, specific language, and to master the village and the novel on their own terms. *Cranford* has some of the sense of Miss Matty's fading letters, "a vivid and intense sense of the present time, which seemed so strong and full, as if it could never pass away," but it also has a sense of constant loss, as if the work of representation, too, was always slipping away. Miss Matty describes the diary her father once made her keep:

> "On one side we were to put down in the morning what we thought would be the course and events of the coming day, and at night we were to put down on the other side what really happened. It would be to some people rather a sad way of telling their lives '—(a tear dropped upon my hand at those words)—' I don't mean that mine has been sad, only so very different to what I expected." (p. 158)

That fluidity, the movement between expectation and reality, the present as it is lived and the past as it is "put down" in literature, with the addition of the softening tear, is what *Cranford* achieves. Its real achievement, as art, is to hold that flux steady for us, and to involve us so completely in its way of reading.

But in imagining the flux, in reimaging it for us, the novel serves also to remind us of the limitations of the languages we choose. Miss Matty says that she loves the stars, but she cannot talk about them with an eager questioner, for, she says, she confuses "astronomy" and "astrology." She asserts further, in the face of all authority, that "she never could believe that the earth was moving constantly, and that she would not believe it if she could, it made her feel so tired and dizzy whenever she thought about it" (p. 127). What *Cranford* must do throughout is move between experience and explanation, as women must reread what they have been told of the world. But here, as before, the novel must remain "dizzy," an unfixable sphere in front of us, which we cannot maneuver as we please but which offers up nonetheless the possibility of fictions of change rather than a literature of definition. The novel as a genre is always already in motion rather than fixed, but in reinventing the novel for women, Gaskell moved the prime movers; she imagined—and made real—the woman writer no longer being read aloud to but writing out (and out of) her own way of reading.

4

"One Continued Series of Oppositions": *North and South*, Marriage, and the Romance of a Common Language

Although *North and South* has received more critical attention than any other Gaskell novel, it seems that much of the complexity of the work and of its social criticism has been lost in annoyance over the novel's heroine and the marriage plot. Critics speak of the book as an industrial novel that narrows into a romance, as if the complexity and richness of the social fabric of *Mary Barton* had been flattened even more arbitrarily than in the earlier novel into a comedy of misunderstanding and marriage. Like the critics of *Mary Barton* who have seen only the novel's division into the separate spheres of public and private, or like feminist critics quick to read the heroine's progress as only into subjectivity and sexuality, they have made of the novel either imperfect social commentary or the mystification of domesticity that its interest in female authority seems to offer. But *North and South* in fact moves in the opposite direction: from the "romance" of the heroine's life and her progress toward marriage into the density of industrial England and its economic and sexual politics, and into an understanding of the complexity of any "resolution," whether romantic, social, or "fictional." The novel began as *Margaret Hale*,[1] and is perhaps the most clearly centered of all Gaskell's novels in its heroine's expanding consciousness, but from that vantage point it comments acerbically on the marriage plot and the romance structure so central to the novel. By placing those critiques deliberately within the transformations of industrialization, it raises anew the question of the novel's (and the heroine's) relationship to social change, and specifically to those changes in publication and publicity that have been our focus so far. Gaskell began the novel with the voices of her critics (primarily the wealthy manufacturers of Manchester, who had seen *Mary Barton* as a betrayal) in her ears, but she began it as well with the progress from *Mary Barton* to *Ruth* behind her, and with a sharper awareness of the complexities of women's lives all around her.

The important question then becomes, how does Gaskell reform the marriage plot (and its work) in this novel? Critics have been quick to assume that Gaskell meant to merge "north and south" (masters and men; new and old) by the sleight of hand of the heroine's choice of a husband; they argue that when Margaret Hale moves from the South of England and marries the industrialist master, John Thornton, the marriage plot is doing (by extension) the work of ideology, softening social critique and reconciling oppositions.[2] But the novel seems to me to have more of what it calls "one continued series of oppositions"—the heroine's progress toward marriage suggests the difficulties of reconciliation and the continuing tensions of those alienated from dominant structures. Further, as I will argue in this chapter, the novel is deeply skeptical about solutions per se, and specifically, about fiction itself as a solution; *North and South* raises its own criticism of the condition-of-England novel it is usually assumed to be, and of the myth of the all-knowing author, who proposes, disposes, and resolves the differences between "the two Nations." The heroine's progress through the variety of plots and discourses offered her (her own "series of oppositions") and the author's parallel progress here reflect both the tensions of industrialization and the difficult resolution of England's, the woman's, and the novel's "condition." More, the explicit "use" of the heroine as textual transmitter—as a kind of interpreter among and between the many discourses of industrialization—suggests a self-consciousness about the text and authorship; in *North and South*, the heroine serves as a translator for the Babel that is industrialization, and her role as mediatrix comes under scrutiny in ways that suggest a new complexity in Gaskell's own relationship to authority and in the novel's status as an interpretive device. What this novel suggests is, at best, a series of uneasy marriages and uncertain alliances, between fiction, romance, and reform.

i

To make an argument for the social content of the romance plot of *North and South*, we must return briefly to *Mary Barton* to note a few things about its plot, its heroine, and its ideological purpose. Its central romance is that of a working-class girl and her working-class lover, her rejection of the "master's" seductive blandishments, and her ascent into the middle-class following her (appropriate) marriage and (unfortunate) banishment from England. Except for a few carefully staged encounters, the novel is not particularly interested in the meetings between the classes, and the primary work of reconciliation is textual: first, the narrator's use of parable (that of Dives and Lazarus) and quotation (Burns's "a man's a man for a' that"); and second, the biblical tag ("they know not what they do") that follows Mr Carson's encounter with the willful child, and his subsequent reading of the family Bible in which he inscribes his son's death. The heroine, and indeed most of the characters, lack any real self-consciousness about their own "inscription," and the ability to draw the analogies on which successful closure depends rests largely with the narrator—and with the implied audience of middle-class readers to whom she speaks, readers with whom she shares a range of textual and biblical examples, as well as the homely experience that will shape an appropriate response to the text.

Mary's plot, then, does not in itself need to do a complicated kind of cultural work; nor would her range of experience (or, indeed, her interpretive skills) allow her to do it. This is the work of the narrator, and it is the work for us, but the work is not mediated by the heroine's romance, as it so centrally is in *North and South*. Where the earlier novel offered seduction and the second, appropriate choice, what this novel offers is a series of adjustments and negotiations, a series of "resolutions." This distinction in *North and South* gives us a way of replaying *Mary Barton*, of seeing both the limitations *within* that plot and what the "fiction" of that plot left out; what the latter novel also gives us, to make the argument most naively, is a more "realistic" version of what Mary's story might have been.

Soon after Margaret Hale moves to the North of England, she meets a worker, Nicholas Higgins, and his daughter, Bessy, who is dying of consumption brought on by her hard work in a cotton mill. The pair, whose initial and primary purpose in the novel is to provide Margaret with the human interest that will begin to integrate her into Milton society and allow her to interpret it, in many ways recall Mary and John Barton: the father's gruff affection for his daughter; the daughter's protective love of her father; the tension between his radicalism and her gentleness, here represented by Bessy's passionate Methodism. If the daughter's fanatic faith seems closer to what we know, historically, of the industrial working class than did Mary's fantasies of romance and rescue, so, too, must Bessy's fate: she became ill working in the factory in which her father placed her out of his desire to protect her. She tells Margaret that though the latter would never believe it now, seeing her ravaged by her illness, she was in fact a beautiful woman, and her father, fearing she would be raped, sent her to work in a "safe" factory—one in which she was unfortunately not safe from the cotton "fluff" that entered her lungs and is now killing her. Bessy's story could come from contemporary factory reports or newspaper clippings; it is hardly the stuff of romance— but neither, in its flatness, is it the stuff of fiction. It could not provide the plot of, say, *Mary Barton*—but it also lacks the range, the social vision, the interpretive power that *North and South* needs.

In this way the political resonance of *North and South* begins to depend on its very different heroine—and its different heroine begins to seem a product of those political subtleties. What Margaret Hale gives *North and South* is both a central consciousness and a plot; what the conflicts of industrialization give the novel that would have been *Margaret Hale* is the richness and power that a more ordinary novel of marriage would lack; what is conjoined, in their coming together, is the erotic power (the force to drive the plot) of the romance, and the political urgency (and interpretive complexity) of the condition-of-England novel. With the revision of Mary's (Bessy's) plot before us, we could argue that a reader of *North and South*, especially one who had read *Mary Barton*, would be already aware of the class-based notion of romance on which its plot and its thematic resolution depended, so that *North and South* explains and implicitly criticizes its own admixture of novelistic possibilities. With the increased complexity of its narrative structure and of the consciousness that organizes it, comes as well an increasing self-consciousness about the uses of plot, and about the ways novels play with and off the desires of readers to see plots "at work"—and working.

This novel works in ways that are new for Gaskell. It lacks the instructive narration of *Mary Barton*, the first-person engagement (however ironic) of *Cranford's* Mary Smith, or even the wisdom of *Ruth's* narration; it is undernarrated, in many sections, except in its pointed transitions, which do the work of the much longer commentaries in *Mary Barton*. And they work more subtly, as in the most pointed of them, when we move from the Hales to the Thorntons with a passage beginning, "We must look at a scene similar but different." The process of drawing analogies ("similar but different") is the stuff not only of social unification but of sexual union, of the novel—it being the job of the marriage plot to convince us of the "similarity" to make possible the wedding of the "different." That doubled consciousness is more complex than anything *Mary Barton* achieves; it is more minimal and more of a risk, but it forces on *us* a doubling of consciousness.

Throughout the novel, in the place of narrative intervention we have the progress of the heroine's consciousness; we also have a new attention to varieties of reading and readers, a range of potential fictional languages, and a progress across England and back again, from London to the South, to the North, back to the South, briefly back North, and back to London—a wider sweep than Gaskell had earlier attempted, and a wide path for a heroine to travel. In contrast to novels like *Middlemarch*, which offer a similar range, we might notice that in Gaskell's, the heroine need not leave England to attain her wider vision; her voyage covers, instead, a range of classes (and discourses) not available to Dorothea, Gwendolen, and others.

To marry off its heroine, this plot must travel an England that is not the normal "plot" fiction traverses. To effect this sweep, the novel needs an intense self-consciousness about both plot and character. The novel that started out as *Margaret Hale* begins with its heroine watching a more conventional heroine, about to be married, as she sleeps; it then sweeps its heroine off into a series of possible plots and encounters, through a series of languages and vocabularies, until a dizzy reader might well wonder where this novel might be going. It is as if the novel must begin by displacing all other plots, chief among them the "more conventional" romance, along with a more conventional heroine. Margaret, from the first, is taller, more queenly, and less submissive than people expect her to be. When she appears in front of her aunt's friends wearing the exotic India-silk shawls that belong to her cousin Edith, it is Margaret whom the shawls become; Edith, about to marry a rather stupid fiancé, cannot quite carry them off. But Margaret also remains untouched by their beauty, admiring their feel while managing not to desire them—or Edith's domesticated happiness. Margaret is a heroine whose mouth is "no rosebud, [formed] to let out a 'yes' or 'no' and 'an't please you, sir'"; instead, she is prone to asking difficult questions, to wondering "why . . . forms and ceremonies [are] to be gone through."

This habit of questioning and speaking out serves her well when the novel begins to jostle her (and the plot) along. Having begun with a marriage and presented us with a beautiful unmarried heroine, the novel has readied us to predict a marriage, and provides a possible fiancé for her within pages. But it also presents us with a series of rapid ruptures within that progress toward romance, which prepare us for a series of changes paralleled in the heroine's "changes," and the "changes" of industrialization. Here the usefulness of the heroine's plot for the representation of industrial transformation becomes clearer than it might otherwise seem. No purely industrial novel could recreate the intense changes of industrialization so assiduously as does *North and South,* which turns out to contain very few initial clues even as to its subject. Not only does it open in London society, move to rural England, then move again, abruptly, to the industrial northern city of Manchester but its thematic concerns seem to change as rapidly. With its geographic movement it moves from a novel of marriage to a novel of religious doubt, from a society novel to a political novel, from family relations to industrial relations, from private to public and back. If the constant within these initially posed variables is the heroine, Margaret Hale, at the beginning of the novel in London, watching the marriage preparations of her cousin and anticipating with pleasure her return to her native village of Helstone, the novel depends on our "anticipating" as well. As canny readers, we can predict the marriage proposal she will receive from Edith's new brother-in-law, perhaps her initial shock but eventual acceptance, and so on—but both her plot and ours are subverted when she goes home to Helstone. Henry Lennox does appear and does propose, but she rejects him; her father announces that his religious doubts have led him to resign from his country vicarship and to move his family to the northern town of Milton, to which we and our heroine repair in a state of confusion.

This suggests a kind of play within the novel between the expectations of earnest readers (quick to pick up on clues, to anticipate plots) and the unsettling nature of the "new" plotting of industrial England.[3] Although no novel can present its heroine's life as already fixed, or there would be no novel, the comforts of genre are usually such that readers can name the plot: Emma Woodhouse will marry someone; Jane Eyre will speak out, and earn her living; Becky Sharp will throw books and manipulate men; and we can watch the variations on these expectations, secure in our sense of the dominant theme. *North and South* is unusually canny about this readerly habit of projection, and works to undercut predictions at every turn, altering plots by putting them in unexpected places: Margaret will find romance in industrialism; the village's vicar will move to Manchester; the heroine's brother will enter the plot by leaving town; and so on. The novel is not so much "new" as it is unexpected.

What is further undercut by these transformations is our notion of a heroine, for the untraditional, questioning Margaret is equally hard to "fix" in the plot. The novel's constant motion suggests the generic nature of the bundle of characteristics we call a character. The novel moves Margaret from situation to situation—literally from place to place—in order, specifically, to move her to Manchester, the "Milton-Northern" of the novel, and within these chapters all other fictional possibilities are closed off as well. The heroine's enclosure re-creates generic limitations; readers, like Margaret, are forced into imagining a new novel. Victorian novels traditionally offer few possibilities for a heroine, and the beginning of *North and South* seems almost a parody of them: the heroine can remain in London society; she can live out her days with her parents in an English village; she can accept an eligible suitor. That is, she can be a social adventurer; she can be a dutiful daughter; she can marry. Each story Margaret rejects—or has taken from her—is also a possible plot for the novel; each, furthermore, is a possible "character" for her. With every one of these characters (the proud and queenly heroine choosing between sweethearts; the parson's daughter, drawing, visiting villagers, growing through her connection with nature; the wife or fiancée of a young attorney, engaging in the battle of wits their initial conversations suggest) we begin to write a novel *for* that character, but each is in turn cut off. Margaret's abrupt and unhesitating dismissal of Lennox, and Mr Hale's announcement that they must leave Helstone—with each of these yet another novel begins, and a new "character" for Margaret must be created. One might know what to expect of the heroine of each of these just-ended stories; it is harder to know what to expect of the heroine of a novel that takes on religious doubts, industrial change, and a fragmented family. It is not that readers do not know what will *happen* to the heroine, for one rarely knows that, but we do not know, any more than she does, what sort of heroine she is to *be*.

To begin a novel with the heroine out of place suggests a deep displacement in the coherence of the novel, one signaled here primarily by the confusion of discourses in the book. A certain incoherence is always at stake in a marriage plot, for romance by definition presents misunderstandings, "differences" to be converted into the "similarity" of marriage. But Margaret's romance with Thornton will suggest the irreconcilability of the industrial North with the South of either country or city; here, the "removal" of the heroine into the conflicts of North and South will mean a linguistic incoherence, shifts in dialects and vocabulary, that will generate the twists and turns of the industrial plot. And what is the work of the romance plot if it requires a new dictionary—if Margaret and Thornton cannot speak to each other, how are they to fall in love?

To understand this, we must rehearse briefly the reasons Milton-Northern is itself incomprehensible to Margaret. Her first view of the city, as she approaches it with her father, is under a cloud of smoke that does *not* mean rain. First, the air is described as having "a faint taste and smell of smoke; perhaps, after all, more a loss of the fragrance of grass and herbage than any positive taste or smell,"[4] but the narrator goes on to point out:

> Here and there a great oblong many-windowed factory stood up, like a hen among her chickens, puffing out black "unparliamentary" smoke, and sufficiently accounting for the cloud which Margaret had taken to foretell rain. (p. 96)

As the narrator moves from a language Margaret could use (the "hen" and "her chickens") to a word that Margaret does not yet know, and in fact later takes some time to understand ("unparliamentary"), she must also both conjure up and dismiss *our* usual associations (black cloud = rain) to suggest the range of what Margaret does not yet "take" correctly.[5] In the succeeding pages we learn that Margaret does not yet know about a "taste" in which the showy is more valued than the modest; an economy in which wages matter more than education; a street life in which women comment freely on one another's dress, and men on women's beauty. To be a heroine in Milton-Northern is to learn a new sign system—and, by extension, then to be a different kind of heroine.

But here the romance plot begins to break down, to fail to work its coherence, for to be such a different (displaced) heroine is also to be part of a different system of sexual symbolism, one that permeates the romance plot, and makes Margaret equally slow to "take" people's meanings. True, part of what Margaret learns is what every heroine of romance must learn (that she is under observation; that she can, as Elizabeth Bennet realizes, be "mortified"; that her parents have somehow failed her and must be replaced by that better teacher, a husband), but much of what Margaret comes to realize is, as it were, industrialized: the lessons of social change and romance come together. The clues in Manchester are even more difficult than the divisions of class that mark a romance like *Jane Eyre*, or of race that mark *Daniel Deronda*. Margaret doesn't see Thornton's hand offered to her as he leaves the room after his visit to take tea at their house, and so he thinks her "proud"; because she does not know until too late the "frank familiar custom" of the place, and because she cannot tell him of her "sorrow" when she recognizes the insult she has inadvertently offered, the two cannot "meet" properly. Here, as elsewhere, the limits of assigned gender roles and social difference conspire to enclose the heroine. Much of her time with Thornton is spent defining their terms: they cannot agree as to what they consider a "gentleman," what the role of a "master" is, how he is to treat his "hands." But more, Margaret is mistaken about the social rules governing heroines in Manchester: she does not realize that she is regarded as necessarily husband-hunting; she does not hesitate to throw her arms around Thornton in the course of protecting him from angry strikers; she is unaware of the rules of sexual desire and "maidenliness" by which she will be judged.

What happens in the novel is that misunderstanding is eroticized, the violence and confusion of the mob increasing the excitement of the marriage plot at the same time that marriage threatens to contain all differences. Any novel must perpetually balance its sameness and differences; what this novel does continually is to read opposition as at once political and sexual. Where it moves beyond the conventional marriage plot is in its focus (always one of Gaskell's strengths) on male desire, and its relation to the authority (again, always limited for her) of the "master"; Thornton must lose authority through desire, so that Margaret can acquire it, while he must simultaneously retain it so that industry (and marriage) remain possible. At the same time, the forces of economic power are constantly intervening in the romance plot, through the strikes, shortfalls, and business failures that essentially run the narrative. Characters in the novel, no less than critics, seem to assume that economic thinking *follows* desire, and that it is love for Margaret that will "soften" the hardened capitalist. What critics have ignored is the way capitalism itself is eroticized in the novel—as, indeed, is the moment of submission, which both characters act out at the close of the novel, as they end, practically kneeling on the floor, in each other's arms.

That sexual desire takes a social twist in this novel is perhaps the most interesting innovation *North and South* makes in its inherited form—that, and the fact that it is the heroine who must learn to read the social landscape. The progress, one of misunderstanding and obstacles, I have been suggesting here is crucial to the progress of any fictional romance: the heroine must misrecognize the hero and his desire; she must unwittingly provoke a response (and a proposal) from him, only to reject it; but his proposal itself must make her aware of herself as a possible object, of both her power (to inspire desire) and her powerlessness (to act on it). Where in *Mary Barton* these tensions depend on modesty to prolong the plot, in this novel, it is a workers' strike that sets off this chain of necessary events, and a crash in the market that makes possible its solution. Similarly, this novel depends as much as does *Mary Barton* on the expansion of the heroine's imagination (she says to her father that Thornton is her "first olive," and he must allow her to make a face "while swallowing") but here it is the heroine's social imagination that most needs expanding. And in this novel, that expansion (the extended growing up and reaching outward that will make possible the marriage) requires that the heroine learn a new vocabulary.

ii

Margaret Hale's adventure in Milton-Northern is largely linguistic: the novel is almost a romance of the languages of industrialization, challenging characters and readers, enlisting a new vocabulary, offering itself as a dictionary, and using its heroine's consciousness to achieve all this. Repeatedly, the novel offers up a new term, runs through a series of definitions, explains what is at stake in each, and then allows Margaret to choose. As she is initiated into Milton (and into its new plot), she becomes increasingly fluent with the vocabulary she must learn there—and increasingly, as she serves as a translator for other characters and for readers, the novel serves as a glossary of industrialization. Take, for example, the question of the strike, which was of such importance to Gaskell that she wrote to Dickens to ask if he intended to have a strike in *Hard Times*, currently running in a serialized version in *Household Words*.[6] When Margaret asks, "What is a strike?" she is signaling her ignorance (with which a London reader might identify) and putting herself in the middle of social forces that shape her (smaller) individual plot; she is both a narrating intelligence (what Wayne Booth might call the reader's friend) and a narrative agent. The strike functions in that double-directional way we have been tracing (it is an agent in the romance plot, literally forcing Margaret into Thornton's arms, and the embrace in turn becomes a force in the "industrial action" of the novel, as the two plots blur), but it is also a linguistic puzzle, forcing new definitions and new "combinations" of words from a variety of characters.

Margaret's characteristic form, the question, with its necessary unsettling of prior meanings, is a question here of linguistic indecisiveness. Margaret must learn what the word *strike* means to a wide range of characters before she can mediate between them, and before they can learn to speak to each other. But the "question" of language is deeply vexed politically, a problem that resounds through *North and South* even more thoroughly than it did through *Mary Barton*. As with the politics of language, so the politics of the heroine's speech: where *Mary Barton* could frame its heroine's speaking out as the heroic moment of connection and communication, no such easy optimism obtains here, and the incoherencies of language parallel some of the difficulties of plot we have been rehearsing.

What I mean to follow here is Gareth Stedman Jones's insight that the language of political debates shapes their content: that "the form in which [Chartist] discontents were addressed cannot be understood in terms of the consciousness of a particular social class, since the form pre-existed any independent action by such a class."[7] The language of any "class" (any social group; any "character") will in turn "speak" that class or that character. Language does not refer back "to some primal anterior reality, 'the social being'" (p. 20); on the other hand, it cannot promise a transhistorical self, being shot through with its own "social being." Class consciousness is "constructed and inscribed within a complex rhetoric of metaphorical association, causal inference and imaginative construction" (p. 102). If my earlier use of Stedman Jones, in discussing *Mary Barton*, was to emphasize the language of representation at the heart of Chartist politics, what I wish to emphasize here is the multivocal nature of *all* discourses of class, and the political nature of all language, particularly the languages of fiction. What *North and South* will suggest is Stedman Jones's warning that even his account of the languages of Chartism cannot be complete, for it is taken from radical literature and speeches reported in the radical press: "Quite apart from the fact that such re-ported speech took no account of accent or dialect, I am not arguing that this is the only language Chartism employed. What is examined here is only the public political language of the movement" (p. 95). Gaskell's account moves between "public" and "private" languages as carefully as it does between the languages of a range of characters, classes, "associa-tions."

It is in this context that we must understand the novel's preoccupation with language. At the time Gaskell was writing *North and South*, her hus-band was offering a series of lectures on the English language; they were published with the fifth edition of *Mary Barton*, along with a glossary for the novel's dialect, which makes linguistic the novel's social argument, that language itself is a social weapon, and that the language of the workers (like the lives they lead) demands both the respect and the special understanding of readers. For the Reverend William Gaskell, language is the "close connection between the present and the past," for language "ever runs backwards," but more appositely, the "slang" of Lancashire is not, "as some ignorantly suppose, mere vulgar corruptions of modern English, but gen-uine relics of the old mother tongue."[8] In a building metaphor that will be resurrected in the factory vision of *North and South*, he adds, these "forms of speech and peculiarities of pronunciation . . . are bits of the old granite, which have perhaps been polished into another form, but lost in the process a good deal of their original strength."

The language that Margaret eventually learns in Manchester is one she praises for its strength, and for its absolute appropriateness to the new world in which she finds herself. Like all lessons of the novel, that of the new language is learned first by the heroine—and largely, at the risk of sounding too abstract, through her body; the strike literally "strikes" Margaret; the angry men throw stones at her; her body's signs are (mis)-read sexually. Her acquisition of a new language is an initiation as central as the sexual initiation it signals; to use the word *knobstick* for a strike-breaker is like swallowing an olive; and to be ready to learn a language is as sure a sign of sexual readiness in this novel as is dancing in a novel by Jane Austen. The phrase "slack of work" that, to her mother, is a "provincialism . . . horrid Milton words . . . factory slang" is to Margaret only natural: "If I live in a factory town, I must speak factory language when I want it," and without "a great many words you never heard in your life," she would "have to use a whole explanatory sentence instead" (pp. 301–302). And the new language is not only economical but "expressive," sensual, usefully concrete, promising some kind of more direct representation. As she goes on to ask Thornton, to excuse herself for calling what she has "picked up" in Milton "vulgarity," "Though "knobstick" has not a very pretty sound, is it not expressive? Could I do without it, in speaking of the thing it represents?"

The slight confusion signaled here between new things and new words—what *knobstick* "represents" is the harshness of relations between workers and masters in industrial England, and the violence directed against the "knobsticks," or scab workers, themselves—is also a way of insisting on the novel's importance. To offer itself as a narrative dictionary of industrialization is both to constrict our point of view to what it can translate for us and to offer us the misspoken or misheard languages *around* Margaret, and the potential violence of these representations. Take again the range of answers Margaret receives to that central question, "What is a strike?" The novel so much expects readers to share Margaret's confusion that a whole chapter takes its title from the question; a reader might further echo Margaret's comment:

> Why do you strike? . . . Striking is leaving off work till you get your own rate of wages, is it not? You must not wonder at my ignorance; where I come from I never heard of a strike. (p. 181)

"I wish I were there," is Bessy Higgins's response, coding our ignorance as truly social bliss; for Bessy, the strike is linguistic hell, "just the clashing and clanging and clattering that has wearied me a' my life long, about works and wages, and masters, and hands, and knob-sticks," and she "could have wished to have had other talk about me in my latter days than just [that]" (pp. 184–185). For Bessy, the strike is only more "talk," and even the by now infamous *knobstick* only one more linguistic counter.

All the answers to Margaret's questions—all attempts to agree on a definition for that one word, *strike*—end in a kind of linguistic "strike" because none of the definers can agree on their terms. For Mrs Thornton, the strike is "uncomfortable work . . . going on in the town," and the men are only striking for "mastership and ownership of other people's property" (p. 162). For Thornton himself, mastery is capital, and the only language available that of captainship: the strike is the workers' "next attack," and it is his "right" as an "owner of capital" not to explain his action to his workers. Margaret, trying to argue with him, invokes another discourse, of "a feeling which I do not think you would share." There is, she says, a "human law" to allow him to "do what you like with your own," but no religious right. In an attempt at least to define his definitions, she declares, "I know so little about strikes, and rate of wages, and capital, and labour, that I had better not talk to a political economist like you" (p. 165). But when she tries out these same phrases (those of political economy) on Nicholas Higgins, asking if "the state of trade may be such as not to enable them to give you the same remuneration," Nicholas replies,

> State o' trade! That's just a piece o' masters' humbug. It's rate o' wages I was talking of. Th' masters keep th' state o' trade in their own hands; and just walk it forward like a black bug-a-boo, to frighten naughty children with into being good. (p. 183)

Here, the masters' abstract language becomes a "bug-a-boo," "humbug," "walking . . . forward" to frighten the workers. But how could such linguistic conflict lead anywhere but to a strike, to the failure of language to do any of the work of reconciliation? The abstractions of trade and wages fade further in the face of Bessy Higgins's account of the workers themselves during the strike:

> Yo'd ha' been deaved out o' yo'r five wits, as well as me, if yo'd had one body after another coming in to ask for father, and staying to tell me each one their tale. Some spoke o' deadly hatred, and made my blood run cold wi' the terrible things they said o' th' masters, —but more, being women, kept plaining, plaining (wi' the tears running down their cheeks, and never wiped away, nor heeded), of the price o' meat, and how their childer could na sleep at nights for th' hunger. (p. 202)

There seems *no* way to reconcile Bessy's account of starving children with the masters' discussion of the strike on "sound economical principles" in which Mr Thornton shows "that, as trade was conducted, there must always be a waxing and waning of commercial prosperity; and that in the waning a certain number of masters, as well as of men, must go down into ruin, and be no more seen among the ranks of the happy and prosperous" (p. 204). The gap between "be no more seen" and the "childer [who] could na sleep at nights for th' hunger" is no more—and no less—than the failure of any one language ever to represent the range of "waxing and waning" in Manchester. The narrator says Thornton spoke "as if this consequence were so entirely logical, that neither employers nor employed had any right to complain if it became their fate," but such suppressed "complaining" of employer and employed sounds far different than the "plaining, plaining" of the grieving mothers; they hardly seem in the same linguistic register—nor do the poetical emphasis of "waxing and waning" and the Wordsworthian echo in Thornton's speech do justice to the violence of class conflict.[9] If what Margaret pleads for at the moment of the strike is for Thornton to go out, like a man, and address his workers, to "speak to your workmen as if they were human beings," to "speak to them kindly," it is hard to see the novel's putting forward any language in which he could speak to them, as she implores, "man to man!"

What ends the strike and its potential violence is not, of course, any language, anything "man to man" at all; rather, it is the stone that strikes Margaret and her silent fall that silence the rioters. One might add, as well, that the inability of the strike to solve the workers' difficulties leaves us without any clearer answer to Margaret's initial question; a strike is leaving off work, but its ends remain as unclear in *North and South* as in more politically reactionary novels. No more than *Hard Times* can *North and South* recommend political action that will end the "plaining." More pointedly, what the novel leaves in question is the possible reformatory power of any language that remains "man to man": as in the gap between Bessy's and Thornton's accounts, the difference between the "strikes" of men and women informs the whole novel. If Margaret's conscious answer to the madness of the crowd is to send Thornton to "go out and speak to them," like *Mary Barton, North and South* is framed around a woman's transgressive movement into the public sphere. Margaret's insistence that her stepping in front of the crowd is only using a woman's "high privilege," the "sanctity of our sex" to do a "woman's work" in preventing "one blow, one cruel, angry action that might otherwise have been committed," allows her to salvage her "maiden pride." But it also suggests again Gaskell's own much beleaguered sense of authorial modesty—one no longer quite in keeping with the authorial assertion of the preface to this novel, which carries into the public her quarrel with Dickens over the novel's serialization in *Household Words*, and one that is as strained as any in the novel over the status of the woman's "plaint."

Margaret's move into the public realm before the angry strikers and the connection between her actions and Gaskell's in speaking out before the crowd suggest again that the linguistic questions under discussion here have a gendered inflection, one that returns us to the question of the social economy of romance. To rephrase this slightly, we might ask, what happens to the tension between male speech and female silence, the masculine "political economy" and female "plaining" when we move beyond the "strike"? Is there a conflict between men and women that registers as deeply—that is, as linguistically—as that between masters and men?

There seems to be such a conflict in Manchester, for if the language Margaret learns is primarily one of labor ("slack of work," "knobstick") there is another language of commodification that is also new to her, and that she hears primarily in the conversations of women. The gendered languages surface at dinner parties as well as on the streets: when she dines at the Thorntons' in Milton, there is a "very animated conversation going on among the gentlemen; the ladies, for the most part, were silent, employing themselves in taking notes of the dinner and criticizing each other's dresses" (p. 215). When Margaret separates herself from the "ladies'" conversation, she catches "the clue to the general conversation," which she notes is "in desperate earnest,—not in the used-up style that wearied her so in the old London parties." Later, she is

> surprised to think how much she enjoyed this dinner. She knew enough now to understand many local interests—nay, even some of the technical words employed by the eager mill-owners. She silently took a very decided part in the question they were discussing. (p. 216)

But Margaret is "decidedly" silent at that moment. Her newfound vocabulary serves her well as a reader but not a speaker; she is no more vocal than she was in London, where the men sat downstairs after dinner, and the women's "fragments of conversation" that she overheard horrified her.

Her accounts of the women's conversations in Milton are hardly more encouraging. As she describes them to her father,

> the ladies were so dull, papa—oh, so dull! Yet I think it was clever too. It reminded me of our old game of having each so many nouns to introduce

into a sentence. . . . They took nouns that were signs of things which gave evidence of wealth,—housekeepers, under-gardeners, extent of glass, valuable lace, diamonds, and all such things; and each one formed her speech so as to bring them all in, in the prettiest accidental manner possible. (p. 221)

The dinner-party conversation in some ways signals the old problem of "signs of things which gave evidence," recalling Margaret's earlier defense of her use of *knobstick*: "Could I do without it, in speaking of the thing it represents?" The dinner party is all "representations," all the "extent" of commodities, most especially in the formal fakery of the "prettiest accidental manner possible." It is as if the women were themselves dressed in language (in nouns, to be precise) that displayed their husbands' wealth even more conspicuously than the gentlemen's conversation "relative to the trade and manufactures of the place"; at the dinner table, the ladies are "employing" themselves in "taking notes of the dinner and criticizing each other's dresses." Similarly, when Margaret returns to London after the death of both her parents, and returns to the Harley Street wealth of her aunt, conversations reflect mere "cleverness" and "relentless ease"; "there might be toilers and moilers there in London, but she never saw them." The conversations, as much as the social whirl itself, exclude any life other than high society (the very servants, Margaret says, "lived in an underground world of their own, of which she knew neither the hopes nor the fears" [p. 458]), and it is only when she receives her inheritance and is free to begin the social work that occupies her until her marriage (and to which I will return) that she hears anything other than "the easy knowledge of the subjects of the day" or meets anyone other than people who "talked about art in a merely sensuous way," "lashed themselves up into an enthusiasm about high subjects in company, and never thought about them when they were alone," who "squandered their capabilities of appreciation into a mere flow of appropriate words" (p. 497). If female conversation is less economical than the men's ("squandered" as it is), it is also less useful; it offers no new words, no metaphors for social union, nothing except the "dress" Margaret is always rejecting. But Margaret cannot use the masculine language for her needs either; the novel seems to need some other language to describe what the heroine is now "silently" so decided about.

The isolation of male and female languages, which the novel in many ways refuses to "solve" artificially, is part of its larger dissatisfaction with old vocabularies, with the "flow of appropriate words," with a language that provides only lists of possessions, with the segregation of the male realm of business and the female world of party dresses; with the inability of conversation to incorporate new languages with which to describe "new things." What had seemed in Milton an anarchy of signification, with no agreement about the relations of words to things, gives way in the second half of the novel to the social stratification of language; men speak only to men, women only to women, and the toilers and moilers only to one another. With the recognition of this division, the novel also begins to express some doubts about its own role as mediator between one language and another, with its own models of reconciliation, with the mythic promise of a common language that will unite the two nations. It will register that ambivalence, as we have come to expect, first, with an attention to the difficulty of shared *written* languages, in which the novel must include itself, and then with its focus on the even more difficult role of the woman as mediatrix, poised between one discourse and another, one England and another, between masters and workers, men and women. It is to the mythology of the condition-of-England novel, the vision of a language that would unite all these Englands, that we must turn. What kind of dictionary is it that this novel tries to be or imagine, if its romance depends on the absence of any shared language at all?

iii

If the literary discourse under investigation in *Ruth* was that of the Romantic poet, and the plot that of the seduced heroine, the discourse that falls under Gaskell's scrutiny here is that of the industrial novel, and the plot of reconciliation it seems to promise its readers. And if its question is, how are we to read during (and about) industrialization, what this novel suggests is a wide range of readers—and hence of potentially different texts. In much the way that the novel could not offer a simple definition of a strike, or propose a single language for the conversation between masters and men, so it reflects a deep-rooted skepticism about the project of the condition-of-England novel, and about the ways texts can work to "unite" their readers.

The model of readerly reconciliation based on a recognition of mutual needs is of course central to the novel, and its reconciliation of masters and men. Take Bessy Higgins's account of how she came to be dying of lung failure: although cotton fluff fills the air in the factory where she works and eventually fills her lungs, the masters resist installing the wheel that would pull the fluff out of the air because it would cost too much. But she adds that the workers fight against the wheel as well because it would remove the fluff they have become accustomed to swallowing and that satisfies their constant hunger. "Between masters and men th' wheels fall through," she explains, and nothing is done—and yet, she adds, she wishes the wheel had been in *her* factory. The invocation of the common selfishness of "masters and men" suggests here its opposite, the possibility of a shared project of social reformation; it also subtly elides the difference between the two groups, that one is greedy and the other is simply starving. But what the novel suggests is that could the masters (or the workers) *see* Bessy Higgins coughing to death, they would abandon their own positions and install fluff-wheels immediately; the novel will overcome all individual (selfish) solutions.

At its most basic, the model of sympathy seems to posit the literary text as the object that moves between masters and men, that will lead them to the sympathy that in turn brings about reform. But two other moments in this long conversation between Margaret and Bessy suggest instead the inability of texts to translate between social groups or groups of readers. Bessy has asked Margaret about her home in the forest, for "I like to hear speak of the country, and trees, and such like things."

> [Margaret's] heart was opened to this girl: "Oh, Bessy, I loved the home we have left so dearly! I wish you could see it. I cannot tell you half its beauty.
> . . . In other parts there are billowy ferns—whole stretches of fern; some in the green shadow; some with long streaks of golden sunlight lying on them—just like the sea."
> "I have never seen the sea," murmured Bessy. "But go on." (p. 144)

The initial pattern of "I cannot tell you half its beauty" is one we are accustomed to taking metaphorically; it is inevitably followed by beautiful language, through which we *are* made to see the scene, or see enough to fill in what we cannot be told. To interrupt Margaret's lovely description of something "just like the sea" with the reminder that Bessy has never *seen* the sea does something else to the indescribability topos: it makes it unmetaphorical, by pointing out that even the metaphors we most take for granted ("like the sea") are class- and geography-bound; to a reader dying in a Manchester slum, nothing can ever be like the sea; she can never quite "see" what Margaret does. The literary language to which Margaret has such easy access (as, of course, do the London readers) is closed to Bessy; how much, in turn, is Bessy's life closed to them?

Gaskell's skepticism about the usefulness of metaphorical writing seems to extend to books in general: the second textual moment in this conversation between the two women also concerns reading, and brings us back to Bessy's poisoned lungs. When Margaret asks Bessy why she was working in the factories, she reports that her father feared "letting me go to a strange place," largely because she was beautiful ("a gradely lass enough") and he feared her being molested. She goes on:

> And I did na like to be reckoned nesh and soft, and Mary's schooling were to be kept up, mother said, and father he were always liking to buy books, and go to lectures o' one kind or another—all which took money—so I just worked on till I shall ne'er get the whirr out o' my ears, or the fluff out o' my throat i' this world. That's all. (pp. 146–147)

Bessy works because she fears looking "soft," because her dead mother valued her sister's education—and because her father likes to buy books and go to lectures. It is possible that the books are the political economy he attempts to make sense of, or the accounts of working-class life John Barton read, but it is also possible that the books are novels like *Mary Barton* or *North and South*—novels that include the "lectures" we are always reading. At the least, the education reformers are always advocating for workers here proves fatal—not to the "men," but to their daughters, who cannot get the "whirr" out of their ears. Even seeking enlightenment is dangerous in this world, and fiction may be part of what keeps workers hungry, choking on "fluff."

Margaret's father's removal to Milton is similarly complicated. The novel fluctuates between Mr Hale's assertion that the study of the classics (in which he instructs Thornton) provides a man (or, more accurately, a master) with suitable models for gentlemanly behavior and a proper relationship to authority, and Thornton's view that "what preparation [were] they for such a life as I had to lead? None at all. Utterly none at all" (p. 126). Mr Hale asks,

> "Did not the recollection of the heroic simplicity of the Homeric life nerve you up?"
> "Not one bit!" exclaimed Mr Thornton, laughing. "I was too busy to think about any dead people, with the living pressing alongside of me, neck to neck, in the struggle for bread." (p. 127)

Later in the novel, Mrs Thornton mounts an even more vicious attack on dead languages. When she is angriest with "those Hales" for rejecting her son, she aims her anger instead at the lessons Thornton receives from Mr Hale.

> She told her son that she wished they [the Hales] had never come near the place; that he had never got acquainted with them; that there had been no such useless languages as Latin and Greek ever invented. He bore all this pretty silently; but when she had ended her invective against the dead

languages, he quietly returned to the short, curt, decided expression of his wish that she should go and see Mrs Hale at the time appointed. (p. 305)

That this attack is linked to the aristocratic notions of Margaret Hale, called by Mr Bell a "classical daughter," by the narrator a "Roman daughter," is certainly true for Mrs Thornton, but the direct "use" of classical languages is more asserted than shown in the novel. And the quiet irony of "Milton" (both Mill-town and an invocation of Satan's Hell) is at once directed at readers and lost to the town's inhabitants; a classical education here can be acquired by those who have acquired other signs of wealth, and Mr Hale can argue that it is the fulfilment of their mercantile selves, but it does, indeed, seem useless.

"I want to learn Latin," asserted the young Jane Welsh Carlyle, "I want to be a boy." The novel's clearest discussion of literary languages is as weapons of power, whether patriarchal or economically paternalistic. Much as Margaret's seemingly innocent oceanic metaphor reveals the inequity between the heroine and the woman to whom she has "opened her heart," so other official languages seem to assert their deadening rather than their unifying power within the novel. To return to William Gaskell's metaphor, the "granite" of languages is more evident than their ability to change or be changed. Nicholas Higgins's attempts to read a book offered him by his employer, Mr Hamper, who has just called him a "noodle," suggests one such failure. He explains to Mr Hale,

> "I took th' book and tugged at it; but, Lord bless yo', it went on about capital and labour, and labour and capital, till it fair sent me off to sleep. I ne'er could rightly fix i' my mind which was which; and it spoke on 'em as if they was vartues or vices; and what I wanted for to know were the rights o' men, whether they were rich or poor—so be they were only men." (pp. 292–293)

What Higgins wants is almost an allegory for capital and labor ("vartues and vices") and a language that will annihilate the difference between them, reduce difference to "rights," and conflict to "only men." When Hale insists that the book "would have told you the truth" if only Higgins had kept at it, the latter objects,

> "Well, sir . . . it might, or it might not. There's two opinions go to settling that point. But suppose it was truth double strong, it were no truth to me if I couldna take it in. I dare say there's truth in yon Latin books on your shelves; but it's gibberish and not truth to me, unless I know the meaning o' the words . . . [though] I'm not one who thinks truth can be shaped out in words, all neat and clean, as th' men at th' foundry cut out sheet-iron."
> (p. 293)

Here again, Latin becomes the image for a closed language, one that is "gibberish" to those who do not "know the meaning o' the words," but even more, the novel opposes any language that would reduce truth to something "neat and clean," cut out in one sheet. The reminder of labor that ran through Margaret's vocabulary lessons surfaces again here, as does an unexpected emphasis on the relativity of truth—or rather, the individuality of ways of "tak[ing] it in." "Folks who set up to doctor th' world wi' their truth," as Higgins goes on, "mun suit different for different minds; and be a bit tender in th' way of giving it too."

Doctoring is very much the goal of *North and South*, as it is of the condition-of-England novel in general, and "tenderness" is an odd invocation in a book that declares it offers "truth double strong," but Gaskell's experience of writing the book in fact refutes any vision of the novel as "truth . . . shaped out in words, all neat and clean" in a "foundry" of fiction-making. More than any other of her novels, *North and South* was for Gaskell a *work* of production, one that found her laboring in another's factory, working by his orders. The experience of writing a serialized novel for Charles Dickens was disappointing, frustrating, and aggravating for Gaskell, and her own participation in "mechanical reproduction" lends a strong element of critique to her depiction of harmonious languages of reconciliation; reconciliation was hardly the "key-note" of her dealings with Dickens.

Gaskell's letters from this period share the concern with language and literacy that runs throughout *North and South*. She seems more concerned than usual with her own prose, even that of her letters, writing to John Forster that it is an effort to "make one grammatical sentence."[10] But this anxiety is interwoven with an increasing sense of her own status *as* a writer. In another letter to Forster, she writes, "Oh! I am afraid this letter is going to be what Dr Holland once called a letter of mine 'a heterogeneous mass of nonsense.' But that was before I wrote Mary B—he would not *say* so now."[11] The author of "Mary B—" is a very different being from the woman who ducked under the tablecloth after its publication. Rather, this authorial anxiety is blended with a broader concern about issues of literacy and reading, as when, in the same letter, she quotes an old song called "Jess MacFarlane," which includes the "naive verse"

> I writ my luve a letter
> But alas! she canna read—
> And I like her a' the better.

She goes on, "I am rather afraid I've heard somebody say it is not a proper song; but I don't know why it should not be for all I know of it, and I am sure my two verses are charming & innocent," but their relevance to the questions of reading that punctuate *North and South* is evident—and not so innocent. Gaskell herself reflects, in these letters, on the possibility of introducing a new woman character to the novel, who "shd not be what people call *educated*, but with strong sense," suggesting that the "luve" who "could not read a letter" (and the pun seems relevant to Gaskell's correspondence) was a necessary character for the novel she imagined.

But the strain that runs most deeply through these letters is precisely that of writing the novel itself. In none of her other letters does Gaskell so worry the details of authorship, and with none of her other novels do questions of plot and structure seem to have disturbed her so. She gives the novel to Mrs Shaen, who liked what was then "M. Hale"; she read it "grunting & groaning when she does not like," but "says it is good—but out of proportion to the length of the planned story, /written or published/—& so cramfull of possible interest that she thinks another character would make it too much—."[12] Gaskell also tries out plot maneuvers on her correspondents ("What do you think of a fire burning down Mr Thornton's mills *and house* as a *help* to failure? Then Margaret would rebuild them larger & better & need not go & live there when she's married."[13]) that suggest both the varieties of endings available to her, and the normative push ("need not go") behind the plotting available to her. Similarly, she writes as she finished the book, "Mr Thornton ought to be developing himself—and Mr Hale ought to die."[14] But the tensions run even deeper than the plot, and seem to have to do with the construction of the story to fit its place of publication. She writes to Dickens, who was editing it for *Household Words*,

> I dare say I shall like my story, when I am a little further from it; at present I can only feel depressed about it, I meant it to have been so much better. I send what I am afraid you will think too large a batch of it by this post. . . .
>
> I have tried to shorten & compress it, both because it was a dull piece, & to get it into reasonable length, but there were a whole catalogue of events to be got over. . . . Therefore I never wish to see it's face again; but *if you will keep the MS for me, & shorten it as you think best for H. W.* I shall be very glad. Shortened I see it must be [emphasis added].[15]

In the "must be" of "shortened," comes the relation between the "compression" of publication and the compulsion of plot; the issue is less the potential perfection of the novel than the present need for a "reasonable length," the "catalogue of events to be got over" that is at once the necessary and necessitated plot. As Gaskell was to recount the publishing to a friend,

I made a half-promise (as perhaps I told you,) to Mr Dickens, which he understood as a whole one; and though I had the plot and characters in my head long ago, I have often been in despair about the working of them out; because of course, in this way of publishing it, I had to write pretty hard without waiting for the happy leisure hours . . . at last the story is huddled & hurried up; especially in the rapidity with which the sudden death of Mr Bell, succeeds to the sudden death of Mr Hale. But what could I do? Every page was grudged me. . . . Just at the very last I was compelled to desperate compression. . . . I can not insert small pieces here & there—I feel as if I must throw myself back a certain distance in the story, & re-write it from there; retaining the present incidents, but filling up intervals of time &c. &c.[16]

Gaskell's representation of herself as diligent worker ("I had to write pretty hard") resisting the demanding taskmaster ("Every page was grudged me") suggests she understands herself as a slave to production, but another metaphor she used for the writing of the book suggests even more strongly its relation to the thematics of language in *North and South*: "If the story had been poured just warm out of the mind, it would have taken a much larger mould. It was the cruel necessity of compressing it that hampered me."[17] The text here becomes consciously a *made* object—one that was not, to return to Nicholas Higgins's metaphor, "shaped out in words, all neat and clean, as th' men at th' foundry cut out sheet-iron," but one cruelly hampered, forced into a mold too small for it. The work of art here is primarily an artifact of "mechanical reproduction," and concerns with printers, copyright, and unexpectedly duplicated pages continue to obsess Gaskell even after it is done. In another letter, she writes, "There is a page in 'North & South' printed *twice* over. *16* lines. Page 262, & Page 312. Mr Gaskell, in returning one of the proofs, requested you to ask the printer to look whether there was not a repetition."[18] Its awareness of its own reproducibility makes *North and South*, for Gaskell, a doubly "industrialized" novel.

Gaskell's sense of herself as a "compressed" laborer and her text as product belies any easy identification of the novelist/novel as "doctoring" *above* the marketplace, and her question to Dickens (if he "meant" "to have a strike") suggests her anxiety, like that of Thornton's workers, about competing *in* the marketplace. Her depression over the writing of the novel left her increasingly uncertain about her own relationship to the reading public:

I believe I've been as nearly dazed and crazed with this c—, d— be h— to it, story as can be. I've been sick of writing, and everything connected with literature or improvement of the mind; to say nothing of deep hatred to my species about whom I was obliged to write as if I loved 'em. Moreover I have had to write so hard that I have spoilt my hand, and forgotten all my spelling. . . .

If all goes on well and my wretched story is done, I think we shall go and escape the reviews, hang 'em.[19]

To feel "deep hatred to my species about whom I was obliged to write as if I loved 'em," with its slight slanginess, is unimaginable in the realms of sympathetic narration ("the improvement of the mind") *North and South* invokes—how much more so is its writer's "escape" from the reviews, from those readers she seems to be trying to improve. Gaskell, writing for the editorial Dickens who threatens to Wills in his despair over Gaskell's overlong and late proofs, "If I were Mr G oh! heaven, how I would beat her," is almost as violently "spoilt" for her audience; the elided curses ("c—, d— be h— to it, story") suggest the impossibility of language to make concrete the anger of the woman writer, the "impressed" "half-promised" producer, the "compressed" fiction-maker at work in the metalworks, longing for a larger "mould."

Gaskell's self-consciousness about "literature or improvement of the mind," I am arguing here, is in fact reflected throughout *North and South* in these debates over language we have been tracing, in its irony about literary forms and the classical inheritance, but primarily in its treatment of Margaret Hale as the translator between these various languages, as the character who carries out the authorial mission of "improving the mind." If one could argue that the rhetoric of the woman novelist as the ideal bearer of the socially enlightening word enacts a kind of mystification of the difficult production of the text, one could argue similarly about Margaret Hale's "function" in the novel that the heroine's role as "perfect listener" subsumes the difficulty of being a daughter, of being a powerless woman, of being economically dependent, that the novel might otherwise describe. Just as Margaret must wear her cousin's shawls, so she must listen to Edith prattle until Edith falls asleep, and then, "in default of a listener, she had to brood over the change in her life silently as heretofore" (p. 36). When she returns to her family, she must "shake off the recollection of what had been done and said through the day, and *turn a sympathising listener* to the account of how Dixon had complained that the ironing-blanket had been burnt again . . ." (65; emphasis added). Later, she must be *"made a good listener* to all her mother's little plans," while her father "sipped his tea in abstracted silence; Margaret had all the responses to herself" (p. 75; 65; emphasis added). What the novel suggests is that Margaret must be "made" a listener, must "turn" to listening; women are not naturally those sympathetic narrators (or readers) upon which texts depend but are *made* sympathetic. But in the scene that follows the violence at the mill, when Margaret has urged Thornton to speak face to face, to listen to his men, she returns home to where her father

> wanted, as Margaret saw, to be amused and interested by something that she was to tell him. With sweet patience did she bear her pain, without a word of complaint; and rummaged up numberless small subjects for conversation—all except the riot, and that she never named once. (p. 248)

Trapped by the "numberless small subjects," Margaret cannot assume her own "subject," which she never names. The "conversation" between masters and men, as a conversation, and perhaps as a novel, seems similarly to silence the woman's "subject."

This brings us back to the question of Margaret's "plot," of the ways the industrial novel and the marriage novel jostle against one another. For the marriage novel to *work* as a symbolic enactment of union, the woman as translator is crucial, bearing the word between masters and men; Margaret's "message" has been read accurately by Thornton, who is now ready to be married. His conversion is at once a consequence of and a sign of his readiness to love Margaret, but their marriage will also reinforce the "message" as well: as Margaret and Thornton could be brought together, so workers and their employers can be "married," learn to see their common goals, the truth that lies *between* "masters and men." But one might argue that as much as Margaret's "subject of conversation" gets lost in the conversation, so the woman's plot is in danger of getting subsumed in the larger plots (the social conversation, the industrial debate, the ideological imperatives of marriage) that Gaskell's "subject" demands. Margaret's silencing might extend to her disappearance from the title of the novel, into the larger thematic concerns of the social plotting of "north and south."

iv

In these ways, Gaskell's critique of the *form* of the industrial novel returns us to the question of the marriage plot, and the ways in which the "romance" offers the central metaphor for union in the novel. A feminist reader might begin with this questioning of the role of the sympathizing woman in reconciling the oppositions of England; a more cynical reader might simply comment that Gaskell's faith in the powers of union is optimistic, at best. Such a criticism makes sense only if we are to make larger claims for the marriage than I think the novel does—and the desire to make those claims (if only to refute them) testifies to the tremendous power both of the marriage plot and our own quest for union(s). If the novel is skeptical about the ability of texts to pose solutions, it is equally so about the capacity of readers to change; no transformation larger than a marriage is, finally, promised, and the lovers' reconciliation takes place in solitude, with only the *imagined* voices of others as commentary—and those voices are, it is worth noting, still skeptical.

But this novel does promise more than some others, and it is important to note the promise that transpires deliberately outside the marriage itself. That promise has something to do with the heroine's *other* life—the story that resists the marriage plot—and with the precise nature of Thornton's transformation; it also has a great deal to do with Gaskell's difficulties in finishing the "c—, d— be h— to it" novel. Much as Gaskell had difficulty imagining an end that would truly redistribute power ("What do you think of a fire burning down Mr Thornton's mills *and house* as a *help* to failure? Then Margaret would rebuild them larger & better & need not go & live there when she's married") and yet leave Margaret free (she "need not go and live there"), so the novel marks the difficulty of bringing characters into that social resolution signaled by the marriage plot and by the heroine's blushing disappearance into the hero's embrace.

The triumph of the ending's embrace is earned by the transformations of both characters, precisely against the social scorn of her aunt and his mother, the erotic triumph mirrored in the overcoming of social opposition. So it seems that the social plot achieves *its* desires precisely through the manipulation of what we might lightly call the reader's "easier" desires, those for sexual union, marital bliss, closure itself; reading for the clinch in this novel becomes reading for the transformation of the masters into a more benevolent middle class. In terms of the substitution of one plot for another with which this chapter began, the novel's final slide is into the plot with the most recognizable—and hence, nameable—solution, that of romantic satisfaction.

Except, of course, that we began with the assumption that the heroine's "slide" into marriage was precisely the problematic to be resolved by the plot. If Margaret's marriage *is* the difficulty, how can it be said to resolve the difficulties of the social plot? Rather, we might turn our attention to the ways *North and South* delays its end in order to make *more* complicated the heroine's wedding—the ways it deconventionalizes its heroine and her desires; the way it reinscribes the plotting of class on the heroine's body in its final chapters; the difficulty with which it marries her off.

These difficulties are as inflected with the class/language problems as what went before. What moves Margaret to marriage, and what keeps her from it, are both read through the social divisions with which the novel has been concerned all along. The chief obstacle to the marriage is the melodramatic misunderstanding consequent upon Margaret's brother's mysterious visit to the family in Milton, and Mr Thornton's observation of the two siblings at a train station, where, on that night, a man meets his death. In conventional terms, the digressive plot provokes jealousy in Thornton, while also making Margaret (and Gaskell's readers) realize how much she values Thornton's opinion of her. It is certainly a credit to the realism surrounding the melodrama that Thornton can actually say, "Your secret is safe with me," without its seeming an exaggeration, but her "secret" is further eroticized when Thornton thinks that "he shared with the mob, in her desire of averting bloodshed from them; but this man, this hidden lover, shared with nobody; he had looks, words, hand-cleavings, *lies, concealment,* all to himself" (p. 387; emphasis added). But its significance for *our* purposes is that the misunderstanding depends on a sentence Margaret *cannot* speak to Thornton: she can never say, "You observed me with a brother, not a lover; I lied to protect him." Margaret's inability to explain her own "honour" involves the plot in a series of lies and missed opportunities that repeat the thematics of inappropriate speech diffused throughout the novel. The fact that it is a sexual secret that remains undisclosable suggests the ways sexual energy continues to be bound within the text, the tension sustained till the end of the novel.

The novel, then, needs to make possible the revelation of the secret (the secret, here, of innocence), but it also needs to move the heroine back to the hero. In this novel both these tasks are accomplished by the insertion of the heroine into the working-class plot of the book. The secret of Frederick's visit, which Margaret hoped would be told by Mr Bell, is in fact disclosed by Nicholas Higgins: without Margaret's friendship outside her class, and without the new arrangements at Thornton's mill (prompted by Margaret's lectures on the subject) Thornton would never learn of Margaret's innocence, and never be prompted to propose again.

But the novel needs more than just the clearing of the heroine's name; it needs to invent a slightly different heroine, to make possible the different ending that might promise social resolution. The most interesting moment of *North and South* in this light is the break in the motion toward marriage, the chapters after Margaret's lonely return to London and before her meeting with Thornton at yet another dinner party. The Margaret who dines with Thornton is not the Margaret who left Helstone. Although the text went to some trouble to make her, in Mr Bell's phrase, "that poor creature there,—that helpless, homeless, friendless Margaret" (p. 437), it does not throw her (helpless) into Thornton's arms. Rather, the end of the novel finds her newly propertied, independent, serene; it returns to her the suitor of the opening chapters; it of course leaves her more beautiful than ever.

But what has happened in between the opening and the close is not just the heroine's growing wisdom (reflected, again, in her deepening beauty) but her very specific education into questions of class and labor. In the chapters after the death of her father and Mr Bell, whose bequest leaves her an heiress, Margaret chooses not to retreat into the wealth of London; instead, she goes out looking for those "toilers and moilers" concealed by (but providing) that wealth. Her independence begins when she learns she is to inherit from Mr Bell; when she hears he is dying, she insists on traveling to Oxford, and is always glad afterward she had insisted on that independent action. The novel is explicit about the ways her money *allows* Margaret this independence (and that explicitness is part of the novel's strength), but it insists also on explaining the details of the independence: she pays for rent, she buys her own clothes (as she makes clear to Edith), and she works to understand her property, "teaching her of what all these mysteries of the law [deeds and papers] were the signs and types" (p. 505). The explicit economies of the novel's conclusion make possible the (different) conclusion of the romance: Margaret must understand her property to propose leasing it to Mr Thornton; it is only the property (the proposal) of a truly independent woman (one who goes into slums, walks alone, takes the physical risks the novel was so explicit about in its opening) that can make possible the (different) marriage that will end the book.

If the way out of the novel is through the propertied heroine, the way to her greater authority was actually through a removal from the middle class that parallels the linguistic contagion of Margaret's conversation. Soon after moving to Milton, Margaret helps her mother by ironing her mother's caps; when she is done, she jokes that she is "no longer Peggy the laundry-maid, but Margaret Hale the lady" (p. 115)—a joke her mother refuses to share. Margaret, fearful of disturbing her mother, is quick to add that she doesn't "mind ironing, or any kind of work, for you and papa," for "I am myself a born and bred lady through it all, even though it comes to scouring a floor, or washing dishes." But her labor threatens to blur those distinctions—in ways different from the blurring that happens when Bessy Higgins hints that Margaret is not "grand" enough to visit the wealthy Thorntons, and Margaret must haughtily insist on her gentility, and on having always "lived among educated people." The possibility of being at once "Peggy the laundry-maid" *and* "Margaret the lady" allows for both irony against the lady and the inclusion of the laundry-maid. Although physical labor is not entirely unheard of among Victorian heroines, no other heroine comes to mind who names (or, rather, renames) herself as a laborer, who proudly wears the lower-class nickname, and whose social work begins with that initial pose of solidarity.

Nor is there another heroine who seems to embrace so even-temperedly the possibility of spinsterhood. Although Caroline Helstone, in *Shirley*, worries that "there [is] a terrible hollowness, mockery, want, craving, in that existence which is given away to others, for want of something of your own to bestow it on," Margaret actually senses that she is in the mood in which women "took the veil." She longs for a life of usefulness, not for another man; the changes of the previous chapters leave her stunned but independent, and she is able to say, even of Thornton and her desire that he know of her innocence, that "this wish was vain, like so many others," and instead she "schooled herself into this conviction [and] turned with all her heart and strength to the life that lay immediately before her, and resolved to strive and make the best of that" (p. 506). Far from assuming that the best of her life was over, or that striving was in vain, the novel offers the possibility of the heroine's independence from male authority and male attention:

> [Margaret] had learnt, in those solemn hours of thought, that she herself must one day answer for her own life, and what she had done with it; and she tried to settle that most difficult problem for women, how much was to be utterly merged in obedience to authority, and how much might be set apart for freedom in working. (p. 508)

After informing her aunt of her choice and "charming" her into acquiescence to her will, Margaret "gained the acknowledgment of her right to follow her own ideas of duty," and goes to work. "Only don't be strong-minded"—Edith's plea, which approximates the social disapproval Margaret can anticipate—is met with Margaret's assertion that "as I have neither husband nor child to give me natural duties, I must make myself some, in addition to ordering my gowns." And the novel effectively dismisses *any* criticism of "strong-minded[ness]," when Margaret teasingly offers to "faint on your hands at the servant's dinner time, the very first opportunity; and then, what with Sholto playing with the fire, and the baby crying, you'll begin to wish for a strong-minded woman, equal to any emergency."

Edith's fear that Margaret will "grow too good to joke and be merry" probably grows out of Gaskell's own visits to Florence Nightingale's family, for it was in their house (as Florence was achieving the fame that would make her even more a stranger to her family) that she wrote much of the novel. But the novel's pleasure in the strong-minded woman "equal to any emergency" is equal to its *need* for a character who is equal to the changes and transformations it depicts; the heroine of the industrial novel, it seems to say, could not be a heroine who would faint at "the very first opportunity." The novel reflects as well as Gaskell's own ambivalence about the balance of work and "obedience," the growing debate in the 1850s about women's work and women's independence. The essays and lectures of the early feminists whom Gaskell knew and respected, particularly Anna Jameson, dwell repeatedly on the failure of English society to present its women with meaningful work (particularly Protestant women who could not "take the veil," as Jameson argues in essays on the need for new "sisterhoods"[20]); what the novel finally makes of its heroine *is* a different kind of "labourer." This new sense of heroineship reflects the novel's attention to Margaret's social placement *and* inner transformations: the heroine's public usefulness, as well as her deep despair, her very real isolation, her quiet conviction that she will never marry or have children. The novel's ending seems to carry out an undoing of the heroine's expectations that parallels its undoing of her expectations at the beginning: none of the old plots, it seems, will quite do.

And this is where the presumed closure of the old marriage plot will offer the least. What the novel needs most from its heroine (and its readers) is an acceptance of *change*—of living in a "whirring" world that will allow the *heroine* to change. When she visits Helstone, Margaret is discouraged by (and frightened by) the changes in the town, and in herself. What she realizes only after she leaves her old home is that the changes in the world are necessary to accommodate the changing desires of a self always whirred, always in motion. She moves from "a sense of change, of individual nothingness, of perplexity and disappointment . . . [of] this slight, all-pervading instability" to the belief that "if the world stood still, it would retrograde and become corrupt" (p. 488). "Looking out of myself, and my own painful sense of change, the progress of all around me is necessary and right," she argues, and notes just a page later, "And I too change perpetually—now this, now that—. . . ."

What the novel accomplishes is the historicizing of that "changing" self; that self always in opposition to itself, to existing social conditions, to the silencing going on around it. What *North and South* establishes is not only the novel *Cranford* proposed, a novel that is open to the changes of a dynamic, historical world, but a novel capable of depicting a world in deep conflict. When Thornton is attempting to explain the changes he has made in his mill, he says he has come to believe no change can happen except when people meet face to face, in "actual personal contact," for "such intercourse is the very breath of life." When asked if he thinks this will prevent strikes, he says (displaying a realism the novel is not often credited with) that he has *no* such expectations, but he hopes the strikes will be less bitter.

The oppositions the novel "resolves" in its other plots seem to me similarly intractable; moderation rather than solution seems the tone of the novel—and more, the novel *enjoys* these oppositions, which are (of course) deeply eroticized throughout the book. When Margaret cares for Edith's son, rejected by others when he indulges in tantrums, she carries him off into a room, where "they two alone battled it out; she with a firm power which subdued him into peace, while every sudden charm and wile she possessed, was exerted on the side of right, until he would rub his little hot and tear-smeared face all over hers, kissing and caressing till he often fell asleep in her arms or on her shoulder" (p. 495). In the same way, what tires Margaret the most in London is "the eventless ease in which no struggle or endeavour was required" (p. 458); not only is the novel not afraid of conflict, or deeply attracted to it, or dependent on it, it *believes* in conflictual models. Not only is there no novel *without* a conflict but the use of the novel seems to be that it can *incorporate* conflict. The "social intercourse" of the novel will be the moderating force of the "strikes" between readers, not in the sense that it will assuage their hostility but that it will force a recognition of conflict, and of the utter necessity for the intercourse in which it involves its readers.

This is at once to criticize the conventional expectations of the industrial novel and its faith in the face-to-face encounter, and to expand those expectations. If the heroine's plot seems to re-create this motion of conflict, intercourse, and less strained conflict, we must note both the variations this creates in the conventions of the heroine's story and the ways the marriage plot remains central to every other concern of the novel. Marriage-with-a-difference will provide the necessary narrative model, as well as the erotic energy (the readerly desire-conflict-and-opposition), that will instruct us. What the novel accomplished with its motion from plot to plot, its transformations of its heroine and our expectations for her, its encapsulation of multiple languages and readerly perspectives, it hopes to hold in place (to the extent that transformation can be held in place) with that poised conflict of marriage as resolution—the resolution of continued oppositions, sexual tension, pleasure and dispersal, which is all the marriage plot ever has to offer.

III

SO MANY VIEWS:
CLOSING AND OPENING
VICTORIAN FICTION

5

"Filled in with Pretty Writing": Desire, History, and Literacy in *Sylvia's Lovers*

"Desire is always there at the start of a narrative," Peter Brooks has suggested: the desire of the reader for movement, of the text for its own end, of the characters for whatever the desideratum of the plot is to be.[1] In both *Sylvia's Lovers* and *Wives and Daughters*, Gaskell's attention moves from the focusing of desire into the marriage plot to the way desire itself is plotted. Where the earlier novels offered fairly conventional progresses of both characters' and readers' desires, here, there is no such easy progression. In these novels, desire is given a gender and a history; it is placed within history (as revolution or evolution) and within gender (in the gothic plot of female desire). In *Sylvia's Lovers*, desire is self-consuming; it loses its place as the force always already (naturally) there. The heroine's plot and its historical analogue (the revolutionary fervor of the Napoleonic wars) take place within a world of doubling, confusion, and narrative self-reflexivity.

Sylvia's Lovers is Gaskell's first historical novel. Although she had written historical fiction previously (*My Lady Ludlow*, a story about the dangers of teaching servants to read in the time of the French Revolution, was published in 1858; *Lois the Witch*, a novella dealing with the Salem witchcraft trials, in 1859), and although *Ruth* was set thirty years in the past, *Sylvia's Lovers* is her most extended venture into the past—and perhaps the most deliberate. The novel not only examines the questions of change and violence these other historical works posed but manages to rephrase as well the question of the relationship between the heroine and the revolutions around her; between individuals and social change; between male and female plots, in a way unique in Gaskell's work. Like

153

Dickens's *A Tale of Two Cities*, published in 1859, the year Gaskell first proposed her novel to George Smith, *Sylvia's Lovers* wants both to trace the passions of individuals at times of intense social change and to understand the parallels between the desires of men and women and the forces of revolution.

Like *Mary Barton*, *Sylvia's Lovers* begins with the need to marry off a spirited, willful heroine; with two men who love her; with her angry, impassioned father, and his dangerous political violence. Like the earlier novel, it asks which "force" it is that collapses into the other; where do the public and the private end and begin? And like the earlier novel, this book seems deeply aware of its middle-class readers, and their complacency about historical change. The Yorkshire of the novel is at once the land of the Brontës, in which Gaskell had been immersed in writing the biography of her friend Charlotte, and the home of much of the radical working-class protests of the 1830s and 1840s; in this novel, it is also a comment on the absence of real change in later Victorian England.

The novel seems to take its energy from the wilds of the Yorkshire whaling village; it announces itself as a novel of desire, with characters who speak out fiercely what they want. But *Sylvia's Lovers* presents a world of constant oppositions, confusions, and reversals; after speaking their desires, characters find they want something else. As soon as they make their bold claims to freedom, they are forced to recant, realizing they have made some crucial interpretive error or do not know how to name what they want. Throughout the novel, desire is articulated only to be contradicted, and each character's desire exists as one plot among many, amid a mesh of conflicting wishes, repetitions, negations, and returns, in which choice seems at once free-floating and forever fixed.

Not only is *Sylvia's Lovers* filled with a confusion of desires, it argues a central confusion in the construction of desire itself, and unfixes desire as a concept from the realm of sexuality. Desire here is a way of structuring and forming identity, a plot in which identity is gained through conflict and opposition. The central "plot," one written by and for men, and acted out primarily through their love of women, depends on the registering of difference between men and women, and its essential progress is one in which men fix their identity by desiring each other's women.[2] In that light, Gaskell's novel begins by asking how women can acquire *any* identity in a plot that requires them to be only objects, never fully formed subjects, free to choose for themselves. How, if they are known through their "lovers," are they to come into being themselves?

It is here, with that question of desire and change, that history and narrative come back together. Narrative, as Tzvetan Todorov has argued, depends on the tension between "two formal categories, difference and similarity"; that is, neither absolute difference nor absolute similarity will generate narrative.[3] *Sylvia's Lovers* suggests that the realms of similarity and difference have culturally assigned, gendered roles: men live in the world of difference, conflict, history; women in the realm of similarity, repetition, myth. Narrative depends on the play between them, the play we conventionally enact through the romance plot, in which women stay at home, and men have adventures. But *Sylvia's Lovers* will also suggest that in times of violent social change, plots of all sorts become more complicated, and the tension that seems to guarantee narrative can come to contaminate it instead. In *Sylvia's Lovers*, the plot of female desire unfixes difference, and works its own narrative transformations; in *Sylvia's Lovers*, the woman writer's concern with the literary, indeed, with literacy itself, asks what it would mean if the woman novelist began to tell a new story; if the density of female desire might, instead, write a new history altogether.

i

At the center of *Sylvia's Lovers* is a very dense romantic triangle. Sylvia Robson, the young, high-spirited only child of Daniel Robson, a sailor-turned-farmer, and Bell, his better-born, educated wife, is adored by her mother's cousin, the earnest, sober Philip Hepburn. But she, barely registering Philip's devotion, loses her heart to the handsome, bold specksioneer Charley Kinraid, who in turn promises his love to her— much to the horror of Philip, who believes Charley to be untrue. The novel seems divided between the passions of these characters, and Gaskell's working titles for the novel suggest her interest in all three. At first the novel was to be called "The Specksioneer," and then it became "Philip's Idol," a title to which she seemed deeply attached. She changed it finally to *Sylvia's Lovers*, the only title of these that includes all three central characters. The fluctuation suggests the focus on character *in relation*: each character seems to take over the novel in turn, not taking it over alone but always as he or she is viewed by or matters to others. Hence, Philip is not "Philip," but "Sylvia's Lover"; Sylvia is important in that she is "Philip's Idol;" even the "Specksioneer," significantly, is noted not for his name but for his representative, "heroic" stature as harpooner. And so, too, within the love relationships of the novel, characters assume charged roles, representative positions; not names but functions.

Further, though the emphasis of the novel, as the final title suggests, is on the two men—what they represent for Sylvia and the ways they represent or imagine her—the novel encloses the relations between the three central characters within larger circles of desire that draw in other characters as well. Philip, obsessed with Sylvia, is the object himself of obsessive love: Hester Rose, the Quaker woman with whose mother he boards, loves him as quietly, as passionately as he loves Sylvia. Hester, in turn, is loved by William Coulson, the other junior partner in the Fosters' shop where Philip works. Coulson, when rejected by Hester, is able to turn to another woman, much as Charley Kinraid, when he discovers that Sylvia has married Philip, marries a rich, beautiful, sheltered girl who has none of the qualities he swore would make him love only Sylvia forever.

Although some of these loves seem not to touch the central relations— Philip does not "learn" from Coulson how to love Hester, for instance— at other times, love seems entirely imitative. When Charley and Sylvia meet, each perceives the other as already desired by or belonging to someone else. Charley is pointed out to Sylvia by Molly Corney, and Molly presents him as already practically engaged to her; when he first sees Sylvia crying at a dead sailor's funeral, he "conclude[s] that she must have been a sweetheart of the dead man."[4] Each act of desire shimmers with the reflection of someone else's (imagined) desire; people are searching for their own image in someone else's story.

This kind of love is always a blending of public and private relations; the novel thrives on eavesdropping, interruptions, trysts, onlookers, and soliloquies, with only the narrator watching all the observers in turn. Yet in this overlapping world, no event takes place only in one person's "story." Even in the scene when Sylvia first speaks to Charley, who thinks her already spoken for, in the presence of Molly, whom Sylvia assumes to be Charley's fiancée, she has been followed in her progress to the speck-sioneer by her cousin Philip, who wants to protect her from the crowd and keep her to himself. But the repeated parallels, here and throughout the novel, are ignored by the characters: the irony of the opposing romances is noted only by the quiet narrator, who juxtaposes them by moving directly between them:

> "Yo'll come and be nursed at Moss Brow, Charley," said Molly; and Sylvia dropped her little maidenly curtsey, and said, "Good-by;" and went away, wondering how Molly could talk so freely to such a hero; but then, to be sure, he was a cousin, and probably a sweetheart, and that would make a great deal of difference, of course.
> Meanwhile, her own cousin kept close by her side. (p. 72)

Each character is caught up in several plots at once—with an array of conflicting desires, so there is hardly an "individual" or "private" plot to be named. Philip may be the tradesman in one plot, the "cousin" in the next, the earnest lover in his own, but only the narrative translates between one plot and the other; the characters seem unaware of the jumble in which they move.

Sylvia's Lovers seems to pose *intentionally* complicated problems of plots, but do we, initially, take seriously its overlapping stories, conflicting aims, doubled desires? These seem at first essentially comic elements, plots of romantic reversals, where we can expect a kind of "Midsummer Night's Dream" in which "Jack will have Jill; Naught shall go ill." The task of fiction, after all, is often to shuffle lovers from inappropriate choice to appropriate choice. One way of reading *Sylvia's Lovers* would be as a romance plot whose tragic—morbid—overtones take over, as another of Gaskell's novels where the domestic plot turns to melodrama and an essentially familiar novel is derailed by the novelist's penchant for overly dramatic contrasts.

Critics have raised this question to focus on the generic switch into melodrama at the novel's conclusion, when the two heroes find themselves at the Siege of Acre and—improbably—recognize each other. But this one melodrama of doubling—the moment when the heroes face unexpected similarities where they had previously perceived difference, and finally see each other as trapped by the same plot—is part of a larger pattern of doubling (formal and thematic) throughout the novel: plots that trap, confuse, and narrate their characters; plots that force on characters unexpected "returns." This doubling, what Peter Brooks describes as narrative that appears "to partake of the demonic, as a kind of tantalizing instinctual play, a re-enactment that encounters the magic and the curse of reproduction or 'representation,'"[5] is part of a larger drama, a plot *Sylvia's Lovers* reads through sexual conflict. And here the "comic" ending is displaced, in favor of a deeper disruption, for although in comic plots there is room for female activity, and female desire can be acknowledged and its threat contained, in nineteenth-century fiction, desire can be expressed only by men. In this novel, the "curse" is the disruptive power of female desire, in the world where Sylvia's lovers, not Sylvia herself, are empowered and—culturally—given textual authority. This is the truly disruptive possibility the novel's dense plot wishes to entertain: that women would write stories of difference, rather than "standing for" that crucial difference against which men will write their stories; that women could desire, and speak out that desire.

This might suggest again the danger of reading too narrowly the (female) plots of romantic desire in the novel, of missing what Eve Sedgwick has argued of desire, that it is a "social force, the glue, even when its manifestation is hostility or hatred or something less emotively charged," that it is a "structure."[6] It is easy to misread "love" in a novel; to see only the confusion we know as plot, only the plot we call "love." What Sylvia wants when she "falls in love" with Kinraid—what that love is another name for—need not be limited to the structures of romantic love but can be linked to a wider field of desire, to which she gains access by "falling in love" with him. And again, in reading the intense relations between Kinraid and Hepburn—Sylvia's "lovers"—we can see that their inter-interpretations, as well as their readings of Sylvia and her character, express desires that transcend any notions of romantic love. In Charley's ways of promising his love to Sylvia, in Philip's interpretive battle about Charley and his dilemma over his promise to present Charley's love (his "truth") to Sylvia, and particularly in Philip's confusion over his marriage to Sylvia, we see the way that romantic desire promises to function for these characters: it will provide them with something they lack, something, most often, caught up with their own sexual identity and self-definition, but something which has little to do with the real experience or identity of the beloved object.[7] The quest to fill that emptiness, then, goes by the name of romantic love; it is their own identities that Sylvia's lovers most lack.

Philip loves Sylvia, most simply, because she is resistant: she is charming, wayward, beautiful, and completely indifferent to him. What he recognizes from the first is their difference, but it is a difference that sparks his passion. What he wants from her must be that resistance. When they are finally married, after circumstances—her father's execution, her mother's illness, the loss of her farm—have moved Sylvia into his arms, he can notice only the gap between what he wanted and what he in fact has:

> He wanted the old Sylvia back again; captious, capricious, wilful, haughty, merry, charming. Alas! that Sylvia was gone for ever. (p. 330)

What he has is a woman under his "influence," who "obey(s) his expressed wishes with gentle indifference, as if she had no preference of her own," "out of the spirit of obedience" toward her mother. What he wanted was a woman who would be "wilful" and at the same time under his influence: whose will, in essence, would be to be his.

But Philip's desire, which is on the one hand for possession of Sylvia, is also, on some level, to be possessed. Of all the characters, he is the one most obsessed with his "idol," most completely defined as a "lover." His passion nears masochism, in his repeated return to her side despite her scorn, his over-reading in her polite "good-nights" an encouragment to

his hopes. Not only does he blur the lines between possessor and possessed, he seems to blur lines of masculine and feminine plots of desire
here. He feels within him "a force of enduring love," which is what marks
him as unusual: the "thought of her was bound up with his life; and that
once torn out by his own free will, the very roots of his heart must come
also" (p. 160). That passivity of "enduring love," the suppressed violence
of tearing up "by his own free will" the "very roots of his heart," the
connection between thinking of her and "his life," are the most violent—
and the most conventionally feminine—statements of desire in the novel.
But they suggest, further, that that aspect of Philip—desiring, where he
seems content; angry, where he seems meek—can, in what are traditionally feminine terms, get expressed only through love. Philip gets a self, as
women customarily do in novels, by being in love.

Charley Kinraid's love for Sylvia takes place equally in terms of desire
and possession, though in a more mutual struggle for power. Both he and
Sylvia enjoy each other's defiance: "they were like two children defying
each other; each determined to conquer" (p. 184). For Charley, Sylvia is a
"pretty girl," whom he claims he will "niver forget," but in fact, she seems
to slide in and out of his consciousness. What he enjoys, most clearly, is
his power over her; what we never know, exactly, is how much he does
think of her when she isn't there.

We do know that the men in the novel think constantly of one another,
and are unable to read the other(s) except as projections of—or in
opposition to—their own psyches. The novel's critique of Charley's "forgetfulness"—and his love for Sylvia—is most clearly in Philip's terms:
when he sees Charley kidnapped by the press-gang, and hears his farewell
message to Sylvia promising to return, Philip thinks of writing to Sylvia
and "telling her—how much?"

> She might treasure up her lover's words like grains of gold, while they were
> lighter than dust in their meaning to Philip's mind; words which such as the
> specksioneer used as counters to beguile and lead astray silly women. It was
> for him to prove his constancy by action; and the chances of his giving such
> proof were infinitesimal in Philip's estimation. (p. 224)

Philip sees Charley, here, not as his own person but as a type, "such as
the specksioneer," rather than this particular specksioneer. (Here Sylvia,
too, becomes a type—one of the "silly women" easily led astray.) But
Philip sees Charley through his own lens: Charley does not express
"constancy" by action such as Philip would choose. Charley *has* just
offered proof, by sending a farewell warning to Sylvia rather than just
disappearing, but Philip will not "estimate" that proof. He has, of course,

just closed Charley's chance of giving any proof, by deciding not to give
the message to Sylvia; clearly, we are to read this as Philip's special
pleading, his own desire blurring his judgment. But this pattern of
reading one's opposite in terms of one's own predispositions continues
throughout the novel: when Sylvia overvalues Hester's courage by imagining what she would do if she loved Philip the way Hester does; when
Hester tries to imagine anything Philip could do to alienate her affec-
tions, as he has Sylvia's; when Philip assumes that he can read Charley's
character as clearly as he does the business information he receives
in London, where he feels himself "fully capable of unravelling each
clue to information, and deciding on the value of knowledge so gained"
(pp. 225–226). Philip "took upon himself to decide that, with such a man
as the specksioneer, absence was equivalent to faithless forgetfulness." He
is leaping from the stories he has heard of Charley's other betrayals to a
notion of character; further, he is leaping from his own desires, what his
absence would mean, to what it must mean for Charley.

Charley—and Sylvia—make similar assumptions about Philip based
on an inability to read a character unlike their own; with Charley and
Philip, competing for Sylvia is as much a battle of character as of wills.
Each asserts a way of being in the world through the ability to win—to
possess—Sylvia. In a sense, each wants her to mirror his success, his self,
back to him, and each wants the other man to register this victory. In a
stunning moment, after the Corneys' New Year's party to which Philip
escorts Sylvia, and at which she first kisses Charley, the Corney family
and Charley himself come into the Fosters' store. Philip watches Charley
"perpetually," "with a kind of envy of his bright, courteous manner, the
natural gallantry of the sailor."

> If it were but clear that Sylvia took as little thought of him as he did of her,
> to all appearance, Philip could even have given him praise for manly good
> looks, and a certain kind of geniality of disposition which made him ready
> to smile pleasantly at all strangers, from babies upwards. (p. 164)

Charley comes to shake hands with him "over the counter":

> Last night Philip could not have believed it possible that such a demonstra-
> tion of fellowship should have passed between them; and perhaps there was
> a slight hesitation of manner on his part, for some idea or remembrance
> crossed Kinraid's mind which brought a keen searching glance into the eyes
> which for a moment were fastened on Philip's face. In spite of himself, and
> during the very action of hand-shaking, Philip felt a cloud come over his
> face, not altering or moving his features, but taking light and peace out of
> his countenance. (p. 165)

That moment of recognition—of mutual desire—is the forging of a bond that encourages not understanding but confusion. Soon after that, Molly tells of Charley's dancing all the rest of the evening at the party, and Philip is deeply relieved, for he says that after Sylvia's departure, "yearning after the absent one would have been a weight to his legs," and he cannot imagine anyone being different. But in their consciousness of each other, and their constant measuring of themselves by the existence of the other, the two heroes remain deeply linked—neither has an entirely separate (individual) desire.

But female desire is inscribed differently and Sylvia's love plot must be read equally differently. The difference is social: the sharp contrast between her love for Charley and the love of both men for her becomes clear when one notes the locations of the repeated confrontations between Philip and Charley. When Philip watches Charley being taken by the press-gang, Charley is about to go out to sea; Philip is on his way to London. At this moment, as at the end of the novel, when both men are at the Siege of Acre, Sylvia is at home, waiting; the plot of female desire differs most clearly from that of men in that men get to go on the road. Men are to some extent free to walk out to meet their destinies; women must wait for their plot to come to them. Nowhere more than in this simple difference do we see what links Philip and Charley: neither need choose a wife to gain freedom.

But to complicate this further, we might note that Sylvia's love for Charley resembles Philip's love for her more closely than it does any other in the novel: Sylvia, like Philip, wants through desire to gain access to some other world. Desire, for her, expresses a lack. Unlike Philip, however, she does not perceive the lack as in herself: there is nothing *in* Charley that she wants, as Philip wants her charm, her willfulness, her sexuality, at one point, it almost seems, the overtness of her desire for Charley. What Sylvia wants, most clearly, is adventure; if she were able to go to sea herself, she would not be in love with "the specksioneer." There is no doubt but that she is attracted to the sailor, who is, as Philip notes, courteous, smiling, sophisticated, worldly—but these terms begin to blend into something he *has done* rather than something he *has*. She wants his sophistication, only in that she wants to be able to do things.

Sylvia's story, then, does suggest a quest for "similarity" rather than difference—identity through emulation rather than opposition—but a similarity already linked to the process of narrative. Although Charley initially comes to Sylvia's attention marked as desirable by Molly's interest in him, he is further marked as a figure of drama, the hero who has resisted attack and won commendation, who bravely mourns his lost comrade. When he enters Sylvia's life more directly, coming to her parents' house, his way in is paved by his stories: he and her father tell stories of their adventures, and "all night long Sylvia dreamed of burning volcanoes springing out of icy southern seas." But, significantly, she recounts of her listening:

> As in the specksioneer's tale the flames were peopled with demons, there was no human interest for her in the wondrous scene in which she was no actor, only a spectator. (p. 106)

Sylvia is "no actor, only a spectator," because she is a woman. The closest she can come to his islands, volcanoes, and seas is her geography lessons from her cousin Philip, which she spends largely

> stooping over the outspread map, with her eyes,—could he have seen them,—a good deal fixed on one spot in the map, not Northumberland, where Kinraid was spending the winter, but those wild northern seas about which he had told them such wonders. (p. 114)

Her desire is not so much for where he is (Northumberland) but where the "wonders" he had narrated are. Here already she confuses narrating with acting, at a moment when she is not herself moving but sits captivated in his absence by his earlier presence as narrator. Sylvia wants not to be with—or even to be—Kinraid but to see things for herself, to be a heroine. The best she can hope for is to be in love with his stories; it is through her love for him that she hopes to gain heroic stature.

But in this way women's desire seems most imitative—or, rather, reduced to the realms of imitation by convention and by narrative itself. While the men wander the world, gaining experience and choosing for themselves, Sylvia stays home and works—and listens. Through the rest of the novel, Sylvia seems singularly hemmed in by stories, and narrative tradition seems to gain in power. Her mother tells her of "poor Nancy," a Wordsworthian abandoned woman who goes mad waiting for her cheating fiancé, but in the story Sylvia hears only a parallel of her own love (a parallel that traps her more deeply in it); the Fosters' story of Alice Rose's bounder of a husband and Coulson's story of his betrayed sister, abandoned by Kinraid, both lead Philip to lie to Sylvia about Kinraid's absence; Sylvia's father's story—his own originating myth—about cutting off his thumb to escape the press-gang leads him to defy them at last, to participate in the rebellion that will lead to his arrest, conviction, and execution by the state. Stories—as cultural truths, as personal history— seem part of the constant repetition that freezes desire, and specifically, that shapes female movement. As stories name things, they limit possibilities: Sylvia's rebellion cannot take a form unimagined by her mother's and father's stories.

In the same way, as Gaskell herself was constantly learning, women cannot always write new plots for themselves. In this novel, as elsewhere in her work, literature itself is implicated in women's inscription into culture. In *Sylvia's Lovers*, we see the traces of this inscription in two places: in Sylvia's battle with literacy, and in Gaskell's commentary on other Victorian women's novels of female desire. The abstraction of theories of fiction on which I have been dwelling (the repetitions and desires of this overdetermined narrative) here focus on the question of female difference and *its* gothic plot—and its relation to the "plots" of history.

ii

Sylvia's Lovers begins with the story that *North and South* left out: that of the illiterate heroine, the "Jess MacFarlane" of the ballad Gaskell cites, who cannot read the letter her lover sends.[8] If Sylvia could read a letter from Charley, she might have a different story; as is so often true in Gaskell, questions of language and linguistic power become questions of plot. But questions of language also *stay* questions of language, unmetaphorized, as they often do *not* in her novels; this is a story about Sylvia's illiteracy, her learning to read, and the relation of what is seen as patriarchal language to patriarchal power. Literacy suggests the larger revolutionary questions of the novel, but the discussion of the literary (of already-told stories) offers an equally powerful critique of state- and gender-systems of authority. It is out of Sylvia's illiteracy (and the cultural disempowerment that represents) that the novel's critique of established plots (and the culturally scripted disappearance of female power) will arise.

It is Sylvia's mother who wants Sylvia to learn to read: Sylvia wishes "the man were farred"—and she is sure it is a man—"who plagues his brain wi' striking out new words" (p. 107). Philip, who wants desperately to teach her to read, both so he can reshape her and so he can be near her, offers her "a pen as'll nearly write of itself," but Sylvia, trying to achieve the right "attitude," bursts out, "What's the use on my writing 'Abednego,' 'Abednego,' 'Abednego,' all down a page?" (p. 93) In that endless repetition of male identity, which Sylvia must copy into a "copy-book wi' t' Tower of London on it, [which] we'll fill . . . wi' as pretty writing as any in t' North Riding" (p. 92), is Sylvia's real "lesson": first, that she cannot speak out against education that she feels to be useless; and second, that the ability of men to make women write out men's names over and over constitutes real, not merely textual, authority. In that drone of patronymics, and in Sylvia's forced participation in the scene of male authorship, Gaskell suggests the text's critique of the constriction of women's lives, and of the endless repetition of male names that makes up history—and of literature's participation in both.

Gaskell will attempt, at the end of the novel, to present a more optimistic vision of women teaching women to read, one that contrasts with Philip's lessons, which are only the repetition of his love for her. She never, in this novel, presents a more optimistic view of women's *writing*. But if one takes up the terms of literary doubling as referring to the text's repetition of other texts, one might locate *Sylvia's Lovers*, and its exploration of female desire and female literacy, in the history of the woman novelist. Gaskell wrote *Sylvia's Lovers* directly after writing *The Life of Charlotte Brontë*, and one can easily see traces in Gaskell's novel of the works of both Emily and Charlotte Brontë, of *Wuthering Heights*, in the ways it rewrites the two-suitors problem, as if imagining an Edgar Linton with passion, and of *Jane Eyre*'s attempt to reconcile passion and both male and female masochism. One might think here also of George Eliot, of whom Gaskell was preternaturally conscious throughout these years, and the problematic passions of Philip Wakem and Maggie Tulliver. Gaskell must have been aware of other women novelists' attempts to give freedom to the sexualized heroine, and it is women writers, rather than men, whom she echoes in this novel. In its insistent use of dialect as well we can see *Sylvia's Lovers* commenting on the works of other women novelists: George Eliot's early realism depends on dialect, and as Charlotte Brontë remarked of her sister's novel, the Yorkshire dialect is what makes the characters in *Wuthering Heights* "graphic"—literally, it makes them signify. The kind of challenge this graphicness represented is suggested, however, by Charlotte's own actions in revising *Wuthering Heights*, for she chose to "modify the orthography of the old servant Joseph's speeches" when publishing the revised edition, out of fear the Yorkshire dialect would be "unintelligible" to southern readers;[9] *Sylvia's Lovers*, as if to force readers to confront the unexpected yet once more, gives even its heroine a "northern" dialect, and the "orthography" to go with it. Gaskell worked to revise the second edition of her novel to be more faithful to the Yorshire accent; and indeed, the revised version looks very different on the page. As frequently happens in Victorian fiction— and particularly, I would argue, for women writers, so often defeated by the conventions of "the real"—the realm of realistic detail becomes almost surreal, pushing at the boundaries of readerly expectation. As is consistent with the naturalized gothicism of the text, too much reality jars the text.

The tension between realism and romance seems particularly to conjure up these other women writers: as in the ghostly interventions of *Wuthering Heights*, the presence of the Great Mother in *Jane Eyre* or in *Shirley*, something supernatural seems always about to rip open the surface of *Sylvia's Lovers*.[10] We might see as well some particular connection of the female novel with the gothic: with the experience of female desire as monstrous, thinking briefly of Mary Shelley's *Frankenstein*, which Gaskell mentions in *Mary Barton*; and of her own gothic stories, with their hauntings, repetitions, and spiritual visitations. Gaskell believed in ghosts (or at least ghost stories), with their invocation of another world, and may have viewed it as a specifically female world, in which the limitations placed on women in the realistic novel did not apply. If a questioning woman is, in Adrienne Rich's phrase, a woman in the shape of a monster,[11] Gaskell's novel might need to include the demonic within it to represent the specter of female passion. But at the least, she can be seen as invoking a literary heritage, that of a world haunted by unspoken female desire.

If Sylvia is a prisoner of the narratives of others, of her "lovers" and of "femininity," she cannot desire without being within a gothic plot, part of the monstrous. What we might read more historically, can also be recast in the terms Luce Irigaray offers:

> One would have to dig down very deep indeed to discover beneath the traces of this civilization, of this history, the vestiges of a more archaic civilization that might give some clue to woman's sexuality. That extremely ancient civilization would undoubtedly have a different alphabet, a different language.[12]

As Irigaray goes on to argue, "Woman's desire would not be expected to speak the same language as man's." Gaskell's deliberate invocation of the "primitive" for Sylvia's story might seem close here to Irigaray's "archaic" civilization, but clearly, this pre-cultural realm cannot be achieved in nineteenth-century fiction—or in eighteenth-century Yorkshire. Once again, historical and fictional constraints meet: Irigaray's "digging" for "a different alphabet, a different language" suggests Sylvia's lessons from Philip—and reiterates the ways they are lessons in femininity, in the postponement of desire. They have nothing to do with Sylvia's boldest statement in the novel: when she stares up at Philip, asking him if Charley is indeed dead, and says, directly, "I thought yo' knowed that I cared a deal for him." This is the kind of statement the novel needs to make room for, what there is rarely a language for.

But literacy extends—here, as in *North and South*—into larger social and economic structure. To borrow again from Irigaray's theoretical restatement of this, "Woman is never anything but the locus of a more or less competitive exchange between two men."[13] Woman, as in this novel of shopkeepers, is "a use-value for man, an exchange-value among men; in other words a commodity . . . whose price will be established . . . by 'subjects': workers, merchants, consumers." Irigaray goes on to suggest that women need to move outside this "marketplace," to move beyond "sexual commerce," to claim "a right to pleasure"; what *Sylvia's Lovers* makes clear is that women do not have the economic power to "own"— acknowledge or possess—anything. Hester Rose, the most competent of the younger people at the Fosters' store, will not be made a partner because she is a woman, and to give her property is to give it to some third person you don't know. In one of the novel's best comic scenes, Alice Rose dictates her will to William Coulson, but she knows nothing of official, legal language and insists more on the rhetorical flourishes than on the fact of money itself. That realm, Gaskell says clearly, is closed to women. Sylvia cannot own and run her father's farm, which would save her from having to marry Philip and move into the store— that is as impossible as her becoming a sailor and traveling to Greenland. She would have to cross as great a divide; it would be just as monstrous for her to be economically independent as to be an explorer.

In that light, the world of male history to which I will turn next is even more fatally closed to Sylvia: the unreality of the scenes of battles, for which characters offer a range of oddly textualized explanations, seems entirely unlike Sylvia's scenes of submissive reading, her fireside lessons with Philip. But they recreate a similar story of male identity, in an alphabet Sylvia cannot read. If this chapter began with the fierceness of individual desire in the novel, we need to turn now to the ferocity of history—and of its melodramatic (and self-consciously literary) inclusion in the gothic (romance) text. We must turn, that is, to the world that belongs only to Sylvia's lovers.

iii

The overarching male realm closed to Sylvia is history, and nothing makes clearer Gaskell's sense of Sylvia's constriction than the interruption of the novel by historical events, the way the novel is, to borrow its terms, "impressed." But for all that, in some ways the novel never seems as interested in "history" as are contemporary works: for all that *Sylvia's Lovers* takes its tone (and some of its urgency) from the French Revolution and its echoes in England, its real urgency is domestic, and its energies seem private. Rather than diminishing romance by placing it in history, as Thackeray does in *Vanity Fair*, Gaskell reduces history to a moment of conflict that can be understood *only* by its role in fictional and sexual doubling.

What the novel does draw on is the interest Gaskell had throughout her career in revolution, mob action, and violent historical change.[14] The novel is carefully set around the events of the French Revolution and the subsequent European wars of conquest: the revolution, the conflict that fuels the press-gangs and the wars in which Philip and Charley fight, remains both a hope and threat of transformation in the novel. It stands behind Sylvia's father's small rebellion against the state, when he stages the riot against the press-gang, and behind his questioning of "representation," in which the government exists to speak only what he believes and "govern me as I judge best" (p. 40), mirroring or reproducing his "vote," and his voice, in a larger sphere. In focusing on English response to revolution, especially the violence of the Treasonable and Seditious Actions Act, Gaskell returns to the link she made in *Mary Barton* between limitations on political and sexual choice. In the execution of Daniel Robson, we see the specter of state repression of all dissent. Nowhere does Gaskell suggest that hanging was the appropriate response to so small a disturbance, and her irony at the expense of contemporary readers ("Will our descendents have a wonder about us, such as we have about the inconsistency of our forefathers? . . . It is well for us that we live at the present time, when everybody is logical and consistent.") suggests some of the progress she has made since *Mary Barton*. The action of the authorities can be justified only "looking back on the affair in cold blood," and the defense of the father made by his daughter ("Why, York Castle's t' place they send a' t' thieves and robbers to, not honest men like feyther") carries the ring of Gaskellian conviction. But where alibis and testimony carried weight in the world of *Mary Barton*, and the heroine could act to save her father and win her lover, this novel offers no relief. The darkness of its political vision and the coldhearted economics of Philip's shopkeeping—which presages the mechanical industrialization in the decades that followed the revolutionary years—serve only to contain more completely the novel's heroine, for the two plots remain linked: through the repressive action of the state and the death of her radical father, Sylvia is left alone, forced to marry the cousin she does not love. History, then, is in some ways most present in the text as a repression of female sexuality. It is the plot's way of moving Sylvia into marriage, but it is left open to criticism.

What happens when we move into the larger historical realm? For one thing, the scale becomes much larger: the battles of Sir Sidney Smith in capturing a lugger at Havre-de-Grace in 1796; the Siege of Acre, in which the British defended the Turks in 1798—the text suggests both the range of Gaskell's research and the desire to escape the provinciality of the novel at the same time. And yet, what happens in the plot is another collapse of the public into the private; in literary terms, what we see is an exposure of the text's habit of doubling, and in that, the return of the romance. In the overlap between the fading out of history and the repetition of the *technique* of repetition, we see the novel producing the unexpected doubling of Philip and Charley—a doubling *so* unexpected that difference seems close to breaking down. At that moment, history and plot both suggest again that essential similarity of male desire, played out against the suppression of female desire.

For this reason, I would argue, and not for melodramatic purposes alone, the novel introduces its coincidence of Philip and Charley at the Siege of Acre—and introduces it precisely as a violation of realism. After Charley returns and accuses Sylvia of betraying him by marrying Philip, and Philip confesses to having concealed the action of the press-gang from Sylvia, Sylvia vows never to forgive Philip, and both men leave. Sylvia makes a life for herself in a community of women, to which I shall return at greater length later, and Philip makes his way out as a soldier, as "Stephen Freeman." We see Kinraid, thinking of his "newly-made wife in her English home," near death on the battlefield, and suddenly a man picks him up, a man with a face "like one formerly known to the sick senses of Kinraid; yet it was too like a dream too utterly improbable to be real." But what this dream figure, this "sickly"-sensed man, utters is Philip's only statement on his *earlier* action: "I niver thought you'd ha' kept true to her" (p. 431). The world of heroism and battle has contracted, unexpectedly, into the realm of romance: it is love, not historical urgency, that haunts men at war.

This is "the coincidence, [which] while limited in extent, is too far-fetched to accept," the "improbable encounter" critics have fastened on as breaking the realism that they loved in the earlier sections of the novel.[15] But the encounter shadows the novel for reasons other than disunity. We, as modern readers, may not be as surprised as these critics seem to be by Philip's reappearance, and further, the dissonance of the return is registered in the text by the varieties of explanations offered by *other* characters when they hear the story. Characters reach into the realm of folklore, typology, system upon system of doubling to explain the unexpected. But it is not so unexpected as all that: we have been told that Philip has gone to be a soldier, and further, have before us the example of Gaskell's sympathy for him. Readers are already positioned, if not willing, not to be shocked at his actions. Yet the text also wants us to see it as unlikely. For Philip's friends back in Whitby, the appearance of Charley Kinraid's wife with a story of Philip Hepburn's saving her husband's life at the battle of Acre is so unbelievable it can be interpreted only by recourse to another realm. Both Kester and Sylvia explain it as a "spirit" that has come to save Charley—a solution suggestive of the superstitious world of Yorkshire but also of their real failure to understand Philip. The doctor on Charley's ship, when Philip cannot be found, suggests that it was sunstroke and imagination, for "faces once seen, especially in excitement, are apt to return upon the memory in cases of fever." An "attendant sailor" suggests it was a "spirit," and adds "it's not th' first time as I've heard of a spirit coming upon earth to save a man's life i' time o' need." Alice Rose invokes yet another sphere of mystery to refute the evidence of Charley's story:

> I can forgive Sylvia for not being over keen to credit thy news. Her man of peace becoming a man of war; and suffered to enter Jerusalem, which is a heavenly and a typical city at this time; whilst me, as is one of the elect, is obliged to go on dwelling in Monkshaven, just like any other body. (pp. 450–451)

This model of "heavenly" and "typical"—that is, perfect—doubling reminds us, clearly, we are reading a novel not in the realm of the gothic but the world of "just like any other body" "dwelling in Monkshaven." Or is it "any other body"? Behind Alice's religious invocation of "credit" lies the realm of women, who cannot enter Jerusalem at all. Charley has said he was bewildered, for "we hated each other like poison; and I can't make out why he should be there and putting himself in danger to save me." But despite Charley's puzzlement, the men are in the same realm at this moment: still free to move, still free to fight, still, in some sense, free enough to be not only subject to the forces of history but the subjects of history. As so often in the novel, moments of opposition between men give way to the deeper similarities of their desires: here, both wish to gain glory so as to be remembered by the "wife in her English home." Charley and Philip, in the Siege of Acre, are more like each other than they are like those they have left behind. They are abroad, carving out identities for themselves through conflict and difference,

translating that initial difference between them (their rivalry in love for
Sylvia) into a cultural difference with the French. Their conflict can be
transcended because there is always another sphere in which men can
posit themselves as agents. Here, difference is resolved into a similarity,
so that larger realms of difference can in turn be posed, an endless "re-
enactment" of Brooks's (Freud's) "instinctual play," in which (to quote
Irigaray's nice summary of international conflict) women are "never
anything but the locus of a more or less competitive exchange between
two men, including the competition for the possession of mother earth."

If Gaskell here collapses history, undoing the novel's careful placement
within the larger conflicts of the French Revolution and Napoleonic
conquest, it is only to place the "more or less competitive exchange" in
the realm of both self-conscious fictionality and the writing of female
desire. The remainder of the novel will be taken up with the reconciliation of Philip and Sylvia, an almost equally improbable reunion, but one
that the text will recognize as improbable by locating it within a *literary*
context: Philip has read, and imagines himself in, the story of Guy of
Warwick in *The Seven Champions of Christendom*, a story in which the
hero returns from fighting the Paynim and disguises himself as a hermit,
winning, on his deathbed, a reconciliation with his lost wife, the countess.
So readers are prepared for the invocation of the "literary" solution—
prepared, of course, in a way Sylvia is not. Sylvia cannot have her
resolution within history without "a different alphabet, a different language." She works her way to the reconciliation not through heroic
stories, heroic conflicts, or these models of historical (national) difference
but through a removal from that world of "established commerce" and a
movement into a world shared by the other "commodities"—women—in
the marketplace. Only by removing herself from this male plot can Sylvia
become her own subject, but Gaskell may further be suggesting why
women, within this plot and this (male) language, can never achieve
anything but a "transaction" value, the value of an object passed from
buyer to buyer. Gaskell needs to suggest, finally, her own market of
fiction, in which her heroine will have her own story: if, unlike Philip,
Sylvia cannot act in history, she also cannot read—or reimagine—her life
in any existing storybook.

iv

Sylvia does seem to end this novel in a different kind of story, with its
own forms of repetition and difference. If the final encounter between

Kinraid and Hepburn works to place them in the same world, the same battle, the same net of historical power, the final setting for Sylvia—before her husband's return—places her within a very different realm of similarity, one that I think held more power and a deeper appeal for Gaskell herself. The end of the novel finds Sylvia in a world composed entirely of women and feminized men, a world in which she and her daughter find a peace that is missing from the rest of the novel. Its peace is not entirely unlike the sterile, cloistered peace that Philip encounters and rejects at the Bedesman's retreat, but Sylvia's is not the same kind of absence from the world: she remains very much in the world, connected with both the nature she requires and the town life she previously shunned. What her retreat seems to offer is a space apart from the world of competitive desire. Sylvia finds, and the novel plays with temporarily, a oneness that does not seek to possess something from the other, in which, using the term loosely, both subjects get to be subjects, without one's becoming an object.

But as the end of the novel makes clear, in the wider world that *Sylvia's Lovers* represents, Sylvia can become a subject only, paradoxically, through submission: the woman in a world of women is still within a world of objects, unable to articulate herself. In an increasingly dense linguistic play of pronouns that slip, nouns that cannot be fixed in meaning, Gaskell imagines what might happen if women were freed from some field of determinism. The novel experiments with a linguistic rearrangement akin to what Irigiray called for in the "different alphabet . . . different language" of women. What the novel reveals increasingly, however, is that women would still have to abandon sexual desire for that unity (that difference) to take place. The world without conflict is not yet a world where women choose their own lives; nor can this novel believe (in a universe where identity, desire, and possession have been so linked) in so fully realized an individual subject, with the firm boundaries and clear "I" we might, in a less complicated novel, expect.

What Sylvia does find in this world-before-conflict is again that language we might connect to the pre-Oedipal, a world of unity with the mother and the end to fixed ego boundaries:[16] a world apart from the domination of history; a world, for Sylvia, where she is returned to maternal love and freed from herself and her own story. After Philip leaves and Sylvia realizes she has been betrayed, she goes with her baby to live with Hester and Alice Rose, supported and aided by the Foster brothers, visited by old Kester, surrounded by the care she lost with her mother's death. This care represents a mirroring that other kinds of love rarely approximate in the novel. Earlier in the novel, in the pivotal moments of her mother's illness before her father's execution, when each admits to the other that she has avoided discussing Daniel's impending death, Sylvia and Bell seem to be in a relationship in which each exactly mirrors the other's needs and essence. Bell Robson has been weakened, made "incapable of argument" or understanding, entirely dependent on Sylvia's care. But as each reveals what "I niver breathed . . . to thee,"

> Sylvia choked with crying, and laid her head on her mother's lap, feeling that she was no longer the strong one, and the protector, but the protected. Bell went on, stroking her head,
> "The Lord is like a tender nurse as weans a child to look on and to like what it lothed once." (p. 310)

But the metaphor of the child who learns to "look on . . . what it lothed" suggests the ambiguity of Sylvia's "feeling that she was no longer the strong one, and the protector, but the protected." At first, the ambiguous "she" seems to be Sylvia herself, who, after weeks of care, can abandon the effort to protect her mother. But more deeply, what Sylvia is "choking" on is the knowledge that, in the long run, the "she" who is "no longer the strong one" is her mother.

What Gaskell intensifies here is the lack of boundaries between the mother and her daughter: not just a Dickensian substitution of caring child for caring parent, but Sylvia's—and her mother's—inability to tell one set of needs from the other. Each here is looking, like the child, on what she loathes: Bell on Daniel's impending execution, Sylvia on her mother's readiness to die rather than live through the shame. But at the moment of severance—Bell lapses into irritability and "inability of reason" almost immediately after this scene—the problem of similarity between women, the inability to locate difference, is registered syntactically by Gaskell. Maternal language and the daughter's imitation (as in the murmuring sounds Aunt Esther makes, recalling Mary Barton's dead mother) have a powerful narrative force here; what they also suggest, frighteningly, is the daughter's tenuous hold on her *own* plot, and the novel's further haunting by still more possible doubles.

While this overlapping of mother and daughter creates an anxiety about identity formation, a sliding of boundaries and confusion of the self rather than a fruitful union, a very different sliding of boundaries, a very different abandonment of self, occurs in the conclusion of the novel. In the eerie scenes where Sylvia learns of Hester's love for Philip and holds the crying woman on the floor, we see a bonding through repetition of desire—at exactly the moment when Sylvia has begun to learn to appreciate Philip—which we can pose against Philip and Charley's reconciliation-through-division. Although Philip and Charley can see in each other only Sylvia's ruin—that is, the ruin of their image of her—Sylvia says, seriously, to Hester,

> "Poor Hester—poor, poor Hester! if yo' an' he had but been married together, what a deal o' sorrow would ha' been spared to us all!" (p. 444)

At that moment, Sylvia comes closest to understanding the key idea of the novel. As she listens to Hester's grief, she

> made no reply, only went on stroking Hester's smooth brown hair, off which her cap had fallen. Sylvia was thinking how strange life was, and how love seemed to go all at cross purposes; and was losing herself in bewilderment. . . . (p. 445)

In Sylvia's silence, lie the novel's doubts: exactly as love seems to go at "cross purposes," so do characters seem to lose themselves, but this is at once the blight and the gift of the novel. To "lose oneself" as Philip does, in lies and self-betrayal, is the deepest sin; to "lose oneself" in Christian goodness or, perhaps, in true love of another, may be to get free of the obsessive need to forge identity through destruction of the other. As Sylvia can recognize in Hester's pain her own—and Philip's as well—so she gains from her "bewilderment." In that awful imposition of *self*—setting up oneself as an idol through one's love of some exterior object who will reflect oneself back—is the worst kind of certainty, a certainty that exists at the expense of others, as Jeremiah Foster describes Philip's lie to Sylvia: "a self-seeking lie; putting thee to pain to get his own ends" (p. 413).

The world of women living together offers an abandonment (for better or worse) of one's "own ends." It is the perfect world for Sylvia, who is "sick o' men and their cruel, deceitful ways," one in which she can finally learn to read, can acquire some of the habits that will allow her movement—in imagination, at least—beyond her own life. Although once she wanted to learn to read so as to learn geography, to find on the map where Charley Kinraid has gone, where she wishes she could go, now she is able to learn only to read the Bible, for to Alice Rose, who begins to teach her to read the first chapter of Genesis, "all other reading but the Scriptures was as vanity to her, and she would not condescend to the weakness of other books." But though Sylvia was "now, as ever, slow at book-learning; . . . she was meek and desirous to be taught" (pp. 421–422).

In her meekness, of course, she is growing more like Hester—more like Philip as well, if not more like what Philip wanted her to be. In part,

Sylvia's desire to be taught suggests the disturbing model of growing accommodation that one might expect a Victorian novel to enact on its heroine: a variant of the process that makes Bella Wilfer a good wife, after her education at her husband's hands. But two things suggest that this novel intends something different. First, Sylvia's softening occurs not through Philip's intervention, that is, through the sexual play of marriage and difference, but through a world of women: a harkening back to Sylvia's mother and her desire that her daughter read, write, understand analogically rather than through (her father's) oppositions. Although this might seem a small distinction—after all, Philip was Bell Robson's choice for Sylvia, and he, further, is identified by the text as the "scholar," even more than Bell—still, the change is specifically marked as one that cannot happen in the world of men, in the world in which Sylvia is still commodity, object rather than subject.

But the further distinction between Sylvia's conversion and the "accommodation" plot is that Philip has undergone a similar process of transformation—and that both plots trace these as en-gendered transformations. If Sylvia is to "grow up" in this female world, Philip's experience is as "Stephen Freeman," a nameless, generic soldier whom even Charley Kinraid—a man among men—cannot locate. Philip has what we might call a representative male experience among men: he comes back, literally, a hero. His adventures are precisely those that would make him more suitable for Sylvia: not only has he become more like the adventuring specksioneer but he, like Sylvia, has found a way of undoing past denials of others. He has rescued Charley, in a sense, from the death he himself had imagined for his enemy, and inflicted it on himself, much as Sylvia, in recognizing Hester's loss, has guaranteed that she herself will live to act out her repentance for "poor Hester, whose life she had so crossed and blighted, even by the very blighting of her own" (p. 422).

The last conversation between Philip and Sylvia suggests some possible union, at least through syntactic mergers and elisions of borders, though it cannot work its union through the magic of plot. This is the last of the novel's odd doublings, "crossings," and "blightings," but like these other moments, through linguistic doublings and ambiguities, it leaves the fields of similarity and difference confused. The transformations, the "difference" revealed—Sylvia's ability to live near and visit her husband without recognizing him; his ability to become the hero she had always needed to love—seems somehow less important than some similarity that gets revealed in turn. Or rather, it is what Philip experiences as similarity. He, "forgetful of himself in his desire to comfort her," says:

"You and me have done wrong to each other; yet we can see now how we were led to it; we can pity and forgive one another. . . . God knows more, and is more forgiving than either you to me, or me to you. I think and do believe as we shall meet together before His face; but then I shall ha' learnt to love thee second to Him; not first, as I have done here upon the earth." (p. 496)

Philip can bridge sexual and romantic differences through a third term in which the key difference of God's knowledge erases the gap between him and Sylvia. And in his dying, as his thoughts move between the oppositions of his mother's love and the love "wiser," "tenderer" than hers to which he goes, he sees in his and Sylvia's "forgive me" the same phrase, the same yearning after that union that can be expressed only typologically in the text: it will have been all right to have had an idol, if one can transform that earthly idolatry into heavenly, perfect love.

Sylvia's final version of unity seems different: the last moments at Philip's deathbed are a confusion of identity, with none of the "bright" certainty Philip saw ahead "in heaven." In the first of these confusions, Hester comes into the room with Bella, hoping to say farewell to Philip. Hester begins to cry, but Sylvia rebukes her, asking,

"Why do yo' cry, Hester? . . . Yo' niver said yo' wouldn't forgive him as long as yo' lived. Yo' niver broke the heart of him that loved yo', and let him almost starve at yo'r very door. Oh, Philip! my Philip, tender and true." (p. 501)

Even here, Sylvia seems to see her crime in hurting him that loved her; she never claims to love him but rather to value his love for her. But the confusion about what one loves is doubled by another *textual* confusion of the object of affection: the very next paragraph begins,

Then Hester came round and closed the sad half-open eyes, kissing the calm brow with a long farewell kiss.

Until the "farewell," Hester could almost be comforting Sylvia who, in her grief, is sad but tearless, staring "as if all sense were gone from her." The "almost unconscious" Sylvia needs that kiss as much as Philip at that moment, and it is she who has made the direct appeal for understanding; the text is effecting a series of substitutions in which "sense" "goes from" more than one character, and *to* more than one character.

In the last sentence of the scene, the last sentence before the novel breaks into historical narrative and the characters stop speaking to us except through reported anecdote, Sylvia again raises the question of

difference—here, the difference between God's mediation and the earthly
idol Philip had asserted Sylvia *had* been to him when he promised to see
her "in heaven." Sylvia's constant fear—what prompted Philip's response, what seems to be prompting her sudden expressions of guilt—has
been that "I think I shall go about among them as gnash their teeth for
iver, while yo' are wheere all tears are wiped away." Even here, we cannot
know if what she fears is punishment or separation, but this distinction is
immaterial. What seems clearest, as throughout the novel, is the fear that
the real punishment *is* separation. Without an other, reflecting identity,
without the "desire" of others, loving or hostile, directed toward you, you
not only are alone but do not exist. To go "about among them as gnash
their teeth" without Philip is to be most truly in torment. And this is what
Sylvia addresses at the novel's end: as Bella clings to her mother, and "the
touch of *his* child loosened the fountain of her tears" (emphasis added),
Sylvia says,

> "If I live very long, and try hard to be very good all that time, do yo' think,
> Hester, as God will let me to him where he is?" (p. 501)

Where Philip saw God and the human as still different, that distinction
has blurred for Sylvia: the statement surely ought to be, if she wants
forgiveness, and wants it in Philip's—God's—terms, "God will let me to
Him where *He* is?" To be where *he* is is where Philip is, not God. Sylvia is
still uniting her destiny—her story—with love, here a suddenly understood love for Philip, but she has so blurred the pronouns as to keep her
real desire unclear. What *does* Sylvia want at this moment? Philip?
Redemption? God? Union? Forgiveness? At this moment, she has rewrit-
ten her life story to be about her eventual death, without any clear goal in
sight; surely, at this moment, she has blurred the lines of her life by
conflating Philip's love with resurrection, by erasing Philip's "lie" and
replacing it with her "sin," as Philip somehow returned her to the twelve-
year-old girl he first met and loved, and called, as he repeatedly calls
her in this scene, "my little lassie." Through the transitory power of
Philip's death and fear of her own impending death, Sylvia seems able to
blend in one sentence, for one moment, heavenly and earthly love, the
realm of individual (transient) identity and the realm of transcendental
(permanent) things.

But what are we to make of this description of blurred difference when
it is put back into the romance—the problem of the desiring heroine—
with which we began? Sylvia seems to have located her problem of
being—of being "very good all that time"—firmly within a romance plot,

merely a deferred plot endorsed by a beneficent God who remains uninterested in the "gnashing of teeth." But questions of how to *be* are still resolved by questions of whom to *love,* and Sylvia (and the novel) seem far away from a plot of autonomous identity. In what way does the novel allow for the "woman who chooses" with which it began? In what way has Sylvia become what we might recognize as a fully recognized subject, with independent desires? If the comic novel (with its heroine's acquiescence in her married fate) in some essential way fails in this novel; if the violent desires of the first half of the novel, and the passionate vows of the second, all suggest a world in which the comic plot is not adequate to explain peoples' action, where can this almost apocalyptic novel end? Gaskell's narrative violence, conjuring up purging fires of destruction, seems to want to leave the world, at the end, ready to begin again. But she also seems to want to begin the novel again, begin it differently, and, most important, to put herself in.

That insertion is what focuses the questions we have been discussing, the tension between difference and similarity, male and female, writing and blurring. In *Sylvia's Lovers* the difference of the woman's story (the narrative poised between these oppositions, questioning the opposition itself) is the (woman writer's) telling not only the story but the story of storytelling, the movement of female desire into myth. The final "plot" of the novel is the accumulation of stories that occurs in the last chapter, where a variety of accounts of the events we have just read come together to suggest the imprecision of all (his)story; the novel's final plot, that is, is Gaskell's plotting of this, her last completed novel, and its displacements, disparities, and disappearances.

v

Sylvia's Lovers ends with a coda, a pulling-back into history unique in Gaskell's work, and particularly unusual in its retreat into gossip, conversation, and anecdote. In a way, the end of the novel forces on us a self-consciousness, if not a skepticism, about storytelling, and the story we have read. It also forces on us, as we might expect, given the double-edged progress we have been reading, both a new beginning (in Bella's move to America) and the endless repetition we have been reading for. The conclusion, which follows a row of asterisks that separates it from the novel "proper," gives us both the "now" of our narrative moment, and the unending pattern of nature and biblical time:

Monkshaven is altered now into a rising bathing place. Yet, standing near the site of widow Dobson's house on a summer's night, at the ebb of a spring-tide, you may hear the waves come lapping up the shelving shore with the same ceaseless, ever-recurrent sound as that which Philip listened to in the pauses between life and death.

And so it will be until "there shall be no more sea."

But the memory of man fades away. (p. 502)

Here, the fading of memory becomes as inevitable—as ever-recurrent—as the sea; the only public memory, which she goes on to recount, is of "Philip Hepburn and the legend of his fate"; "our" narrative is rendered as transient as the sounds the dying man heard.

But in this first of several narratives offered in these concluding pages, we begin to see the failure in the patterned story. The "legend" repeated by "a few old people" describes a man who

died in a cottage somewhere near about this spot,—died of starvation while his wife lived in hard-hearted plenty not two good stone-throws away.

This, we are told, "is the form into which popular feeling, and ignorance of the real facts," have "moulded the story," though the "bathing woman" did know "an old man when I was a girl" who "could niver abide to hear t' wife blamed." "He would say nothing again' th' husband; he used to say as it were not fit for men to be judging; that she had had her sore trial, as well as Hepburn hisself." But despite this emendation—which comes closer, if not closest, to our sense of the novel—the "legend" of Philip Hepburn is about *Sylvia's* guilt, not Philip's lie. Sylvia, not herself but "a pale, sad woman, allays dressed in black," is said to have died "before her daughter was well grown up," leaving her child to Hester Rose, who founded alms-houses for "poor disabled sailors and soldiers" and named them for "P.H." Philip, in short, gets all the decent epitaphs; Sylvia's story, that of the woman who tried to *have* a story of her own, cannot be told. No wonder critics have neglected to read that story into the novel: the conclusion cannot frame it, for it is a story about stories that cannot get written. How could they, when women like Sylvia cannot write? If women are taught to read by men like Philip, and are not free to write their own narratives, then the stories they leave behind will bear only men's initials.

But what is most striking about the novel's end, and its reflections on female texts, is that it is a female conversation that gets the last word in *Sylvia's Lovers*. The last paragraph of the novel concludes the conversation between an unnamed "lady" who went to the "Public Baths" on the "very site of widow Dobson's cottage" and, "finding all the rooms engaged" sat down to talk to the "bathing woman." That "lady," reminiscent of Kinraid's "lady-wife," asks questions about the women in the "legend". It is she who asked "what became of the wife," then asks, "Miss Rose?" after being told it was she who took the daughter, and finally asks, "And the daughter?" Significantly, it is the daughter's story that breaks the seemingly endless "similarity" of the woman's story. In the closing paragraph, we are told by the "bathing woman" that

> one o' th' Fosters, them as founded t' Old Bank, left her a vast o' money; and she were married to distant cousin of theirs, and went off to settle in America many and many a year ago. (p. 503)

This seems to undo much of the novel's chronology, which began overprecisely with "the end of the last century" and only now invokes the storybook time of "many and many a year ago." Bella's departure further reverses the story of origin told in the book's first paragraph, the "traditions of [Monkshaven's] having been the landing-place of a throneless queen." In the possible reversal we can hear the novelist saying, what if there were a strong woman not empowered by law ("throneless"), and what if she began to move?

Bella's departure does not quite add up to all that; what it suggests is, rather, that even to begin to act freely, a daughter would have to be orphaned, become rich, and reside in another community.[17] We want, I think, to read this as an act of freedom, Bella's movement to the uncharted American continent echoing something of her implied spiritual father (Kinraid) in her voyaging, and perhaps fulfilling her mother's desire to go to sea. But even here, she is able to move only toward marriage: an arranged marriage into the Quaker family of the Fosters. She is perhaps less Sylvia and Charley's child—via Philip—than Philip and Hester's—via Sylvia. Bella cannot fulfill both Philip's and Sylvia's plots—or can she, for she does get to go to sea at last, even if it is only to sail into another ordered plot, and that a plot with an adequate bankbook.

If what is hopeful about Bella's departure is its departure from what we have been reading (that she is leaving *some* old plot, *some* old history, behind her, and opening some new possibilities), what seems even more encouraging is the way the final conversation recounts at least part of the story from Sylvia's (imagined, muted) point of view. It seems, again, to render problematic views of history, while vindicating a different kind of romance. One could read the conclusion as merely tying up the loose ends of plot, while suggesting, à la Billy Budd, the skewed ways that facts make their way into legends. But I choose to read in that last story something about the way legends make their ways into novels. The "lady" who comes down to hear the old woman's story, who keeps asking the next question (and that always a question about women) seems to me a figure for the novelist herself: Gaskell, who, turning from her desperate desire to make Charlotte Brontë's hidden life into a legend, chose the life of an unknown, almost unimaginable, completely silent woman on a quest to make her own life significant; Gaskell, who did as much serious research on *Sylvia's Lovers* as on the *Life of Charlotte Brontë*; Gaskell, who may be asking, where in all these cultural stories, these legends of wronged men, the book of Genesis which Sylvia is taught to read, where are the stories of women, the stories they must learn to tell (for) themselves?

She may be asking that question for herself in new ways as well. Edgar Wright has suggested, somewhat cavalierly, that Gaskell "would have been passing through the 'change of life' at this period, with its accompanying restlessness."[18] But we need not read this as a menopausal novel, hence a "mediocre" work, betraying fatigue, concentrating on "gloom and morbidity." The gloom, which resembles not so much morbidity as the conscious claustrophobia of *Lois the Witch*'s plot, may reflect Gaskell's restlessness not at the "change of life" but at the inability of Victorian formulations of the novel to take in those "changes" she herself was going through. When Elizabeth Gaskell went to Rome in 1857, she was sought out by a young American, Charles Eliot Norton, who had met her years before and been charmed by her. Their friendship, which was immediate, continued till her death: he named his second daughter after her (he would have so named the first, but Gaskell's written approval reached him after the baby's birth); they corresponded regularly with hopes of meeting again; there seems little doubt that, in an unexpected and indescribable way, they had fallen in love. She wrote to friends on her return to England that

> it was in those charming Roman days that my life, at any rate, culminated. I shall never be so happy again. I don't think I was ever so happy before. My eyes fill with tears when I think of those days, and it is the same with all of us. They were the tip-top point of our lives. The girls may see happier ones—I never shall.[19]

In those years, Gaskell was to worry increasingly about her daughters' marriageability; indeed, two of her daughters never married, which to Gaskell, ever a defender of marriage, was a sad end indeed. But she is facing some end of her own here: "The girls may see happier [days]—I never shall." What Sylvia faces at the end of the novel named after her lovers is the end of her own story: she dies soon after, but the bleakness of what she faces, in the death of her now-dear husband and the defection of her adored Charley, is her own movement out of the only possible female plot. What Gaskell may have been living is the failure of that plot to give to her daughters (or even to her) the richness she could imagine.

Gaskell ends *Sylvia's Lovers* with an image of women alone, women in conversation, women retelling history. None of these women fit easily into a marriage plot, any more than did Charlotte Brontë, whose marriage Gaskell, like most of Brontë's friends, thought a mistake, and whose entrance into the true female plot ("wives and daughters," as Gaskell will call it next) leads to her death of "pregnancy-sickness" at thirty-nine. *Sylvia's Lovers* offers several visions: a world of desire crossed by history, which Gaskell read as primarily a world of men forging identity through sexual conflict; a world of isolated women, learning to read but forced to read the Bible and Eve's fall over and over; a world of understanding found "too late," defensible only if submerged into God's plot. In the last scene, as the women tell each other unfinished stories, we might see something else, but we are not yet offered that other novel: it might be Bella's "American novel," where she "went off to settle in America many and many a year ago," and may have found something better; it might be Hester Rose's world of usefulness, writing the piece of stone that says "this building is erected in memory of P.H.," the only edifice that survives the novel; it might be Sylvia's imagined adventure.

Where that difference may reside in this novel is in the voice of storytelling, in the vibrant direct address that Gaskell uses to begin this epitaph to the novel: "Yet, standing near the site of widow Dobson's house on a summer's night, . . . *you* may hear the waves . . . and so it will be until 'there shall be no more sea'" [emphasis added]. That moment of speaking to "you," reminiscent of the engaged fiction of *Mary Barton*, draws *us* back into the narrative: it is the passionate voice of the characters, and the self-conscious reflections of the novel's coda. In the questioning woman who asks, "What became of the wife?" "And the daughter?" one could imagine a new reader, one ready to take on the generic challenge of the female narrative, ready to continue the questioning of culture, history, and myth implicit in the "story" that Gaskell will take up critically in *Wives and Daughters*, but that she could read only tragically in *Sylvia's Lovers*.

6

Telling Tales: Every-day Life, Secrets, and the Woman's Story in *Wives and Daughters*

Scherzade in the Marketplace

—Hilary Schor

Wives and Daughters begins with the rare assurance readers love novels to begin with, and it locates that assurance as much in its fictional voice as in its content. Subtitled "An Every-day Story," the novel places us from its first sentence not so much in the "every-day" of life but in the "every-day" of fiction. "To begin," the novel begins, "with the old rigma-role of childhood," summoning up the conventions for us, reminding us of their constant presence. This novel opens with a young girl on her first adventure, and asks us to follow a kind of Cinderella story—that is, it puts us in a fairy tale and gives us the voice we expect. But it does so while drawing our attention to that voice. Critics who speak of this as Gaskell's most confident novel, her finest achievement, must have this in mind: the novel's voice is self-consciously fictional, and it announces its place in the tradition of bourgeois realism.

But it takes its place with a difference, a difference inevitable after the variations and transformations of novels like *North and South* and *Sylvia's Lovers*. Not only does the novel open by talking about its own beginnings, it places itself in a line of beginnings, which it can dismiss. The novel will be about fictions of origins: it begins with the "fiction" of "origins," the novel of beginnings.[1] And as such, it notices from the beginning what its readers expect. Gaskell has learned, through attempting "unfit subjects for fiction," what the rules of fiction are—and how readers are shaped. We are offered what we want at the moment we are told that we want it. Readerly desire, at that moment, is the ironic subject of the novel. We cannot be naive readers when the text calls up our desire only to call it to our attention. *Wives and Daughters* evokes our most easy ways of reading, fairy tales and family histories, only to make us aware of our ease, and make the old narratives impossible: we will be at once comfortable and self-conscious, at home in and estranged from our readings.

Were we more careful readers, we might have been divided readers from the beginning—or, as it were, before the beginning. If the novel is to locate ways of reading by making us feel "read," it will do so by placing us—consciously—as readers within a culture. Specifically, the novel is placing us by reminding us of how social roles—readerly roles, roles as recipients of stories—locate us. Gaskell re-creates throughout the novel the ways this feeling of writing and reading (being and being described) go on contiguously and continuously. The title, even before the subtitle, seems to place us inside and outside at once; our initial assumption must be that one is "born" a daughter and "made" a wife, the one state natural, the other constructed. We are offered two alternate states of being, around which we will create stories of relation. Women, we will probably say, can avoid being wives; they can never avoid being daughters. This, then, may be the "every-day" story the novel will tell, if, as this ghost of a progressive narrative suggests, the necessary chronos of beginnings is that daughters become wives, so that there are always more daughters, so that. . . . But this novel will not only give us that progress, it will concern itself with naming the states within it. By giving us a daughter and making her a wife, the novel offers us "the old rigmarole" with a vengeance, and then asks us not to take it so seriously—or is it, not to take it so lightly? Further, it places the daughter within the dual structures of society and fiction, for just as the novel will be "about" the marrying (wiving) of the daughter, complicating our initial reading of the title, so, too, being a daughter will not prove, after all, a blank slate, that mythical state we call nature. Here, daughters are as much born into culture as they are placed into fictions. In the novel, then, Gaskell's recurrent concerns with the way cultural meanings shape our understanding—and the complicity of fiction with ideology—connect with that fictional "assurance," her own power over the slippery functions of narrative.

The ease of narrative progress here must be connected with not only the heroine's progress and romance but broader cultural stories: all the stories of origin that offer systems of meaning, a way of reading growth, progress, change, those key elements of Victorian science and Victorian fiction. At the novel's center are systems of information, ways of organizing thought and judging behavior—and the age's most characteristically male system of thought, the scientific thinking associated throughout with the heroine's doctor-father and her lover, Roger Hamley, the biologist who goes off on a Darwin-like excursion to gather objects for a new local museum. This scientific structure echoes and expands the "fictional" structure of the novel, for it includes both history—the concern with the origins and stories of families and of community—and, in its widest form, the "origin of species," the entire evolutionary model. But if we take both biology and history as ways of organizing what we see, of constructing narrative around facts, we are led to a parallel system in the novel: the female world of gossip, courtship narratives, and blackmail; the treacherous world of village women who create their own originating stories, and who deny, as fiercely as any of Darwin's bulldogs, the possibility of free movement and choice. Although the female world does not put itself forward as constructing reality in the way the Darwinian story does, it nonetheless shapes and explains behavior, particularly the behavior of women. In this novel, culture—in both its broadest and its narrowest sense, from biology to manners—becomes an imprisoning narrative. Gaskell is writing an early, specifically feminine version of *Civilization and Its Discontents*.

It is in its attention to systems of knowledge that this novel's real achievement lies. Consistently, it locates science within a structure of stories of origins within the novel, a placement not unlike the movement of *Origin of Species*, or the movement Foucault traces throughout *The Order of Things* from the eighteenth-century's obsession with classification to the nineteenth's with historicity. Natural history takes its place with other languages or ways of ordering, but as Foucault suggests, in terms strangely like Gaskell's, "Natural history did not become possible because men looked harder and more closely"[2] but because it deliberately restricted the area of experience, what it attempted to perceive. What Foucault has called the "mutation of Order into History" (p. 220) is man's coming into being and studying in "origin" not "the beginning— a sort of dawn of history" but the way he "articulates himself" (p. 334); he then studies "life, labour and language" within a "stratum of conduct, behaviour, attitudes, gestures already made, sentences already pronounced or written" (p. 354). The scientist, in Foucault's critique, looks outside because he wants to see, to name himself, but he cannot do so, because he is always already in society, in language.

This doubling of the self in science echoes what we might say of the novel as a method of ordering, for within the novel as well, men are represented back to themselves within a "stratum of conduct, behaviour . . . already pronounced or written." *Wives and Daughters* seems to be commenting on itself as both history and museum, but even in this self-articulation we can see a tension between a generic notion of "man" and an idea of specific historical origins. That is, we might argue either its complicity with placing "man" at the center, and assert that Gaskell saw her novel as genuinely organic, or we might link its fictional self-aware- ness ("beginning with beginnings") to an awareness of the "history of origins" as traditionally written by men—or, equally, to the heroine's history conventionally written by women. It is in the juxtaposition of that range of histories (the heroine's, the species', the woman's novel) that *this* novel is written: the museum and the novel trade places, comment on each other, deconstruct each other. This novel offers to rewrite the fiction of the every-day itself, and through that revision, enacted through the self-conscious progress of the heroine's plot, to erect a different kind of museum exhibition.

i

"Am not I a grand young lady to have a doom?"

The certainty with which *Wives and Daughters* begins marks not only its quality of being "already told" but its cultural status: this is not only the age-old story of daughters turning to wives, with which every heroine's fairy tale is concerned, but a story of how a girl becomes a heroine. It is lodged with some confidence, like most nineteenth-century novels, be- tween the etiquette book and the guidebook, but its make-believe is the "what if" of what it carefully wants to present as ordinary life—or would, if it weren't so self-consciously fictional. The beginning of the novel, like the beginning of so many Victorian novels, easily assimilates its own fairy tale: not only does it play with its own assurance, it plays with what it will reveal to us. In the first paragraph, it localizes its heroine within fiction as much as reality:

> To begin with the old rigmarole of childhood. In a country there was a shire, and in that shire there was a town, and in that town there was a house, and in that house there was a room, and in that room there was a bed, and in that bed there lay a little girl; wide awake and longing to get up, but not daring to do so for fear of the unseen power in the next room— a certain Betty, whose slumbers must not be disturbed until six o'clock struck.[3]

That little girl, at once a fairy-tale princess and a very real girl afraid of a very real Betty in the next room, goes to a castle (the Towers, the "great family mansion,") and is lost in the woods. There, she is rescued by a (wicked?) fairy named Clare and brought back to the castle, where she falls asleep, only to sleep too long, miss her ride back home, and be shut up in the castle, frightened by gruff adults, and spoken to in French. Just as she despairs, she is rescued by her (also gruff but loving) father, who takes her back to her humble home, which she will never try to leave again. That structure, of the heroine who goes out, is overwhelmed, and must be rescued, "sets" Molly's character: the "fairy tale" becomes fixed even as we watch. If the novel is a heroine's case history, Molly has just displaced her dead mother's abandonment onto that of the castle's governess, Clare, who eats Molly's lunch, leaves her to sleep too long, and then forgets to tell anyone in the castle that it was her own fault and not Molly's that Molly has become the unwelcome and unwilling guest she is. And Molly has also been fixed as unable to speak up to female domination, forced to wait for the father's word to free her, her only choices to mimic Clare's violent activity or to remain a passive princess.

Given the quiet darkness of this scene, even with its return of the heroine to her father's side, we are not surprised to see the novel's turn into comic unhappiness when Molly's father marries again; we could not expect him to marry anyone *but* the careless governess, Clare, now a widowed Mrs Kirkpatrick. But it is here that the novel's attention to the "ordinary" deepens; with Mrs Kirkpatrick, now Mrs Gibson, comes her daughter, Cynthia, exactly Molly's age but with a range of experience far removed from our initial fairy-tale structure. It is Cynthia's "novel" that makes Molly's seem less transparent. Whereas Molly's life fits itself easily into the first narrative, being, as it were, an open book, Cynthia's life is a secret—in fact, is the secret of the novel, giving rise to the complications that keep the novel going. It is Cynthia's childhood that challenges the ease of representation Molly's life presented; Cynthia's that invokes the plots of blackmail, broken promises, and hidden correspondence; Cynthia's that is the pathology of the fairy tale, the trauma at which Molly's abandonment only hinted. The challenge of the one story by the other is made especially clear by the placement of the two girls' stories within the same over-riding narrative—the quest for husbands, for the security marriage signals in a novel—and the way the differences in their initial "tales" continue to shape them both. The movement between the good and bad princesses—one blessed, one blighted at birth—creates a story of social counterpoint, at exactly the moment the princesses enter the marriage plot, the larger "tale" of social determination, within which the elements of secrecy and detection dovetail with those of Molly's secure and readable past.

With Cynthia, left at school by her mother, unwelcomed on her arrival at Hollingford because her mother doesn't "like to expose [her] feelings to every passer-by in High Street" (p. 252), full of those "French airs" the family at the Towers had expected in vain from Molly during her stay, another marriage plot is put in place, and we are offered a way of reading human character that departs from the straight, uni-originary tale Molly's introduction suggested. Whereas Molly was just given to us, presented straight, Cynthia is introduced through her mother's accounts, her character suggested through her mother's inattention. Her character, unlike Molly's, is presented from the first not as her own but a result of her upbringing. The first criticism we hear of the new Mrs Gibson comes from Lady Cuxhaven at the Towers, who says, "The only thing that makes me uneasy now is the way in which she seems to send her daughter away from her so much," though we are reminded immediately that as a "poor dear woman trying to earn her livelihood, first as a governess, . . . what could she do with her daughter but send her to school?" (p. 125). Cynthia's arrival on the scene marks the inscription of Molly's plot into this larger world of "poor dear women," a world of economic necessity and forced choices—like the orphans Mrs Gibson always calls "poor dears."

The novel in many ways fights against this plot; in part, it wants Mrs Gibson to stand as evil, unadulterated by her own necessities, born into some primal vulgarity. In such a world, Molly can be originally good, not through education or even something so subtle as influence but through some supra-environmental quality of her own, that inherent mark of a lady readers are always instructed to notice in Victorian fiction. This is a reading Cynthia at times allies herself with, even when Molly insists that, despite her moral qualms, she would have behaved exactly as Cynthia did: "No, you would not. Your grain is different, somehow" (p. 535). But what Cynthia's entrance on the scene does is rewrite the early chapters: with the beginning of the socially determined plot, we see the socially determining nature of Molly's childhood.

Molly's only griefs, we are told explicitly, are the "small grievances of a very happy childhood," but a happy childhood seems a mixed blessing in this novel. Molly is seventeen when the real story of the novel begins, but seems in some key ways unsocialized. She is a sweet girl, a village favorite, and wins the heart of Squire Hamley and his invalid wife when her father sends her off to visit them. But she is sent off because she has also won the heart of one of her father's resident medical students, a red-haired Mr Coxe, who writes her a surreptitious note declaring his eternal passion, "with a very proper admixture of violent compliments to her beauty. She was fair, not pale; her eyes were loadstars, her dimples marks of Cupid's finger, &c" (p. 81). Mr Gibson calls her "quite a baby" at "sixteen and three-quarters," though he remembers "poor Jeanie was not so old, and how I did love her"; but her tumble into the realm of desire, her unknowing movement, prompts his remarriage. Until then, Molly had been entirely her father's: when he brings her back from the Towers, she declares,

> "I should like to get a chain like Ponto's, just as long as your longest round, and then I could fasten us two to each end of it, and when I wanted you I could pull, and if you didn't want to come you could pull back again; but I should know you knew I wanted you, and we could never lose each other." (p. 58)

What this plan involves is a link not only of presence but of consciousness: the father and daughter in constant connection. And in some odd way, Mr Gibson's marriage is to protect that connection; rather than let it be dissolved by her marriage, he will dilute it by his own marriage, as if keeping Molly sexually untouched is more essential to their intimacy than keeping himself single. She is to remain all his; he is no longer all hers.

What the novel accomplishes here is a denaturalizing of this state; Molly's inscription into daughterhood becomes more pointed in light of Cynthia's orphanhood. "I wish I could love people as you do, Molly," says Cynthia.

> "It's very shocking, I daresay; but it is so. Now, don't go and condemn me. I don't think love for one's mother quite comes by nature; and remember how much I have been separated from mine!"

Cynthia's narrative provides an alternative version of what it means to "part" from one's parent, of being a "trouble":

> "Mamma had to go out as a governess; she couldn't help it, poor thing! but she didn't much care for parting with me. I was a trouble, I daresay. So I was sent to school at four years old; first one school, and then another; and in the holidays, mamma went to stay at grand houses, and I was generally left with the schoolmistresses." (p. 257)

Initially, the passage seems to suggest that Cynthia's inability to love is a warping of nature: without that initial separation, without the evidence of her mother's inability to care for her, Cynthia would be as sweet as Molly is. But the novel begins to suggest this from the other side: that "sweetness" itself is a cultural construct. Cynthia says to Molly,

> "I'm not good, and I told you so. Somehow, I cannot forgive her for her neglect of me as a child, *when I would have clung to her*. Besides, I hardly

ever heard from her when I was at school. And I know she put a stop to my coming over to her wedding. I saw the letter she wrote to Madame Fléchier. A child should be brought up with its parents, if it is to think them infallible when it grows up."

"But though it may know that there must be faults," replied Molly, "it ought to cover them over and try to forget their existence."

"It ought. *But don't you see I have grown up outside the pale of duty and 'oughts'*. Love me as I am, sweet one, for I shall never be better." (p. 261; emphasis added)

Even within this passage, stronger than most Victorian fiction in its sisterly indictment of parental "faults," the emphasis shifts from what all children will do (cling) to what children need equally to be taught to do. Why should children go on loving where there is abuse? Why should we cover faults? What is it that makes us love "naturally"? Only if we are already inside the "pale of duty and 'oughts'" can we claim this as "nature."

If Cynthia's education has been (mis)shaped by parental neglect, Molly's has been formed by parental, specifically paternal, attention: her father kept her from learning too much, saying to her governess,

"Don't teach Molly too much; she must sew, and read, and write, and do her sums; but I want to *keep her a child*, and if I find more learning desirable for her, I'll see about giving it to her myself. After all, I'm not sure that reading or writing is necessary. Many a good woman gets married with only a cross instead of her name; it's rather a diluting of mother-wit, to my fancy; but, however, we must yield to the prejudices of society, Miss Eyre, and so you may teach the child to read." (p. 65; emphasis added)

She is, the narrator says, "daunted by her father in every intellectual attempt," and "only by fighting and struggling hard" does she persuade him to let her have French and drawing lessons. Her father's impatience with her needs leads him to snap, "I wish girls could dress like boys"; he seems near, at moments, to wishing she were a boy, while continually limiting her movement because she is a girl.

The most important fact of their relationship is its exclusivity, and the shared joy in what seems its repetition of marriage: when she goes to the Hamleys, Molly wishes she were not going, and her father replies, "Nonsense; don't let us have any sentiment. Have you got your keys; that's more to the purpose." But she drives off,

looking back and kissing her hand to her father, who stood at the gate, in spite of his dislike of sentiment, as long as the carriage could be seen. (p. 93)

The ostensible excuse of this exclusivity—and its reward, in the novel's terms—is the *moral* life the father and daughter lead, one we presume to be strengthened by the lunches of cheese they eat alone together in the kitchen before his arriviste wife forces them to eat inconvenient, formal midday meals. Mr Gibson's strongest disappointment in his wife is that "the wife he had chosen had a very different standard of conduct from that which he had upheld all his life, and had hoped to have seen *inculcated in his daughter*" (p. 432; emphasis added). As events turn out, in *Wives and Daughters*, Mr Gibson's "standard of conduct" seems far preferable to Mrs Gibson's, but Molly, rightly, differs with him on several occasions, to his bitterness. Her testing of his understanding, particularly in her defense of Cynthia's privacy and suffering, suggests that what Mr Gibson had loved about Molly is that he *could* "inculcate" conduct in her. Daughters arrive unformed, wives with their own opinions. Molly's formation by her father seems for the best in this novel, but the emphasis on Cynthia's malformation reminds us of the dangers of "forming" one's children. If there is no such thing as an originary self, much of Molly's passivity, as I suggested earlier, comes from her assumption that her father will know best; his encouragement of her docility has left her better able to act on behalf of others than for herself.

The deepest lesson of femininity in the novel, and it is both Gaskell's recurrent fear and the lack that haunts most of her fiction, is the absence of a loving mother: Cynthia becomes entrapped by Preston literally because her mother departed without leaving a forwarding address; Molly's mother, dead since she was a child, exists only as a memory of perfect love, a woman who brushed and played with the wet curls that are a constant torture to Molly's stepmother.[4] But the lesson of the dead mother, and of the few living mother figures in the novel, is that to be female is primarily to be an invalid, to be passive, to suffer victimization. This is what both women try to overcome: Molly, by defying Preston and, eventually, her father; Cynthia, by trying to write her own marriage plot, choosing and jilting men. But like most "lessons" in the novel, it is taught both by social example and by literary exemplum.

Molly's transition from the "girlhood" her father sees and the prospective wifehood her stepmother sees is her trip to Hamley Hall—the trip undertaken at the moment when she is first seen by her father as desirable to men. The world she enters in those scenes, especially her time with Mrs Hamley, is explicitly presented as a *maternal* daughterhood she lacked: "You're a blessing to mothers, child," Mrs Hamley says to her, and Mrs Hamley's world of invalidism, poetry, family portraits, and quiet rooms is part of that socialization Molly has missed. But in the other scenes in this passage of the novel, specifically the scenes where she sobs over her father's remarriage, only to be comforted and advised by Roger, what she learns is to "think of her father's happiness before . . . her own" and to "hope for the best about everybody, and not to expect the worst." But we might note that the key lessons are all framed by books—specifically by Molly's reading of Felicia Hemans's poetry and *The Bride of Lammermoor*, that nightmare novel of parental betrayal—on the day when someone first mentions that her father might remarry. Her introduction to this world of sexual choice and matrimonial blight, as Gaskell and Scott present it, is through her father's claim to be betraying her for her own good: "I've taken a step which will, I hope, make us both happier." Like Cynthia, Molly is offered what can only be a "substitute" mother; unlike Cynthia, she is quieted by domestic instruction into believing (or pretending to believe, to appease her furious father, who walks off in the middle of their conversation when she questions him) that what is being done to her is for her own good. Her reading can only encourage her to obedient passivity or (like Lucy Ashton) to self-destructive rebellion.

If the novel sets up so schematically the differences—and the structural similarity—between Molly's and Cynthia's education, it traces the effects of that education by placing the girls in the marriage plot, and following the specific results of Molly's over-inscription into the "pale of duty and 'oughts'" and Cynthia's absence from the "natural" love of mother. With this shift from the world of familial relations—and it is really Cynthia's presence, with her secrets, that introduces the sexual plot—the novel moves most completely into the social world. The familiar overlapping worlds of Victorian fiction—here, the "family" at the Towers, the squirearchy at Hamley Hall, the spinsters of the village, the mercantile class of Mr Preston, and the distant glamour of London relations—are called into unity, become one plot, with the introduction of marriage; they were exterior to the original family but essential to the foundation of new families. If the novel's plot exists to turn its "daughters" into "wives," it needs to invoke a larger society to endorse or condemn the match. Characters who had served minor functions in the novel before—the Misses Browning, to watch Molly and her father; Mr Preston, to be a subject of tension between Cynthia and her mother; Lady Harriet, to comment on Mrs Gibson and comfort Molly—are pressed into more active service in this plot, as marriage proves not only social but narrative glue, attaching characters in new ways to one another. But the other "glue" of this plot, what begins to connect its movements, is a series of secrets (primarily sexual secrets, secret negotiations between mothers, daughters, and their lovers) that threaten again the presentation of the ordinary.

Desire, as we saw, was the hidden motivation for Molly's exile to Hamley, and for her father's remarriage—the latter being, we might argue, a double secret, for although he claims to himself and keeps secret from Molly Mr Coxe's offer as a reason for marriage, his own sexual desire is the motive the villagers assume, and which we would be wrong entirely to discount. Molly's desirability—woman's openness both to rape and seduction—is what is really hidden in the novel, and her father's desire to keep her "hidden" is at the heart of his moral "inculcations." But there are two specific sexual secrets in the novel, both part of the marriage plot. The first, that Osborne Hamley is already married, is a secret Molly stumbles on early and one that she protects until after his death. The second, and more interesting, is Cynthia's secret engagement to Mr Preston, which she does not tell in the hopes she can escape it; to protect that secret Molly herself is caught up, almost fatally, in the plotting, secret meetings, and clandestine payments of the blackmail plot.[5] Mr Preston's name evokes anxiety from the start, in both Cynthia and her mother; Lady Harriet warns Molly not to trust him; he is the character most clearly marked as dangerous; he is also the dark space the plot must pass through to come out in light at the other side. Mr Preston, and his violent desire for Cynthia, suggests that the secret of passion is what the *socialized* novel must both invite, to initiate its heroines, and fight off, to keep them marriageable.

Cynthia's entrapment by Preston echoes Molly's betrayal by Mr Gibson, for both are introduced in terms of being a "heroine," being placed into the feminine, the realm of socialization. Cynthia declares to Molly,

> "Perhaps I might be a heroine still, but I shall never be a good woman, I know."
> "Do you think it easier to be a heroine?"
> "Yes, as far as one knows of heroines from history. I'm capable of a great jerk, an effort, and then a relaxation—but steady, every-day goodness is beyond me. I must be a moral kangaroo!" (p. 258)

"Steady, every-day goodness," what we might think the ideal of a novel subtitled "An Every-day Story," is what Molly has: the novel has suggested that that "every-day" daughter, though not heroic, has her own tragedy. But further, the novel argues that being in the every-day and having that "steady goodness" is a luxury, or at the least a construct, rather than its own state of nature. Molly's vision initially claims that "love" is an absolute: one's tastes are organic, intrinsic. Desire can be recognized as easily as Mrs Hamley states when she says of Molly, "I like your face, and I always go by first impressions," or when Molly herself announces that nothing could have made her like Mr Preston. But this world of reliable impressions and natural "tastes" is put into question exactly by Cynthia's entrapment by Preston. Cynthia's engagement takes place not in a world of "liking" or of "steadiness" but of exchange and "trading in daughters," as the novel calls it later. Molly comes on the two of them holding hands, and Preston attacks Cynthia, saying, "I do not know what you will say at home; but can you deny that you are my promised wife? can you deny that it has only been at your earnest request that I have kept the engagement secret so long?" Cynthia replies,

> "Since you will have it out—since I must speak here, I own that what you say is literally true; that when I was a neglected girl of sixteen, you—whom I believed to be a friend, lent me money at my need, and made me give you a promise of marriage." (p. 511)

This promise and loan, the conflation of friendship and sexuality, the buying of Cynthia's marriage, begins an examination of the social place of this marriage plot. When Preston says, "You seem to imply you sold yourself for twenty pounds," and Cynthia answers, "I did not sell myself; I liked you then. But oh, how I hate you now!" the question of "like" no longer seems part of the organic plot of tastes but, rather, creates a plot of need, contingency, secrecy, abandonment—a plot dangerous to both women.

Molly's view—of "liking," of "steady goodness," of reliable impressions—makes her the obvious "heroine" of an every-day story; except that in this novel, the every-day is a very complicated, and not easily interpreted, realm. Molly herself is secretly in love with Roger Hamley, who is in love with Cynthia; she is in on the secret of Osborne Hamley's marriage; further, even her affection cannot decipher Cynthia's secret or, more significantly, protect Molly from being the victim of random, vicious gossip in the village. Cynthia's inability to extricate herself from her engagement, to hide her own letters, to return money to Preston, to gain the protection of Mr Gibson, all suggest the vulnerability of the melodramatic "heroine"; Molly's inability to tell her own story straight suggests that all heroines exist in a shady world of information, gossip, secrets, and promises. Further, as must be obvious by now, the "every-day" novel is a more complicated genre than it looked. The narration of this novel itself depends on these same networks of knowledge and secrets. If neither heroine can escape cultural formation, neither, of course, can the novel or the novelist. In its attention to the structuring of (in)formation, *Wives and Daughters* begins to discover its own relationship to the problematic making of the "heroine(s) from history."

ii

If the heroine's plot suggests a movement (a tension) between the "ordinary" and the transmission of information, a tension signaled by the dependence of plot on secrecy, the larger question (to return to the terms Foucault suggested) is of the relation of novelistic information (letters, blackmail, gossip, memories, family history) to its scientific counterpart in the novel (museums, genealogical history, scientific reports). If these reports are a factor in the love plot (the movement that will bring Roger from being Cynthia's to Molly's suitor) it will also become clear that the scientific report is not exempt from sexual tension; the "history" that science seems in this novel to support is a precarious construct as well, and plots of female desire (flirtation, seduction) have the power to disrupt the certainties of (masculine) knowledge as well.

Not that the men aren't all initially certain of their knowledge and the view of the world it endorses, but the novel is considerably more skeptical than that. (*Wives and Daughters* features three scientists prominently: Mr Gibson, Lord Hollingford, and Roger Hamley. It seems initially to separate them and their world of detailed observation from the world of romantic love, with its accumulation of feminine detail.) The slippage between one world and the other terrifies Mr Gibson, whose most passionate outburst in the novel comes when he discovers that his wife has overheard his consultation with another doctor about Osborne Hamley's failing health, and has altered her plans for her daughter Cynthia's marriage accordingly. This movement amidst his professional secrets seems to the doctor the most serious possible violation of trust, but it reflects also his concern with (male) authority, and with protecting a realm for unmanipulable, pure knowledge. Mrs Gibson not only overheard the conversation but looked up the words in his dictionary, appropriating his knowledge. She then "traded" in that knowledge, attempting to "trade in a daughter's affection."

But it is not only Mrs Gibson who views scientific knowledge as part of a larger realm of secrets that are "traded," nor is it only medical information that the novel treats as part of a larger power structure.[6] The whole quest for scientific information and certainty, and the need to assemble details into a system, are considered on the one hand as part of assembling and bolstering patriarchal authority, and on the other as structurally similar to the female world of detail and romance, in which, as Lady Harriet tells Mr Preston, "You give rise—you have given rise—to reports."

Officially, the "reports" of the novel are those of Roger Hamley, who goes to Africa, whence he sends back letters with "many curious particulars" to an "annual gathering of the Geographical Society," and about whose discoveries "all our scientific men are so much excited." Roger, for much of the narrative, is the romantic object of both heroines, and the solid information in his letters to Cynthia goes unread, except by Molly, for his fiancée reads only for compliments to herself. But his scientific progress carries a great weight in the novel: he is removed from the scene for two years, sent off by Lord Hollingford on a scientific expedition. His travels do more than provide for absence in the plot; they seem a trope for the disinterested curiosity. In her original sketch of the novel, Gaskell wrote to George Smith that

> Roger is rough, & unpolished—but works out for himself a certain name in Natural Science,—is tempted by a large offer to go round the world (like Charles Darwin) as naturalist,—but stipulates to be paid *half* before he goes away for 3 years in order to help his brother.[7]

But within the text, his departure is announced in a slightly different way, and signals more than his concern for his brother and the difference between them; it invokes thematically, in its connection with "the authority of experts," the question of why men need scientific knowledge:

> "Didn't you hear of that rich eccentric Mr Crichton, who died some time ago, and—fired by the example of Lord Bridgewater, I suppose—left a sum of money in the hands of trustees, of whom my brother is one, to send out a man with a thousand fine qualifications, to make a scientific voyage, with a view to bringing back specimens of the fauna of distant lands, and so forming the nucleus of a museum which is to be called the Crichton Museum, and so perpetuate the founder's name? Such various forms does man's vanity take. Sometimes it stimulates philanthropy; sometimes a love of science!" (p. 405)

Mr Gibson calls this "love of science" a "very laudable and useful object," but in the original description, which comes, in a rather cumbersome sentence, from Lady Harriet, the museum is more a monument to one man's memory than natural history, leaving open the question of what the role of science in man's memory—and man's vanity—is to be.

Throughout the novel, science has functioned as the realm of serious thought. Roger's superiority to his brother Osborne, both as moral arbiter and as romantic choice, has been signaled by his interest in science, and one could read in his devotion to his work both Gaskell's own interest in nature and in the naming of natural phenomena, and her familial relationship to and interest in Darwin.[8] Gaskell had met Darwin several times, and his sister had traveled with Gaskell's daughter Meta to the Alps on a sketching tour. But Gaskell's other interest is in the relation of women to scientific knowledge. Molly's depths, moral and emotional, have been spelled out in her careful reading of scientific texts and her attention to Roger's lessons. When Lord Hollingford, the other serious scientist of the novel, is forced by his sister to dance with Molly, he announces her "a charming little lady . . . intelligent and full of interest in all sorts of sensible things; well read, too—she was up in *Le Règne Animal*" (p. 339). Her intelligence, of course, is marked by her having "a mind so well prepared for the reception of information" that Lord Hollingford believes himself interesting; we know, further, that her interest is sparked by his beginning the conversation by telling her that Roger, whom she loves, has published a paper in some scientific periodical. But no one seems to consider that Molly herself might have the vision of a scientist; science could not be a realm of pure thought for women. It has been marked as such, however, for men: both Roger and Lord Hollingford are socially awkward, redeemed by—at ease only in—scientific faith.

Men in the "scientific world" are "odd-looking, simple-hearted men, very much in earnest about their own particular subjects, and not having much to say on any other," and seem to live far removed from the social and domestic worlds of the novel. When Molly reads Roger's letters from his travels, she thinks,

> Perhaps the details and the references would make the letter dull and dry to some people, but not to her, thanks to his former teaching and the interest he had excited in her for his pursuits. But, as he said in apology, what had he to write about in that savage land, but his love, and his researches, and travels? There was no society, no gaiety, no new books to write about, no gossip in Abyssinian wilds. (p. 460)

Nothing could seem further from the female world—exactly society, gaiety, and gossip—than his "researches and travels." Molly's interest in his "pursuits" may be romantic, but his interest in them seems to give him access to a wilder realm of pure thought, a region that is "savage," other, closed to women and civilization. But the terms we invoked earlier from Foucault might put into question that putative separation between male and female information, between "savage" and civilized. In *The Order of Things*, Foucault recounts that the first item "excluded" from the realm of science is gossip: "hearsay is excluded, that goes without saying" (p. 132). But natural history is itself a language, and at that a language much like what we have been reading:

> Natural history is situated both before and after language; it decomposes the language of everyday life, but in order to recompose it and discover what it has made possible through the blind resemblances of imagination. (p. 161)

The recomposition of the "everyday" into language is the "field report" of the novel, enacted by "imagination": the language of science must be regrounded in lived experience, removed from the myth of the removed observer. To recall his earlier description of the scientist's study of "origins," he examines "life, labour and language" within a "stratum of conduct, behaviour, attitudes, gestures already made, sentences already pronounced or written" (p. 354). That sense of the "already pronounced" is strong enough in this novel—what Roger's scientific experiments suggest again is at once the prefixedness, and the always-invented quality of his own (as well as Abyssinian) culture. Roger's "museum" is never that far from the world of gossip, of decomposition, of disrupted (female) every-day life.

Where the museum enters the every-day is in the world of local history, the realm of imitation ("fired by the example of Lord Bridgewater") where men "perpetuate" the male "name." In this account, history is hardly the transhistorical realm to which it sometimes aspires; more than recounting stories of origin, it is itself a story, an artifice, an attempt at "*making* history." Seeing this artifice connects the museum to family histories, that need to "make history" by providing an heir, a young double. As Squire Hamley says of his children,

> "There's Osborne, who takes after his mother . . . he takes after madam's side, who, as I said, can't tell who was her grandfather. Now, Roger is like me, a Hamley of Hamley, and no-one who sees him in the street will ever think that the brown, big-boned, clumsy chap is of gentle blood." (p. 106)

But no one will ever think he is anyone else's son, either. When Lady Harriet describes Lord Hollingford's choice for the expedition as "Hamley of Hamley," she assumes Roger to be the oldest son—which he is not—somehow admitting that fitness to the title, eliding the biological obstacle. A history written through biological resemblances, the certainty of "like me," insures paternity; the novel, by killing Osborne, seems to echo the squire's sense of "likeness" as appropriate succession. It is at that moment that science and romance (report and gossip—and their evil relation, blackmail) come together. The danger that Cynthia's flirtation represents—her approachability, her inability to "fix" herself on one man—is as threatening as it is because it reminds men that the proof of paternity is harder to "fix" than that of maternity, and that female betrayal unfixes sexual and historical certainty.

The connection between romance and history fades into this novel's obsession with community itself, the organic life so often associated with Victorian fiction. In the squire's certainty of "Hamley of Hamley" he does more than re-present himself; he embodies local history:

> He and his ancestors had been called squire as long back as local tradition
> extended. . . . His family had been in possession [of his land] long before
> the Earls of Cumnor had been heard of; before the Hely-Harrisons had
> bought Coldstone Park; no one in Hollingford knew the time when the
> Hamleys had not lived at Hamley. "Ever since the Heptarchy," said the
> vicar. "Nay," said Miss Browning, "I have heard that there were Hamleys
> of Hamley before the Romans." The vicar was preparing a polite assent,
> when Mrs Goodenough came in with a still more startling assertion. "I
> have always heerd," said she, with all the slow authority of an oldest
> inhabitant, "that there was Hamleys of Hamley afore the time of the
> pagans." . . . At any rate, the Hamleys were a very old family, if not
> aborigines. (p. 72)

To be Hamley of Hamley is to be not only a museum piece but a museum: the land is a monument to the village's sense of its own history, of the tribal life extended into prehistory through one person's presence. What the time "afore the time of the pagans" would look like, of course, it is up to Charles Darwin to imagine. But in village time, the "oldest inhabitant" knows the most important thing about it: if Hamleys of Hamley were there, so was she, in some form. Her personal history, like the squire's, has a place in larger history. Because she knows and can name local history, she is in it; her naming, as well as their presence in the past, is a founding act.

This larger scope of history, of Romans, the "Heptarchy," the time "afore pagans," bears an uncertain relation to the immediate histories of the novel, in which the "dead hand of the past," as another novel puts it, suggests that history will intervene in "every-day life" not as a nightmare but as a trivialization of real stories of origin. What has Mr Preston's blackmail of Cynthia to do with either Darwin or the landed gentry? In Cynthia's ironic "am not I a grand young lady to have a doom," aren't we meant to read the deliberate leveling of every-day history, in which "doom" belongs more appropriately to melodramatic fiction, to *The*

Bride of Lammermoor? Doesn't Gaskell's classification of her novel as an "every-day story" remove it from "history"? Isn't Molly's growing up "among these quiet people in calm monotony of life" deliberately separate from Roger's report, Lord Hollingford's "information"?

Or is Gaskell, in her concern with secrets and revelation, connecting all these "reports" with her own reporting, suggesting that these larger studies connect with the ways that the village society—which the novel observes as if it were as alien as Abyssinia—makes narratives out of women's lives? *Wives and Daughters*, like the gossip it collects and the secrets it reveals, is the "report" that comes from studying every-day life, the report of the "mysterious implications" that will make the novel a different kind of museum of culture.

iii

Local history and natural history are primarily ways of organizing the evidence that lies in front of the observer, of making randomness coherent, of adducing origin and predicting conclusion, converting the world into narrative and placing it into a museum, thereby preserving both the ordered evidence and the ordering intelligence of the observer. Gossip, the ongoing female history of the village of Hollingford, serves exactly the same purpose: in searching out the meaning of the random observation of Molly Gibson with Mr Preston, the women of the town validate their own methods of observation and views of the world, and they make coherent events that otherwise might baffle them. By passing gossip along, they turn their speculation into fact; by seeing in these events a *larger* narrative, that of courtship, deception, and marriage, they attach their own small histories to a larger order. Gossip is the history of the powerless, suggests Gaskell; but more, it is a microcosm of the larger world of plots and "doom" that beset a heroine trying to make her way through romance, deception, and marriage.[9] "Never be the heroine of a mystery," Molly's father advises her, too late; to be a "heroine," Gaskell seems to suggest, is to be the object of mysteries more complex than a woman like Molly can decipher.

When she comes into her sister's plot, and begins to act for her, Molly begins to understand what deception and concealment Cynthia has been acting out and acting under, but that is merely the darker side of her own deception, which has involved hiding her love for Roger, protecting Osborne's secret, shielding her father from her awareness of her stepmother's foolishness. This constant silence is seen as essential to women's lives, but the policing of silence is also feminized. Throughout, it is specifically female instruction that keeps Molly's instincts in check—the "little bird" of gossip that the Misses Browning invoke and that Molly has wanted to strangle since she was a child; the constant small affectations of Mrs Gibson. Gossip here seems a form of social control, a small, constant voice of reproach, a way of orderi⁻ the behavior of others that increases the power of those who advise and monitor. In the powerless world of Hollingford women, those who can speak for society have the only authority; much of the gossip of the novel, in fact, is generated out of the need to prove one's right to speak up, the married women arguing with the spinsters, the "old inhabitants" with the newcomers. Those who have seen the most, those who construct the most impressive narrative, speak for the other women.

But both Molly's "good" concealment of suffering and Cynthia's more suspect deception about past failings suggest that in this world of limited female power, most women must lead painfully silent lives. Cynthia's initial sin with Mr Preston was to reveal her unhappiness at her poverty and her inability to pay for the welcome reprieve of a vacation with a wealthier family: she cannot write to her mother for money, for her mother has not relayed her temporary address; she cannot cry; but she can mock her own suffering, leading him to lend her the twenty pounds out of which he will extort the marriage promise. But more, and more sad, he can continue to blackmail her with letters she wrote in which she spoke too freely of her contempt for her mother and her affection for him—calling him "My dearest Robert" (p. 522) and saying "things in those letters about mamma" (p. 523).

> Those unlucky letters—written when I was not sixteen, Molly—only seven of them! They are like a mine under my feet, which may blow up any day; and down will come father and mother and all. (p. 523)

The sadness of these letters as Molly describes them is that they were "written, when she was almost without friends, to you, whom she looked upon as a friend!" (p. 532). But if Cynthia's was originally a fall into confidence, into mistaken revelation, that mistake has destroyed her ability to be confiding, and threatens to destroy Molly's:

> Unwillingly, Molly was compelled to perceive that there must have been a good deal of underhand work going on beneath Cynthia's apparent openness of behaviour; and still more unwillingly she began to be afraid that she herself might be led into the practice. (p. 525)

After she enters into this plot—and perhaps, as she realizes its implication for her own life—Molly cannot speak up either. She must conceal things from her father; she is silent before the Misses Browning; she recognizes but dares not question her own ostracism.

Another way of explaining gossip is the process of a woman's becoming a heroine of a story she cannot rewrite: Molly knows that she is not in love with Mr Preston, but she cannot know that that is being said of her.

> All these days the buzzing gossip about Molly's meetings with Mr Preston, her clandestine correspondence, the *tête-à-tête* interviews in lonely places, had been gathering strength, and assuming the positive form of scandal. The simple innocent girl, who walked through the quiet streets without a thought of being the object of mysterious implications, became for a time the unconscious black sheep of the town. (p. 557)

The "buzzing" grows from fact, ignoring character and history, but it exists in "positive form" because there is a form already existing for it. Even Molly's father reminds her,

> "I hear of this from the town's talk. . . . Everyone makes it their business to cast dirt on a girl's name, who has disregarded the commonest rules of modesty and propriety." (p. 568)

Molly, as we know, has not violated these rules in spirit, but the mere appearance of disregarding the "commonest rules" casts her into the "commonest" story. The "town's talk" suggests those eighteenth-century literary exempla, *The Tatler* and *The Spectator*: just as we can find the roots of the novel in conversation manuals and guidance books, organized talk and story transformed into narrative, so here Molly's "heroine-ship" grows out of gossip, the novel only a step away from "dirt on a girl's name." As her father protests:

> "It's all a mystery. I hate to have you mixed up in mysteries."
>
> "I hate to be mixed up. But what can I do? . . ."
>
> "Well, all I can say is, never be the heroine of a mystery that you can avoid, if you can't help being an accessory." (p. 571)

How Molly is to avoid this "heroine-ship" is not clear. She is more than an accessory, of course, as soon as she falls in love and has her own story; what she does not have, in the world of the town's talk, is the ability to tell her own story.

Significantly, Molly cannot undo the false narrative for herself. Again her father urges her to full disclosure, but she insists,

> "I have told you all I can tell; all that concerns myself; and I have promised not to say one word more."

"Then your character will be impugned. It must be, unless the fullest
explanation of these secret meetings is given." (p. 569)

She cannot give "the fullest explanation," for the secret is not hers, but
this means she cannot rewrite the gossip. Cynthia discovers the same
thing: she must undo her engagement to Roger, for she cannot imagine
telling him her history, and only after releasing herself from the engagement, and from the obligation to confess, can she tell Mr Gibson the
whole story. Molly's reputation is cleared through a series of almost
accidental repetitions and rightings of the truth. Only Lady Harriet's
courage and confidence in her young friend could be labeled an active
cause for Molly's salvation; the rest seems as accidental—as incidental—
as the original chain of events. Lady Harriet hears the "buzzing" from the
Misses Browning and confronts Mr Preston with the accusations in front
of her father, who repeats the rumors to Lady Cumnor, who in turn
upbraids Mrs Gibson with her daughter's "Jilting Jessie" ways. It is only
when Mrs Gibson returns home furious with having "one's child's name
in everbody's mouth" that the truth comes out; it is only when Lady
Harriet calls on Molly and "take[s] possession of her, like an inanimate
chattel," marching her through the whole town in front of the whole
town, that the town "veer[s] round" in Molly's favor, and, specifically, it
is only because Lady Harriet is "from the Towers" that she has this power
over gossip, a power Molly and Cynthia lack.

What Molly's inability to set herself right suggests is that quality of
already formed narratives, structures looking for women to fill them, we
have seen so often in Gaskell's novels. It is time, perhaps, to turn to the
consideration first of the heroine and then of novel-writing itself that we
find in *Wives and Daughters*. The concern with beginnings both as
natural origins and social "inculcation" can be read as planting the
woman's life (both in culture and in narrative) within a realm of mediation, a realm in which she cannot name her desire or shape her story.
When Cynthia bewails the "doom" that she cannot escape, when she
names herself a "moral kangaroo," capable of the great jerks of "heroines
from history" rather than "every-day goodness," above all when she
constantly attracts and refuses suitors, she is imagining and rejecting
different fates, trying to imagine herself outside the "steady" life of a
woman. This, a pattern in Victorian fiction we might trace to its finest
depiction in Gwendolen Harleth, is the plight of the woman with energies
she has no realm for, the potentially tragic version of Gaskell's refrain,
from *Mary Barton* on, ". wish I were a sailor and might go to sea!" The
greatness of *Wives and Daughters*, the perception in which it surpasses

Daniel Deronda, is that the woman with no visible desire to go to sea, or, in Cynthia's only verbal dream of escape, no wish to go to Russia as a governess, cannot have her own story, either. The good daughter, no less than the desirous imp, finds herself continually blocked and silenced into passive heroineship. Like the gentle Lucy Ashton, whose story she reads at the Hamleys, Molly is inscribed into the father's marriage plot (here, literally, the plot of her father's marriage) and faces being either "traded" into marriage, or, as women fear most in this novel, left unsold at the end of the season.

Molly is inscribed into the heroine's life in several ways, then: through her father's plan for her education; through her stepmother's marriage dreams; through her own reading; through the town's "buzzing" around her; through the novel's careful, self-conscious placement of her within a complicated construct of stories, mediations, and archeologies of femininity. If to be a woman is, as the "talk of the town" and her father's strictures suggested, to be an "object," then Molly's peaceful girlhood and tumultuous romance, her life as a heroine, stands in a representative place, much as Ruth's did, as the observed female who gets her story by being seen. But in *Wives and Daughters*, more than in any novel since *Mary Barton*, Gaskell connects her observed heroine with her own status as novelist, both, in *Mary Barton*'s phrase, "all in print."

The scene in town where Molly is "observed" being indiscreet, handing Cynthia's money back to Mr Preston, takes place in the shop of Grinstead, the bookseller, who serves as "agent" for the Hollingford Book Society, his "agency" an echo of Mr Preston's work for Lord Cumnor and of the sexual mediation that agency invokes. But the novel places Molly's entrapment in the village's plot for her in a world of plots—of marketed literature that serves, ironically, more for social placement than aesthetic pleasure. Grinstead's shop is

> the centre of news, and the club, as it were, of the little town. Everybody who pretended to gentility in the place belonged to it. It was a test of gentility, indeed, rather than of education or a love of literature. No shopkeeper would have thought of offering himself as a member, however great his general intelligence and love of reading; while it boasted on its list of subscribers most of the county families in the neighbourhood, some of whom subscribed to it as a sort of duty belonging to their station, without often using their privilege of reading the books; while there were residents in the little town, such as Mrs Goodenough, who privately thought reading a great waste of time, that might be much better employed in sewing, and knitting, and pastry-making, but who nevertheless belonged to it as a mark of station, just as these good, motherly women would have thought it a

terrible comedown in the world if they had not had a pretty young servant-
maid to fetch them home from the tea-parties at night. (pp. 546–547).

Literature is put forward here as, potentially, "a great waste of time,"
specifically of women's time, because they might be "better employed"; it
is a tool of class, serving to keep the desirous away from both books and
"privilege"; the book shop is a kind of marketplace of information, where
everyone gathers, where gossip spreads, where women, particularly,
watch others choosing books, and comment on those choices. Nowhere
does Gaskell seem to be more conscious of the complicity of fiction, of
her fiction, with ideology, and nowhere more ironic about the impossibility of rewriting fictions, in a world where novels exist *only* as status, with
no possibility for transforming women's lives, or of themselves being
transformed.

But no other Gaskell novel has so consistently a relativist position on
all structures of ideology, fiction, and conversation. As always, the relativism is placed in Cynthia's mouth, in a discussion with her mother about
the gossip at the Towers:

> "They felt for me, for it is not pleasant to have one's child's name in
> everybody's mouth."
> "As I said before, that depends upon how it is in everybody's mouth. If I
> were going to marry Lord Hollingford, I make no doubt everyone would be
> talking about me, and neither you nor I should mind it in the least."
> (p. 594)

"Talk," here, is relative: to be in "everybody's mouth," to be in the realm
of fiction, depends on "how," and Gaskell is at once entirely serious, and
capable of quiet laughter, about the talk of, and talk about, her writing.

But there is a more direct comment on the role of narrative within the
novel: Lady Harriet is imagining, along with her brother, that Molly will
marry Roger, and perhaps they will inherit, and perhaps. . . . But as she
goes on, he stops her, saying,

> "Hush, Harriet, that's the worst of allowing yourself to plan ahead for the
> future; you are sure to contemplate the death of someone, and to reckon
> upon the contingency of affecting events."
> "As if lawyers were not always doing something of the kind."
> "Leave it to those to whom it is necessary. I dislike planning marriages,
> or looking forward to deaths about equally." (p. 677)

Gaskell, too, in her final rebellion, seems to "dislike planning marriages
or looking forward to deaths," and there is no finer comment on the two
ends possible for the Victorian heroine. In *Wives and Daughters*, as in all

her fiction, Gaskell suggests how the two fates are interwoven, marriage often a kind of death; death the basis, in this novel as in *Mary Barton,* for the heroine's marriage. Taking death and marriage as the two possible "plots," always framed, in this novel, by the legality of information, the structures of law, inheritance, gossip, history, we might wonder once more at the novel's own lack of conclusion, at Gaskell's dying rather than ending the novel in marriage, at Mrs Gibson's sleep-induced silence at the end of the novel, which might suggest the silencing of the bad narrator, of the novelist gone bad, of the wild plot-maker, who, at the last minute, allows her heroine to sneak off to one side, into a narrative silence that remains, perhaps uniquely, unbroken.

But what is the relation between the heroine's plot, the mad narrator, and the larger project of the novel I am trying to account for here, that in which origin and ending become narrative, in which realism organizes the information of every-day life into a cultural monument? What I want to propose here is a rethinking of the model of the novel as museum, to suggest that Gaskell was engaged in such a rethinking, for a museum, as Susan Stewart notes, "seek[s] to represent experience within a mode of control and confinement. One cannot know everything about the world, but one can at least approach closed knowledge through the collection."[10] The museum ("the central metaphor of the collection," as Stewart calls it) "strives for authenticity and for closure of all space and temporality within the context at hand." As she quotes Eugenio Donato, "The set of objects the Museum displays is sustained only by the fiction that they somehow constitute a coherent representational universe. . . . Such a fiction is the result of an uncritical belief in the notion that ordering and classifying, that is to say, the spatial juxtaposition of fragments, can produce a representational understanding of the world."

The conventional view of the woman's novel, in particular, is that it preserves that "classification scheme" in which the world exists "'all at once' in a way in which it could not otherwise exist"—that is, as it "must exist." The novel, as a museum of culture, enshrines through the order of realism both the values of the day and the details that give them resonance and status—and, of course, stasis, as well. In this view, the "everyday" both lives in and defines the woman's novel. But in *Wives and Daughters,* the real is not only increasingly relative ("reported," in "mouths," in "circulation") but increasingly provincialized; to be relative is to lose its status as revelation, as guarantor of value, as representative fiction. This was a move implicit in Gaskell's turn to the "fiction" of evolution—what Gillian Beer reminds us is a "determining" fiction—and one equally clear in her revisions of another woman's novel of courtship, deception, and sisterhood: Maria Edgeworth's *Helen*. If the invocation of Darwin leaves us with the plot of origins and kinship, the male "reports" that tend to give way to anxiety about female flirtations, I want to turn now to Gaskell's final evocation of the woman's romance, and the implications of her self-conscious placement of *Wives and Daughters* within a tradition (looking backward and forward) of women novelists, to ask once more, what is the "museum" of women's culture that her novels create and transform?

At the center of Edgeworth's *Helen* is the destruction of one woman's hope of marriage at the hands of another. As in *Wives and Daughters*, the innocent virgin believes (and lies for) her less innocent sister, and has her own honor maligned in return. When the orphaned Helen lies for her best friend, Cecilia, she causes her own exile (from London and from the marriage plot), an exile that can be repaired only by the return of the good mother, and the full confession of the wicked but lovable sister. The differences between this novel and *Wives and Daughters* are important: Cecilia is married, pregnant, in danger of being perceived as an adulteress, and it is her husband's (over)strict sense of justice that she fears. Helen is more free than Molly, for she has no parents, but also more alone, dependent on the families of others. But, like Molly, she signals her femininity in an excess of modesty, blushes, and fevers; and like Cynthia, Cecilia's charms—the excess of her love for her friend—are at once the evil of the false Duessa and the promise of a freer, more knowing sexuality, which the heroine needs to acquire (if only by proximity) to make her way into the marriage plot. In both novels, the fallen woman's desire at first denies and then rewards her more passive sister's desire.

What the novels share most deeply is an anxiety about women's "telling stories": Cecilia's mother, Lady Davenant, sees her daughter's duplicity as a punishment for her own interference in political machinations; Cynthia's inability to confess the truth grows clearly out of her mother's inability to speak any truth "straight." In both novels, one might see the woman writer's anxiety about the pleasures of narrative. As Miss Benson put it, in *Ruth*, inventing is so pleasant, and to have a talent for it (as she did, as Gaskell did) is threatening to any account in which truth as moral certainty is paramount. Certainly, it is not women writers alone who fear the deceptive potential of novel-writing, and I would hardly want to ground a history of women novelists in the poetics of deception, but the anxiety about dangerous (sexual) secrets and duplicitous narratives that one sees in all of Gaskell's novels, and that I am suggesting in *Helen* as well, offers another way of formulating the critique of cultural "truth" I am identifying in *Wives and Daughters*. If the woman's novel is con-

cerned with the safe marriage and enclosure of its daughters, and the
protection of its wives from the dangers of adultery, it is also concerned
with the stories they tell and are told; the story, in all these novels, of how
daughters become wives.

Put another way, Gaskell's transformation of *Helen*'s central plot
suggests her particular awareness of the woman's tradition in fiction, and
her own relation to that central cultural plot. Take another reference in
the novel: Molly's governess, who wants her to read more books than her
father desires, is named Miss Eyre, in what must be a tribute to Gaskell's
dead friend and literary sister, Charlotte Brontë. In a scene where Betty
criticizes Miss Eyre, however, Molly flies at her in a violent passion—her
passion an exact echo of Jane's "flying" at John Reed in the opening of
Jane Eyre.[11] The sin of which Jane is accused, remember, is of lying, but
her perfect truthfulness, like Molly's, consists in revealing what others
would as soon keep hidden—and by the time she wrote *Villette*, Brontë
would certainly have moved toward a world in which female silence and
duplicitous narrative *are* more true than speech.

But what is the relation of Gaskell, of *Wives and Daughters*, to a
tradition of female narrative, to those same issues of female speech with
which we began? A letter that Gaskell wrote to George Eliot after the
publication of *Adam Bede* suggests the shift from *Mary Barton* to the
late novels: mistaking the name as Gilbert Elliot, Gaskell writes,

> Since I have come up from Manchester to London I have had the greatest
> compliment paid me I ever had in my life, I have been suspected of having
> written "Adam Bede." I have hitherto denied it, but really I think, that as
> you want to keep your real name a secret, it would be very pleasant for me
> to blush acquiescence. Will you give me leave? . . .
>
> After all it is a pity so much hearty admiration should go unappropriated
> through the world. So, although to my friends I am known under the name
> of Mrs Gaskell, to you I will confess that I *am* the author of Adam Bede,
> and remain very respectfully & gratefully
>
> Yours,
Gilbert Elliot.[12]

In writing to Eliot, in whose chosen pseudonym Gaskell might have read a
reference to the name Jane Eyre assumes when she leaves Thornfield Hall,
"Jane Elliott," Gaskell displays a new humor about authorship, and even
about truth-telling: gone is the language of alibis and mysteries; present,
rather, the language of modesty, the "acquiescence" of the "blush." What
one might almost see here is a pleasure in mysteries, in the romance of
authorship and admiration, which recapitulates the female plot.

"There is very little to be known; no mysteries, that is one comfort," says a character at the end of *Helen*;[13] a similar sigh of relief is breathed at the end of most courtship novels—though not, of course, at the end of *Wives and Daughters*, which lacks an ending, breaking off when Mrs Gibson, the archetypal deceptive, tattling, female narrator, goes off to dream of shawls, allowing her stepdaughter to sneak out, to dream her own plots. The irony with which *Wives and Daughters* ends (or doesn't end, because Gaskell died, midsentence, while at tea with her daughters, before finishing the novel) suggests a different relationship between the novel and the museum, a different twist on its organization of knowledge, one in which the limits of every-day life (and of "every-day stories") are tested. Without reading into the novel the complacency of the wise novelist, looking back on a self-consciously crafted career, having reached the aforeplanned apex of novelistic knowledge, we might still see in her last book some reflection on her earlier work, on the traditions on which she drew, on the novels this book (and her earlier work) made possible.

When Virginia Woolf invokes Gaskell at the beginning of *A Room of One's Own*, she claims, with customary irony, to offer a summary of "women and fiction": "a few remarks about Fanny Burney; a few more about Jane Austen; a tribute to the Brontës and a sketch of Haworth Parsonage under snow; some witticisms if possible about Miss Mitford; a respectful allusion to George Eliot; a reference to Mrs. Gaskell and one would have done."[14] If the purpose of this book has been to dispel the place of Gaskell at the end of the line, as the most easily dismissed of women novelists, Woolf in fact offers what might serve as a summary of the tradition this book has itself so often invoked. In much the same way, I might (particularly through *Wives and Daughters*) offer my museum tour of Gaskell's fiction: the class struggles of *Mary Barton* giving way to the passionate social criticism *cum* aestheticism of *Ruth*, giving way in turn to the years of engagement with the marketplace and the industrialization of the woman writer, the sociologies of *Cranford* and *North and South*, the violent desires of *Sylvia's Lovers*, the hard-won wisdom and affectionate detachment of *Wives and Daughters*. Or we might see our shy but fierce heroine, battling her way through the courtship plot, emerging at the end of every novel with the always ambivalent triumph of successful marriage, and the promise of the daughters to which it will give birth. If the ironic "evolution" and the romantic "circulation" of *Wives and Daughters* give us pause in this progress, it ought to be as checks on our certainties, moments when our placement—as well as hers—within plot becomes clear to us; the self-consciousness of the every-day life of

Wives and Daughters offers us a new realism, a turn in our walk through the museum, a brighter light (or a darkness visible, to echo *Mary Barton*) on our tour.

Gillian Beer recounts that Francis Darwin commented that his father had the quickest eye for exceptions of any thinker he knew, and Beer connects that "strength of mind" with the first sentence of chapter 1 of *The Origin of Species*:

> When we look to the individuals of the same variety or sub-variety of our older cultivated plants and animals, one of the first points which strikes us, is that they generally differ much more from each other, than do the individuals of any one species or variety in a state of nature.[15]

In her summary, the recognition of the exception, the anomalous, "comes from a highly developed response of individuation as well as from an irresistible power of perceiving patterns" (p. 42). If this might stand as a definition of realism, it stands in particularly well for the "reports" that make up *Wives and Daughters*, which holds before us both the "patterns" of culture, and the "variety or sub-variety" of individuals and their responses. The reports that Gaskell sends back, from the boundaries of her culture, are not quite the origin of a new species. The woman's novel cannot offer that, working as it does within the "collection" that is its inheritance, the culture that is its workshop. If the novel's skepticism—about ideology and romance—offers anything, it is that twin motion of recognition and transformation that has always marked Gaskell's fiction, and the slight dismissal that the absence of an ending marks anew: the dismissal of the napping bad mother, and the daughter's hope of escape into another story.

In the larger schemes of *Wives and Daughters*, its reports of the time before the heptarchy, the progression of daughters into wives, we might be reminded of other schemes of history: of Darwin's origins and descents; perhaps even of Freud's most vivid pictorial image for the individual psyche, the archeological buildings and ruins of Rome and London, the vast city that is human consciousness. It is toward those vaster, universalizing structures that the novel is always tending, and from which our novel is also receding. This novel seems to make more modest claims for itself—though again, even its modesty might strike a familiar chord. "Men," Freud announces magisterially at the beginning of *Civilization and Its Discontents*, "are accustomed to moderate their claims to happiness": under the influence of the "more modest reality principle," "a man thinks himself happy merely to have escaped unhappiness or to have survived his suffering."[16] Something like that moderation—Freud's "happiness of quietness" (p. 24)—might seem the end of *Wives and Daughters*, and of the accommodation of so many Victorian endings, endings in which, as Freud again argues, the rule of the community is not to be broken for the individual. Its reading of culture is at once recuperative and subversive; the achievement of *Wives and Daughters* is to make those rules clear, and to trace the individual's progress into that community marked by "planning marriages and looking forward to death."

But the novel does not only call up the rules, and its openness suggests the other aspect of Gaskell's fiction that has been before us throughout this study: again to invoke Darwin, who (as Beer asserts) "shares with Carlyle and Dickens that use of the prophetic present which leaves no space between us and the future and poises us on the edge of the unknown,"[17] the space of the sleeping narrator is the unknown of the novel, the "prophetic present" of realistic fiction. The desire of fiction to escape the rules represents the desire for transformation, the prophecy that here goes unspoken—but does not go unsignaled, and that carries a particular potency for the woman novelist. If Woolf's vision of Shakespeare's sister is that she must await *our* working for her arrival, Gaskell's Scheherezade might be similarly enchanted. It is in the expectation of other endings that the silence at the end of *Wives and Daughters* gives way to the dream of another storyteller—and of another story waiting to be told.

NOTES

I have consulted a variety of editions of the novels in writing this book; the texts cited are given in the relevant chapters. All references to Elizabeth Gaskell's correspondence are from *The Letters of Mrs Gaskell* (hereafter *GL*), edited by J. A. V. Chapple and Arthur Pollard (Cambridge: Harvard University Press, 1967); letters are identified by number, date, and page.

Chapter 1

1. For a summary of these accounts, see Stephen Gill's introduction to the Penguin edition of *Mary Barton* (Harmondsworth, England: Penguin Books, 1970). The more sympathetic readings are for the most part those of Marxist critics; the best of them is John Lucas's "Mrs Gaskell and Brotherhood," in *Tradition and Tolerance in Nineteenth Century Fiction* eds. David Howard, John Lucas, and John Goode (London: Routledge & Kegan Paul, 1966), which follows on and complicates Raymond Williams's seminal discussion in *Culture and Society* (New York: Columbia University Press, 1958, 1983). The only account of the novel to consider formal, social and political concerns together is Catherine Gallagher's, in *The Industrial Reformation of English Fiction: Social Discourse and Narrative Form, 1832–1867* (Chicago: University of Chicago Press, 1985), which places *Mary Barton* in the Victorian debates on free will and determinism, and reexamines the conflicts between genres and modes of representation in the novel. Although our discussions differ on many points, I find hers the most intriguing and enlightened consideration of *Mary Barton*. For a discussion of "paternal" politics, see Rosemarie Bodenheimer's fine *Politics of Story in Victorian Social Fiction* (Ithaca: Cornell University Press, 1988), especially pp. 21–68, and her account of *Mary Barton* in "Private Grief and Public Acts in *Mary Barton*," *Dickens Studies Annual* (1981): 195–216.

2. Teresa de Lauretis, "Desire in Narrative," in *Alice Doesn't* (Bloomington: Indiana University Press, 1984), p. 139. For a compelling account of female and male plots, which this chapter in many ways follows, see Nancy K. Miller, "Emphasis Added: Plots and Plausibilities in Women's Fiction," *PMLA* 96 (1981): 36–48.

3. Dorothy Sayers, *Have His Carcase* (New York: Avon Books, 1932), p. 149. See Ruth Bernard Yeazell's fine discussion of the "love interest," in "Why Political

Novels Have Heroines: *Sybil, Mary Barton* and *Felix Holt*," in *Novel* 18 (1985): 126–144.

4. *GL* 42, ?early 1849, p. 74.

5. Gill, p. 22.

6. *GL* 48, 29 May 1849, p. 82.

7. Williams, p. 89.

8. Bodenheimer, "Private Grief, Public Acts," p. 213.

9. Stedman Jones, "Rethinking Chartism," in *Languages of Class: Studies in English Working Class History* (Cambridge: Cambridge University Press, 1983), pp. 90–178. This is the finest recent discussion of Chartism, and an example of how an historian can use literature to understand political change, and in turn add to our understanding of literature like the condition-of-England novels; his use of the concept of a "fiction" of politics is central to my analysis. He asserts that "Mrs Gaskell" saw Chartism "solely in terms of anger, distress and the breakdown of social relationships," in his terms, "not as a political movement but a social phenomenon," but his account of the workers' faith in political language (in the fictions of class) is exactly her understanding in *Mary Barton*.

10. *Mary Barton*, ed. Gill, p. 141. All subsequent references to the novel are to this edition and are included in the text.

11. *The Life and Struggles of William Lovett*, in *From Cobbett to the Chartists*, ed. Max Morris (London: Lawrence & Wishart, 1948), p. 229.

12. *The Northern Star*, March 24, 1838, in Morris, *From Cobbett to the Chartists*, p. 235.

13. For Richardson, the right of women to vote was as obvious as the rights of working men: "I believe from this reason," he says, "that she ought to partake of his councils, public and private, that she ought to share in the making of laws for the government of the commonwealth" (*The Early Chartists*, ed. Dorothy Thompson [Columbia: University of South Carolina Press, 1971], p. 124). John Watkins, another Chartist who addressed this question, wrote in his *Address to the Women of England*, "So far from being excluded from taking part in politics, women ought to be allowed to vote; not wives—for they and their husbands are one, or ought to be as one—but maids and widows" (*English Chartist Circular* 1, no. 13 [April 1841], quoted in Dorothy Thompson, *The Chartists: Popular Politics in the Industrial Revolution* [New York: Pantheon Books, 1984], p. 125). Lovett's *Chartism, A New Organization of the People*, ed. Asa Briggs (New York: Humanities Press, 1969), calls for the education, the taxation, and the representation of women (p. 62), but though Lovett and his supporters received suggestions to include in the People's Charter a call for women's suffrage, they rejected these, to quote F. C. Mather, "not from any objection of principle, but from fear of inviting additional opposition to the Charter" (*Chartism and Society: An Anthology of Documents* [New York: Holmes and Meier, 1980], p. 117).

14. *The Northern Star*, 9 May 1845, quoted in Thompson, *The Chartists*, p. 136.

15. "The Politics of Seduction in English Popular Culture, 1748–1848," in *The*

Progress of Romance: The Politics of Popular Fiction, ed. Jean Radford (London: Routledge and Kegan Paul, 1986).

16. de Lauretis, p. 239.

17. Sandra M. Gilbert and Susan Gubar, *The Madwoman in the Attic* (New Haven: Yale University Press, 1979), pp. 153–155.

18. *GL* 150, [early February] 1850, p. 223.

19. *GL* 55, 26 November 1849, p. 91.

20. *GL* 93, 7 April 1851, pp. 147–148.

21. *GL* 68, February 1850, p. 106.

22. "Introduction" to Gaskell *Letters*, pp. xi–xii.

23. *GL* 13, 19 August 1838, p. 34.

24. Elizabeth Gaskell, *My Diary: The Early Years of my Daughter Marianne* (London, Privately printed by Clement Shorter, 1924), p. 5. All subsequent references included in text.

25. *GL* 8, May 1838, p. 14.

26. *GL* 12, 18 August 1838, p. 33.

27. Mary Howitt, *An Autobiography* (London: William Ibister, 1889), 2:28.

28. *GL* 15, late 1841, p. 44.

29. Quoted in Winifred Gérin, *Elizabeth Gaskell* (Oxford: Oxford University Press, 1980), p. 94.

30. *GL* 30, 11 November 1848, p. 62.

31. *GL* 1, 13 November 1848, p. 63.

32. Quoted in Gérin, p. 83.

33. Julia Swindell, in *Victorian Writing and Working Women: The Other Side of Silence* (Cambridge: Polity Press, 1985), has much of value to say about female authorship and pseudonyms, although she wrongly asserts that Gaskell published *Mary Barton* as "Mrs Gaskell," and that Gaskell never used a male pseudonym.

34. *GL* 34, 7 December 1848, p. 65.

35. *GL* 33, 5 December 1848, p. 64.

36. *GL* 36, late 1848, p. 67.

37. *GL* 87, ?December 1850, pp. 140–141.

38. *GL* 71, 28 April 1850, p. 115.

39. *GL* 26, 10 July 1848, p. 58.

40. *GL* 22, 21 March 1848, p. 54.

41. *GL* 23, 2 April 1848, p. 55.

42. *GL* 24, 13 April 1848, pp. 55–56.

43. *GL* 26, 10 July 1848, p. 58.

44. Prostitution, as Judith Walkowitz suggests in *Prostitution and Victorian Society: Women, Class and the State* (Cambridge: Cambridge University Press, 1980), provided the central imagery of contagion associated with the "Great Unwashed": "Pollution became the governing metaphor for the perils of social intercourse between the 'Two Nations'" (p. 4). Aunt Esther's role in the novel as "connection" echoes what Walkowitz claims for the Victorian prostitute: "Literally and figuratively, the prostitute was the conduit of infection to respectable

society. She was nonetheless an object of class guilt as well as fear, a powerful symbol of sexual and economic exploitation under industrial capitalism." Here, the "conduit" is narrative, much as Peter Brooks suggests in his chapter "The Mark of the Beast: Prostitution, Serialization and Narrative," in *Reading for the Plot* (New York: Knopf, 1984).

45. See Walkowitz generally on surveillance: on the collaboration between police and streetwalkers, and on the difficulty of naming, limiting, and proving the act of prostitution. She stresses that traditionally British prostitution resisted the model of "continental" prostitution, "where the regulation system fostered police corruption, women's dependence on pimps, and on organized brothel systems." English prostitutes tended to live with two or three other women in dwellings that resembled "low class lodging houses," and in other ways maintained a "'quiet' truce with the police" (p. 24). But with the new emphasis on "humanitarian reform and on greater efficiency," came increased bureaucracy and regulation (p. 74). *Mary Barton* reflects that new concern, and the intensified scrutiny that came with it. The discussion that follows, of Aunt Esther and the role of surveillance in connecting the two halves of the novel, focuses not just on sexual politics but on narrative self-consciousness: the two plots are unified by both thematic and formal concerns. My treatment of narrative surveillance obviously owes much to D. A. Miller's crucial "Discipline in Different Voices: Bureaucracy, Police, Family, and *Bleak House*" (*Representations* 1 [February 1983]: 1), though I would resist seeing a novel like *Mary Barton* as imposing quite so fierce a discipline as he suggests Victorian fiction must. In *Mary Barton*, one might argue, the struggle to "maintain" discipline is so evident as to put discipline more firmly in question.

46. Mary Jacobus, "*Dora* and the Pregnant Madonna," in *Reading Woman* (New York: Columbia University Press, 1986), pp. 145, 148. For a further discussion of these issues, see Margaret Homans, *Bearing the Word: Language and Female Experience in Nineteenth-Century Women's Writing* (Chicago: University of Chicago Press, 1986), especially pp. 29–32.

47. Julia Kristeva, "Motherhood According to Giovanni Bellini," in *Desire in Language: A Semiotic Approach to Literature and Art* (New York: Columbia University Press, 1980), p. 238.

48. Ibid., p. 239.

49. Judith Lowder Newton, *Women, Power and Subversion: Social Strategies in British Fiction, 1778–1860* (Athens: University of Georgia Press, 1981), p. 5.

50. See Robyn Warhol's discussion of direct address in Gaskell, in "Toward a Theory of the Engaging Narrator: Earnest Interventions in Gaskell, Stowe and Eliot," *PMLA* (October 1986): 811–818.

51. For a compelling discussion of these questions, see Elizabeth Deeds Ermarth, *Realism and Consensus in the English Novel* (Princeton: Princeton University Press, 1983).

52. *GL* 72a, 16 July 1850?, p. 119.

53. George Levine, *The Realistic Imagination: English Fiction from Franken-*

stein to Lady Chatterley (Chicago: University of Chicago Press, 1981), especially pp. 7–8, 15–17.

54. Quoted in Gérin, p. 89.

55. See *GL* 33, 5 December 1848, where she declares, "In the midst of all my deep & great annoyance, Mr Carlyle's letter has been most valuable; and has given me almost the only unmixed pleasure I have yet received from the publication of MB," and *GL* 34, 7 December 1848, where she says she values "Mr Carlyle's note" because it "bears the stamp of honesty and truth," and because he dares to tell her her faults, without flattery.

56. Gérin, p. 100. Gaskell, in a letter to an unknown correspondent, referred to his "friendly warning against being 'lionized,'" and hopes "I might not be materially altered for the worse by this mysterious process of 'lionizing.'" *GL* 40, ?8 March 1849, p. 71.

Chapter 2

1. W. R. Greg, "Prostitution," *Westminster Review* 53 (1850): 448–506. Sally Mitchell (*The Fallen Angel: Chastity, Class and Women's Reading, 1835–1880* [Bowling Green, Ohio: Bowling Green University Popular Press, 1981]) argues that Gaskell borrowed many of the terms for her discussion of *Ruth*—her emphasis on "grinding poverty," on the need for social acceptance—from Greg's review, which she would have seen because of its inclusion of *Mary Barton* (a long quotation about Aunt Esther's "haunts") and since she was "planning" *Ruth* at the time.

2. *GL* 61, 8 January 1850, p. 91. Gaskell wrote to Dickens for advice because he was involved with Angela Burdett-Coutts's "refuge for female prisoners," Urania Cottage, which rescued fallen women and helped them emigrate.

3. *GL* 148, before 27 January 1853, p. 220.

4. See variously Angus Easson, *Elizabeth Gaskell* (London: Routledge & Kegan Paul, 1979), who asserts Gaskell "knew she was tackling a subject likely to bring adverse, even painful criticism on herself, yet felt she was called to do something" (p. 110), and Gerald deWitt Sanders, *Elizabeth Gaskell* (New Haven: Yale University Press, 1929), who declares that the novel "teems with Christian thought," that the heroine is a "blameless and wholly lovable woman," and that "so strong was convention that no writer before Mrs. Gaskell had dared utter such opinions in fiction as she uttered here" (p. 48).

5. Michael D. Wheeler, in "The Sinner as Heroine: A Study of Mrs Gaskell's *Ruth* and the Bible," *Durham University Journal*, 6 (ns37), 1976 (pp. 148–161), discusses Gaskell's habit of allusion, specifically biblical quotation, to build mood and thematic significance in the text, but he does not observe that specific contemporary literary languages are both parodied and absorbed in the novel. Donald Stone, in *The Romantic Impulse in Victorian Fiction* (Cambridge: Harvard University Press, 1980), pp. 149–153, discusses the novel's debate between

Romantic and Victorian views of will. Rosemarie Bodenheimer, in *The Politics of Story in Victorian Social Fiction* (Ithaca: Cornell University Press, 1988), pp. 150–164, discusses the work as a revision of the "pastoral," which in turn revises the "conventional story" of the fallen woman in order to negotiate between social and "natural" views of female sexuality.

6. For a recent treatment of this subject, see Helena Michie, *The Flesh Made Word: Female Figures and Women's Bodies* (New York: Oxford University Press, 1987). While Michie's general discussion is relevant to my argument, her only discussion of *Ruth* is of Ruth's "temptation" by finery, a point I argue is of more relevance to Esther in *Mary Barton*. Michie is not, in general, concerned with Victorian aestheticism. My own discussion moves between aesthetics and power, drawing as well on the work of Michel Foucault on the textualizing of the body.

7. Mitchell, pp. 22–31.

8. Raymond Williams, "Forms of English Fiction in 1848," in *Literature, Politics and Theory: Papers from the Essex Conference, 1976–84*, ed. Francis Barker, Peter Hulme, Margaret Iversen, and Diana Loxley (London: Methuen, 1986), p. 6.

9. George Henry Lewes, "*Ruth* and *Villette*,"*Westminster Review* (1853).

10. T. W. Adorno, "Cultural Criticism and Society," in *Prisms*, trans. Samuel and Sherry Weber (Cambridge: MIT Press, 1981), pp. 30, 32.

11. Judith Walkowitz, *Prostitution and Victorian Society: Women, Class and the State* (Cambridge: Cambridge University Press, 1980), p. 33.

12. Greg, p. 491.

13. Pierre Macherey, *A Theory of Literary Production* (Routledge & Kegan Paul, 1978), p. 195; all subsequent page references included in the text.

14. *GL* 61, 8 January 1850, p. 99.

15. *GL* 42, ?early 1849, p. 74.

16. *GL* 12, 18 August 1838, p. 33.

17. For an interesting discussion of this phenomenon, and of the connections between Wordsworth and Tennyson, as well as Wordsworth and *The Germ*, see Carl Dawson, *Victorian Noon: English Literature in 1850* (Baltimore: Johns Hopkins University Press, 1979), particularly the chapter on *In Memoriam*. Dawson reports that Wordsworth's commercial success was higher in the 1850s than the 1830s, despite his fall in critical reputation. "When Moxon issued *The Prelude*, he printed two thousand copies, a sizable edition even for an established poet. He needed a second edition by 1851" (p. 37). Even more, as Matthew Arnold recounts, of the period of Gaskell's early reading, "Wordsworth had never, either before or since, been so accepted and popular, so established in possession of the minds of all who profess to care for poetry" ("Wordsworth," in *Poetry and Criticism of Matthew Arnold*, ed. A. Dwight Culler [Boston: Houghton Mifflin, 1961], p. 331).

18. *GL* 139, 28 October 1852, p. 207.

19. See Margaret Homans, *Bearing the Word: Language and Female Experience in Nineteenth-Century Women's Writing* (Chicago: University of Chicago Press, 1986), for a discussion of Gaskell's use of Wordsworth in those years. My

discussion will follow some of the same concerns as Homans's treatment of Dorothy Wordsworth, and particularly of George Eliot, of whom she argues, "It is precisely the literalness of Eliot's transposition of Wordsworthian themes—her effort to be a docile student on the model of Wordsworth's implied sister—that constitutes her subversion of them" (p. 122). To the extent that Gaskell's is a literalization of Wordsworth's "naturalism," her novel will be a critique of it.

20. *The Letters of William and Dorothy Wordsworth; The Middle Years, Part I, 1806–1811*, ed. Ernest de Selincourt, 2d ed. rev., ed. Mary Moorman (Oxford: Clarendon Press, 1969), p. 335. I owe this reference, and a greater understanding of the difficulties of this problem, to Peter J. Manning, "Placing Poor Susan: Wordsworth and the New Historicism," *Studies in Romanticism* 25 (Fall 1986). For a slightly different argument, one in which Wordsworth more easily "reasserts and solidifies the priority of male needs and desires" (a reading that I argue presumes a more solid status as subject than Wordsworth ever acquired), see Marlon B. Ross, "Naturalizing Gender: Woman's Place in Wordsworth's Ideological Landscape," *ELH* 53 (Summer 1986). One might amend his attempt to gender Wordsworthian readings with Alan Liu's account of Wordsworthian denial: "Wordsworthian 'nature' is precisely such an imaginary antagonist [as Napoleon's diversionary force in the Simplon Pass] against which the self battles in feint, in a ploy to divert attention from the real battle to be joined between *history* and self" ("Wordsworth: The History in 'Imagination,'" *ELH* 51 [1984]: 505–548). The "subjectivity" Ross declares women are denied is not readily available to male subjects (or poets) either.

21. All references to Wordsworth will be from the Riverside edition of *Selected Poems and Prefaces by William Wordsworth*, ed. Jack Stillinger (Boston: Houghton Mifflin, 1965), except those to "Ruth," for which I have consulted *The Complete Poetical Works of William Wordsworth* (Boston: Houghton Mifflin, 1904). For the text of "The Mad Mother," which was retitled "Her Eyes Are Wild" in 1815, I have used R. L. Brett and A. R. Jones, *Wordsworth and Coleridge Lyrical Ballads* (London: Methuen, 1963), as well as Stillinger, and on all poems, have profited from *William Wordsworth*, ed. Stephen Gill, Oxford Authors Series (Oxford: Oxford University Press, 1984), as well. Since all the poems quoted in this chapter are short and well known, I have chosen not to clutter my text with line numbers.

22. Laura Mulvey, "Visual Pleasure and Narrative Cinema," in *Narrative, Apparatus, Ideology*, ed. Philip Rosen (New York: Columbia University Press, 1986), p. 199. On this necessary silencing of women, see Nancy J. Vickers, who argues in an essay on the fragmented female body, that "bodies fetishized by a poetic voice logically do not have a voice of their own; the world of making words, of making texts, is not theirs" ("Diana Described: Scattered Woman and Scattered Rhyme," in *Writing and Sexual Difference*, ed. Elizabeth Abel [Chicago: University of Chicago Press, 1982], p. 107).

23. By *poet* I mean the poet-figure in the poem; neither the narrator within the poem nor the "poet" narrating the entire poem is to be equated with Wordsworth.

24. In Stillinger, p. 510.

25. Ibid.

26. S. M. Parrish (*ELH* 24 [1957]: 15–63), quoted in Stillinger, p. 510.

27. For an interesting discussion of this, see Carol Christ, "The Feminine Subject in Victorian Poetry," *ELH* 54 (Summer 1987), pp. 385–401.

28. *The Germ: A Pre-Raphaelite Little Magazine*, ed. Robert Stahr Hosman (Coral Gables: University of Miami Press, 1970), p. 1.

29. *The Germ*, pp. 23–33. See also James Sambrook's reprint, with notes, in *Pre-Raphaelitism: A Collection of Critical Essays* (Chicago: University of Chicago Press, 1974), pp. 45–56.

30. Alexander Welsh, *The City of Dickens* (Oxford: Clarendon Press, 1971), especially pp. 180–196.

31. Gaskell was a great admirer of Ruskin's, and she and her daughter Meta were reading *The Seven Lamps of Architecture* in these years. (Her daughter went on to study art with Ruskin.) Interestingly, Gaskell went to school with Ruskin's wife, Euphemia Gray, and once noted, somewhat viciously, that she "really is very close to a charming character; if she had had the small pox she would have been so" (*GL* 195, 17 May 1854, p. 287). Gaskell seemed, too, to sense the deeper dilemmas of Ruskin's relationships with women, saying that "I can not bear to think of the dreadful hypocrisy if the man who wrote those books is a bad man." But in terms of *Ruth*, one might note her recounting of how Effie, during her marriage, used to "come down to *breakfast* with natural flowers in her hair, which he also objected to but she continued the practice" (*GL* 211, 11 to 14 October 1854, p. 311).

32. John Ruskin, *Modern Painters*, vol. 2 (New York: Wiley, 1899), p. 181.

33. Much of my discussion of the transformation from Romantic problems of individual perception to Victorian problems of shared vision grows out of Richard Stein's study, *The Ritual of Interpretation* (Cambridge: Harvard University Press, 1975), which I find the most interesting and useful book on Ruskin and Rossetti.

34. Elizabeth Gaskell, *Ruth* (Oxford: Oxford University Press, 1985), p. 2. All subsequent references are to this edition and are included in text.

35. George Watt, *The Fallen Woman in Nineteenth Century Fiction* (Totowa, N.J.: Barnes & Noble, 1984).

36. Among the more interesting of these is a review by W. R. Greg, "False Morality of Lady Novelists," *National Review* 8 (1859): 144–176, in which he comments on the contradiction between Ruth's much-insisted-on innocence and her need for repentance and redemption. His review stands as a reminder that Gaskell in many ways departed from "liberal" views of the time.

37. I have continued to use the distinction between *plot*, *story*, and *discourse*, in an attempt to account for the dissonances in the narrative, but I do not intend my discussion to be limited to the traditional structural uses of these terms. Although one can learn from the haunting of one term by another, in the constant syntactic echoes of structuralist theory, this incessant, unrelenting similarity

suggests a more closed text than I feel *Ruth* finally *is* for a reader. The terms most useful here might be those of Roland Barthes in *S/Z* (New York: Hill & Wang, 1974; French edition, 1970), and I have always in my mind his play with the "writerly" text, in which the "tutor text" is constantly "broken," but I prefer Macherey's sense of the making of the text to this kind of critical game/engagement.

Further, there seems little space for social readings in traditional narrative theory, and my goal here is to recapture formalist concern for the socially committed critic. For these reasons, my sense of narrative is closer to what Peter Brooks describes in *Reading for the Plot* (New York: Knopf, 1984) as "the play of desire in time that makes us turn pages and strive towards narrative ends" (p. xiii). In his discussion of "prostitution, serialization, and narrative," with its connection between the "thematics of the desired, potentially possessable body, and on the other toward a readerly experience of consuming . . . bound to take on commercial forms" (p. 143), he suggests more, I think, of what narratology has to offer readers. Brooks defines his work as psychoanalysis of narrative, an "erotics of art," but when he suggests that the text's "potentialities are transformed by the proliferation of narratives it provokes" (p. 166), we are as close to the politicized as the psychoanalyzed text.

Following through briefly on his example, for instance, it is interesting to note that although Gaskell was careful not to make Ruth a prostitute—she is a scaled-down test case, as it were—we can locate in her the same narrative energies Brooks locates in the figure of the prostitute; we can, in short, realize the power of this novel to shock by the narrative trope Gaskell invokes, and the powers of desire the novel focuses. Only by placing the (formalist) structuralist terms back in the twin contexts of our desirous and socially placed reading, can we sense the power of narrative.

38. Virginia Woolf, *To the Lighthouse* (New York: Harcourt, Brace & World, 1927), p. 46.

39. Quoted in Winifred Gérin, *Elizabeth Gaskell* (Oxford: Oxford University Press, 1976), p. 132. Terry Castle, in *Clarissa's Ciphers* (Ithaca: Cornell University Press, 1982), discusses a similar tension in the initial response to *Clarissa*, and specifically Richardson's dismay at the tendency of female readers particularly to "yearn for a 'happy' ending." She quotes a letter in which he asserted,

> I intend another Sort of Happiness (founded on the Xn. System) for my Heroine, than that which was to depend upon the Will and Pleasure, and uncertain Reformation and good Behaviour of a vile Libertine. . . . But I find, Sir, by many Letters sent me, and by many Opinions given me, that some of the greater Vulgar, as well as all the less, had rather it had had what they call, an Happy Ending.

Castle goes on to say that Richardson

> patronizingly ascribes to his female readers precisely that sort of flighty bad judgment and sexual *faiblesse* that his heroine's fictional persecutors be-

labor her with—and his remarks carry an unpleasant burden of unacknowl-
edged, almost Lovelacean misogyny. . . . It does not occur to him, obviously, that a female reader—even a moderately pious one—might not
necessarily take an unalloyed pleasure in seeing one of her sex made over
into a decomposing emblem of Christian womanhood, or respond wholly
favorably to that equation between sexual violation and death which he
seems unconsciously to have accepted as a given. (pp. 172–173)

Note again that Gaskell's angriest readers (at least on this point) are women—and
that Gaskell seems to shy away from seeing in her murdering of Ruth the need to
impose "authority" on her text, much as Richardson did in his revisions of
Clarissa. Castle's reading suggests that Gaskell, as well, may have wanted to close
down the interpretive play of *Ruth*.

40. Quoted in Gérin, p. 140.

41. Garrett Stewart, *Death Sentences* (Cambridge: Harvard University Press,
1984), p. 50. Stewart notes later that Gaskell considered titling *North and South*
"Death and Variations" (p. 105). The pure formalism of that title suggests some
of the connections I have in mind between plot and possibility, and I think he is
right to read this as a narratological issue rather than (in the critical truism) as an
outgrowth of Gaskell's "morbid" nature.

42. Patsy Stoneman, in *Elizabeth Gaskell* (Bloomington: Indiana University
Press, 1987), has argued that Ruth dies insane, in a state of "ideological incoherence and madness" resulting from the failure of the "'redemptive' process, based
on 'repentance' which is really repression," for Ruth was "led, while childishly
irresponsible, into a sexual bond which she can now neither forget nor responsi-
bly continue" (p. 115). I do not agree that Ruth in any way wants to continue that
bond, or that Ruth dies divided because she is "aware of her sexuality, [yet]
unable to accept her sexuality because unwilling to be 'sinful,'" (p. 117), but I
agree with Stoneman's suggestion that Ruth dies "as a 'dislocated subject,' [with]
no social identity." The point of the novel, as I read it, is precisely to "dislocate"
social identity.

43. See especially *GL* 153, 7 March 1853, p. 226.

44. *GL* 148, before 27 January 1853, pp. 220–221.

45. *GL* 140, 15 November 1852, p. 209.

Chapter 3

1. Critics have argued against this view, while being taken in by it in subtler
ways. Edgar Wright says that it is "over simple to accept *Cranford* as a nostalgic
idealization, though to some extent it has this quality," yet in the next sentence,
he refers to its "lightness of treatment" (*Mrs Gaskell: The Basis for Reassessment*
[London: Oxford University Press, 1965], p. 108). Both Dale Spender (*Man
Made Language* [London: Routledge & Kegan Paul, 1980]) and Patsy Stoneman
(*Elizabeth Gaskell* [Bloomington: Indiana University Press, 1987]) have discussed

the ways the (deliberate) reshaping of what woman's literature *should* look like (flowery, pastoral, elegiac, local) shaped a reevaluation of Gaskell's canon, leading to the preeminence of *Cranford*. (Stoneman usefully offers Lord David Cecil's praise in *Early Victorian Novelists* of Gaskell's femininity, quoting his description of her as a "domestic, tactful, unintellectual . . . typical Victorian woman.") In an attempt to shed the "lavender scented" school of criticism, recent critics have stressed connections between this novel and Gaskell's more explicitly political works. Making *Cranford* a problem novel can, I argue, extend our definition of that genre, but only insofar as we are willing to accept formal literary transformations as an integral part of any attempt at rewriting society. My reading of the novel *begins* with the assumption that Gaskell was using this "light treatment" as part of a larger critique.

2. Luce Irigaray, "This Sex Which Is Not One," in *This Sex Which Is Not One*, trans. Catherine Porter (Ithaca: Cornell University Press, 1985), p. 25.

3. Hélène Cixous, "The Laugh of the Medusa," in *New French Feminisms*, ed. Elaine Marks and Isabelle de Courtivron (Amherst: University of Massachusetts Press, 1980), p. 245.

4. Mary Poovey argues, in *The Proper Lady and the Woman Writer* (Chicago: University of Chicago Press, 1984), p. 44, that parody "can be seen as the expression of a desire to retain *both* the inherited and the revised genre," a doubling that Poovey argues is "more in keeping with the model of female psychological maturation proposed by feminists such as Nancy Chodorow and Juliet Mitchell." She might be seen as expanding George Levine's comment, that "parody is a necessarily self-contradictory form" (*The Realistic Imagination* [Chicago: University of Chicago Press, 1981], p. 69), into an argument that it thus by its nature fits a woman writer's self-contradictory position. Something of this sort is, at any rate, the basis for my argument that Gaskell saw herself, in writing the divided narrative of *Cranford*, carrying out what Levine notices in Austen's attempt in *Northanger Abbey*: that she did not "pretend to be writing a true history, but is a novelist writing a novel," and, to advance his argument a step, sees her self-consciousness as a feminine position.

5. "The Last Generation in England," in *Cranford and Cousin Phillis*, ed. Peter Keating (Harmondsworth, England: Penguin, 1976), p. 319. (All subsequent references included in text.) I have also consulted the Oxford University Press edition of *Cranford* (edited by Elizabeth Porges Watson, 1972), which has fuller annotation on "The Last Generation."

6. For a general history of publishing and of changes in publishing in this period, see J. A. Sutherland's masterly *Victorian Novelists and Publishers* (Chicago: University of Chicago Press, 1976), especially pp. 62–68. Many of these changes, among them the circulating libraries, predate the innovations of railway publishing; see Frank Arthur Mumby, *Publishing and Bookselling: A History from the Earliest Times to the Present Day* (London: Jonathan Cape, 1930), especially pp. 176–177.

7. See *The Story of W. H. Smith & Son* (London, 1921), p. 11.

8. See *GL* 382, 26 November 1857, to George Smith; *GL* 486, 27 April 1861, to Frederick Chapman.

9. John Ruskin, "The Lamp of Beauty," in *The Seven Lamps of Architecture* (New York: Farrar, Straus, Giroux, 1977), p. 117.

10. *The Interpretation of Cultures* (New York: Basic Books, 1973), p. 20. All subsequent references included in text.

11. See *GL* 562, late February 1865, p. 748.

12. This passage is quoted in Hazlitt's "On Familiar Style" (Essay VII in *Table Talk*, 1822), an essay that in style and tone is very close to *Cranford*—and which contains a critique of Johnson that in many ways anticipates hers. "Words, like clothes, get old-fashioned, or mean and ridiculous, when they have been for some time laid aside"; a similar critique seems to me to be at the heart of *Cranford*. The grace and humor of the Romantic essay—and its ambivalent reading of every subject—seem to me similarly close to Gaskell's fictional intent, especially in the very essayistic *Cranford*.

13. See Winifred Gérin, *Elizabeth Gaskell* (Oxford: Oxford University Press, 1980), pp. 125–126, and, for an interesting treatment of the history of Gaskell's relationship with Dickens, A. B. Hopkins, *Elizabeth Gaskell: Her Life and Work* (London: John Lehmann, 1952), pp. 135–157.

14. Dickens to Wills, 30 July 1854, in *Charles Dickens as Editor*, ed. R. C. Lehmann (New York: Sturgis & Walton, 1912), p. 134.

15. *The Nonesuch Dickens: The Letters of Charles Dickens*, ed. Walter Dexter (Bloomsbury: Nonesuch Press, 1938); 31 January 1850, 2:202.

16. *Nonesuch Letters*, letter misdated 5 (actually 4) December 1851, 2:361.

17. *Nonesuch Letters*, 13 April 1853, 2:457.

18. See Anne Lohrli, *Household Words, passim* (Toronto: University of Toronto Press, 1973).

19. Here we might invoke Bakhtin and the concept of heteroglossia. One can see the Bakhtinian enterprise in this discussion of the layering of voices and texts that, I agree, *is* essential to the novel, which must be dialogic, which must be a reservoir of cultural voices and literary echoes, but I mean something at once not limited to and much more limited than that. The literary echoes I am tracing here are part of a specific literary battle, Gaskell's movement toward her own voice, and must be read in the realm of male/female relations, the marketing of women's fiction, the power dynamic between Gaskell and Dickens. (See Mikhail Bakhtin, "Discourse and the Novel," in *The Dialogic Imagination*, ed. Michael Holquist, trans. Holquist and Caryl Emerson [Austin: University of Texas Press, 1980].)

20. Garrett Stewart, *Dickens and the Trials of Imagination* (Cambridge: Harvard University Press, 1974), p. 13.

21. Wolfgang Schivelbusch, *The Railway Journey: Trains and Travel in the 19th Century* (New York: Urizen Books, 1979); see especially chap. 3, pp. 41–50.

22. Siegfried Kracauer, *History: The Last Things before the Last* (Oxford: Oxford University Press, 1969).

23. Lennard Davis, *Resisting Novels: Ideology and Fiction* (New York: Methuen, 1987), p. 55.

24. Susan Stewart, *On Longing: Narratives of the Miniature, the Gigantic, the Souvenir, the Collection* (Baltimore: Johns Hopkins University Press, 1984), p. 63. All subsequent references included in the text.

25. For a similar discussion, see Joseph Allan Boone, *Tradition Counter Tradition: Love and the Form of Fiction* (Chicago: University of Chicago Press, 1987), pp. 295–304.

26. Stewart, pp. 1–29 especially; Steven Marcus, *Dickens from Pickwick to Dombey* (New York: Norton, 1965), pp. 13–53, and further, "Language into Structure: Pickwick Revisited," *Daedalus* (Winter 1972).

27. We might here connect Gaskell's "Mary Smith" with Virginia Woolf's "Mary" ("call me Mary Beton, Mary Seton, Mary Carmichael") in *A Room of One's Own* (New York: Harcourt Brace and World, 1929), p. 5. Woolf's use of "Mary" as a signifier for the common woman, the "'I [which is] only a convenient term for somebody who has no real being," that is, the perfect, transparent narrator who gets more and more life as the text continues, is much like Gaskell's "Mary Smith," with the plainest name imaginable, an almost balladic simplicity. I would argue, though, that the parallels run further, perhaps to the extent of an arguable influence. Woolf's discussion of women bound in by texts sounds much like Gaskell's discussion of "affairs of the alphabet," and her treatment of the novelist echoes much of *Cranford*'s enterprise. "Mary Carmichael," as Woolf remarks at the end describing her imaginary new woman novelist, "will have her work cut out for her merely as an observer" (p. 92). In that description of what women might write, we can hear many echoes of *Cranford* itself: the new novel's unexpected strength is its portrait of female friendship; it attempts a new sentence, breaking up "Jane Austen's sentence, and thus giv[ing] me no chance of pluming myself upon my impeccable taste, my fastidious ear." But finally, Mary Carmichael has—and this might stand as an epigraph to my discussion of *Cranford*—"gone further": she has

> broken the sequence—the expected order. Perhaps she had done this unconsciously, merely giving things their natural order, as a woman would, if she wrote like a woman. (p. 95)

Woolf's description of the difference between male and female values and fiction further reminds one of Gaskell:

> It is the masculine values that prevail. Speaking crudely, football and sport are "important"; the worship of fashion, the buying of clothes "trivial." And these values are inevitably transferred from life to fiction. This is an important book, the critic assumes, because it deals with war. This is an insignificant book because it deals with the feelings of women in a drawing-room. A scene in a battlefield is more important than a scene in a shop—everywhere and much more subtly the difference of value persists. (p. 77)

I would like to think that Woolf was thinking of *Cranford* when she wrote these words. I am reminded of the quiet irony with which she first commented that "too great a refinement gives 'Cranford' that prettiness which is the weakest thing about it, making it, *superficially at least*, the favourite copy for gentle writers who have hired rooms over the village post-office," and then went on, in the next sentence, to remind us that "when she was a girl, Mrs Gaskell was famous for her ghost stories" ("Mrs Gaskell," *Times Literary Supplement*, 29 September 1910; reprinted in *Women and Writing*, ed. Michele Barrett [New York: Harcourt Brace Jovanovich, 1979], pp. 48–49; emphasis added). Woolf, no "gentle writer" herself, saw through Gaskell's cover immediately.

28. For Gaskell's interesting references to Adam Smith, whom she clearly respected and feared, see especially *GL* 93, 7 April 1851, where Gaskell recommends that her daughter read *The Wealth of Nations* before she forms opinions on protectionism and trade, but that she not "confine" herself "to the limited meaning which he affixes to the word 'wealth'" (p. 148). There are strong points of connection between Gaskell, John Ruskin, and Karl Marx (especially the Ruskin of "The Nature of Gothic" or *Unto This Last* and the Marx of the *Philosophic and Economic Manuscripts of 1844*) that mark all three as readers of Adam Smith, with shared concerns about alienated labor, useless work, rules of exchange.

29. Margaret Homans, in *Bearing the Word: Language and Female Experience in Nineteenth-Century Women's Writing* (Chicago: University of Chicago Press, 1986), poses some suggestive ideas about Gaskell's heroines and their roles in "bearing" (carrying) letters, transmitting words between men; unfortunately, she does not consider *Cranford*, with its feminizing of letter-writing.

30. It is interesting that we never get the text of the letter itself; presumably, the story Peter hears is the story we have just read, and at this moment of narrative fixity (a solid text, a letter, meeting the perfect reading audience) the storytelling could extend infinitely. This suggests what Tzvetan Todorov has called the "embedded" text, which "reaches its apogee with the process of self-embedding, that is, when the embedding story happens to be, at some fifth or sixth degree, embedded by itself," as when Scheherezade tells the story of her own storytelling. As Todorov quotes Borges, "On this night, the king hears from the queen's mouth her own story. He hears the initial story, which includes all the others, which—monstrously—includes itself. . . . If the queen continues, the king will sit still and listen forever to the truncated version of the *Arabian Nights*, henceforth infinite and circular" ("Narrative-Men," in *The Poetics of Prose* [Ithaca: Cornell University Press, 1977], p. 73). The embedding narrative, as Todorov asserts, is the "narrative of a narrative"; in *Cranford*, this brief suggestion of the repetition of the story we are reading is the narrative of a narrative of narrativizing.

31. *The Pickwick Papers*, ed. Robert L. Patten (Harmondsworth, England: Penguin Books, 1972), p. 896.

Chapter 4

1. Winifred Gérin, *Elizabeth Gaskell* (Oxford University Press, 1980), p. 150.

2. The classic attack on the marriage plot as solution to social problems is Raymond Williams's in *Culture and Society* (New York: Columbia University Press, 1958), pp. 87–109. See also Nancy Armstrong's discussion of nineteenth-century fiction's tendency to "bring order to social relationships . . . by subordinating all social differences to those based on gender." The examples Armstrong cites are *Wuthering Heights* and *Jane Eyre*; her conclusion is that "the power of the middle classes had everything to do with that of middle class love." *Desire and Domestic Fiction: A Political History of the Novel* (New York: Oxford University Press, 1987), p. 4. For my discussion of the way these quick solutions become problematic in the light of gender relations, see chapter 1.

There are three important recent discussions of this problem in *North and South*, which must be labeled *the* sticking point of the text for modern critics. Interestingly, all three discussions are by women. The most general of these is Deirdre David's, in *Fictions of Resolution in Three Victorian Novels* (New York: Columbia University Press, 1981), which is most sympathetic to the sexual plot but argues "the fiction of resolution of sexual tension between her lovers seems more plausible than the fiction of resolution of class conflict," because the industrialized working class did not enjoy the "freedom of her heroine" (pp. 48–49). That is, she accepts as unproblematic the sexual freedom of Margaret, and sees no connection other than plot between the two resolutions. Judith Lowder Newton's *Women, Power and Subversion: Social Strategies in British Fiction, 1778–1860* (Athens: University of Georgia Press, 1981) argues that "despite the fact that we are made to *feel* class divisions, they are divisions which we are ultimately compelled to accept" (p. 166), and that "the love plot *is* initiated at the moment of her most dramatic exercise of power" but that "Margaret must marry" (p. 167). Finally, Newton argues, the novel "never protests the economic inequities which restricted the middle-class women to the self-sacrificing role which it implicitly recommends." This is all one version of the truth, and to some degree convincing, but I cannot agree with Newton that Gaskell "celebrates the ideology of women's sphere." I believe she registers the restrictions on women's speaking out and resents them; further, as I argue throughout, she makes more problematic the novel's relationship to the realm of power and to ideology.

My argument converges most closely with Catherine Gallagher's, in her chapter "'Relationship Remembered against Relationship Forgot': Family and Society in *Hard Times* and *North and South*," in *The Industrial Reformation of English Fiction: Social Discourse and Narrative Form, 1832–1867* (Chicago: University of Chicago Press, 1985). Gallagher describes the marriage plot as intertwining "social and familial themes and plots so thoroughly that the very conventional resolution of the novel's love plot appears to be a partial solution to industrial social problems," and she connects this to Gaskell's "use of Margaret Hale to control the novel's point of view," the comparison of "public and private plot episodes" and Margaret and John Thornton's function as "actual representatives of the English upper classes," which "thereby endow[s] their marriage with practical social consequences." She further asserts, and here again I agree, that "the novel provides its own counters to these associative techniques." (p. 170). Where I differ from Gallagher is first in seeing the "private" in the novel as fundamentally concerned with issues of marriage rather than the family; that is, Gaskell's concern is with female sexuality, with modes of union and intimate relationships of power, which do not exist as much in the "private"—that is, a separate sphere—as do Gallagher's "family" questions. Further, I do not see the primary model of the novel as "associative"-metonymic, in Gallagher's terminology-so much as "conversational," that is, always in conflict, always pulling away as much as pulling together. To see these conflicts as linguistic, and as linguistically registered, is to see the novel as much more aware of the partialness of its own solutions, and, in fact, as taking that imperfection of resolution as its subject. (See my discussion of self-conscious representation, below.) Gallagher comes close to this understanding in two statements: first, that "according to this novel and to the ideology that informs it, all women must be strangers to the industrial society they seek to reform" (p. 178), and second, that "the book thus suggests a kind of anarchy of signification, and the sense of anarchy is reinforced by the way the book dwells on the difficulties that northerners and southerners have in understanding one another" (p. 181). I do not read this "anarchy" as incidental but as integral to the novel.

3. See Gallagher's discussion of the tension between "the need to explain events (to make them intelligible) and the need to capture the character's sense of free choice" in *The Industrial Reformation of English Fiction*, pp. 34–35, and, further, W. J. Harvey, *Character and the Novel* (Ithaca: Cornell University Press, 1965).

4. *North and South* (Harmondsworth, England: Penguin Books, 1970), p. 96; all subsequent references are to this edition.

5. On the difficulty of reading the industrial city, see Steven Marcus's "Reading the Illegible," in *The Victorian City*, ed. H. J. Dyos and Michael Wolff (London: Routledge & Kegan Paul, 1973), pp. 257–276.

6. *GL* 191, 23 April 1854. Gaskell reports to John Forster that she had asked Dickens "& he says he is not going to have a strike,—altogether his answer sets me at ease" p. 281.

7. Gareth Stedman Jones, "Rethinking Chartism," in *Languages of Class* (Cambridge: Cambridge University Press, 1983), p. 95. Joan Scott has argued convincingly that Stedman Jones's practice lags slightly behind his theory, inasmuch as his notion of "politics" still depends on "readings" derived from more conventional models of intellectual history than his poststructuralist notions of language would suggest, but his is still the most compelling effort to redefine the relation of class consciousness to language. See Scott, "On Language, Gender

and Working-Class History,' in *Gender and the Politics of History* (New York: Columbia University Press, 1988), particularly pp. 56-60.

8. "Two Lectures on the Lancashire Dialect," by the Reverend W. Gaskell, M.A., in *Mary Barton*, 1854 (fifth) edition, pp. 9-10.

9. I owe these suggestions to Donna Landry and Peter Manning.

10. *GL* 191, 23 April 1854, p. 281.

11. *GL* 195, 17 May 1854, p. 286.

12. *GL* 192, ?8-14 May 1854, p. 282.

13. *GL* 211, 11 to 14 October 1854, p. 310.

14. *GL* 217, 27 October 1854, p. 321.

15. *GL* 220, ?17 December 1854, p. 323.

16. *GL* 225, January 1855, pp. 328-329.

17. *GL* 227, 30 January 1855, pp. 325-326.

18. *GL* 235, 25 April 1855, p. 340. My reference in this paragraph and throughout the chapter is to Walter Benjamin's "The Work of Art in the Age of Mechanical Reproduction," in *Illuminations*, trans. Harry Zohn (New York: Schocken Books, 1969), which has shaped much of my thinking.

19. *GL* 222, 24 [25?] December 1854.

20. See Anna Jameson, *Sisters of Charity Catholic and Protestant, Abroad and at Home* (1855) and *The Communion of Labour: A Second Lecture on the Social Employments of Women* (1856). In her lectures, Jameson appeals to the image of Florence Nightingale, and argues that there exists "at the core of our social condition a great mistake to be corrected, and a great want supplied . . . men and women must learn to understand each other, and work together for the common good. . . . In the most comprehensive sense of the word, we need Sisters of Charity everywhere." In terms that sound very much like Gaskell, she argues that we need not "amateur *ladies* of charity, but brave women, whose vocation is fixed and whose faculties of every kind have been trained and disciplined to their work" (*Sisters*, p. 111).

Chapter 5

1. Peter Brooks, *Reading for the Plot: Design and Intention in Narrative* (New York: Knopf, 1984), p. 38.

2. The essential reworking of the Freudian Oedipal myth into (literary) mediation is René Girard's account of triangular desire in *Deceit, Desire and the Novel: Self and Other in Literary Structure* (Baltimore: Johns Hopkins University Press, 1965). We might here borrow Lacan's rephrasing of the Freudian problem: "desire becomes bound up with the desire of the Other, but . . . in this loop lies the desire to know" ("The Subversion of the Subject and the Dialectic of Desire in the Freudian Unconscious," in *Écrits* [New York: Norton, 1977], p. 301). Interestingly, Lacan posits that the desire for the "other" is the desire for "a presence in

that beyond-the-veil where the whole of Nature can be questioned about its design": the epigraph for *Sylvia's Lovers* is a passage from Tennyson's *In Memoriam*, which reads,

> Oh for thy voice to soothe and bless!
> What hope of answer, or redress?
> Behind the veil! behind the veil!

Like post-Freudians, Gaskell made an essential connection between the desire to possess (identity) and the desire to know (to question)—or, perhaps more accurately, Freud made an essentially *Victorian* connection between the quest for self-knowledge and sexual happiness. Gaskell, Tennyson, and Freud are, of course, all writing about quests that can end (that are defined by ending) only in death.

3. Tzvetan Todorov, "Narrative Transformations," in *The Poetics of Prose* (Ithaca: Cornell University Press, 1977), p. 232.

4. *Sylvia's Lovers*, ed. Andrew Sanders (Oxford: Oxford University Press, 1982), p. 71. All subsequent references are to this edition and are included in the text.

5. Brooks, p. 100.

6. Eve Kosofsky Sedgwick, *Between Men: English Literature and Male Homosocial Desire* (New York: Columbia University Press, 1985), p. 2. My sense of the centrality of the relationship between Philip and Charley must be informed by Sedgwick's provocative thesis, which might pick up on the class argument so well laid out by Terry Eagleton in his essay "*Sylvia's Lovers* and Legality," in *Essays in Criticism* (1977) 26: 17–27.

7. See Kaja Silverman, *The Subject of Semiotics* (Oxford: Oxford University Press, 1983), especially chapters 4 and 5. The discussion of the site of the female gaze (p. 223) to which I refer specifically here, draws on the work of Laura Mulvey in "Visual Pleasure and Narrative Cinema" (Silverman cites its original publication in *Screen* 16, no. 3 [1975]: 6–18), to which I have referred in chapter 2 of this volume, in discussing the relationship of women to aesthetic perception in *Ruth*. My discussion of that novel is in part relevant here; in *Sylvia's Lovers*, I think, we see a more wide-ranging analysis of the workings of desire than we did in *Ruth*, but the concern with the construction of female sexuality (of female desire) remains the same.

8. Gaskell quotes from this ballad in chapter 8, stating Philip "could almost have echoed the words of the lover of Jess MacFarlane," R. K. Webb has also noted the connection to *North and South* in "The Gaskells as Unitarians," in *Dickens and Other Victorians: Essays in Honour of Philip Collins*, ed. Joanne Shattock (London: Macmillan, 1988), p. 162.

9. *The Brontës: Their Lives, Friendships and Correspondence*, ed. Thomas J. Wise and J. A. Symington, 4 vols. (Oxford: Oxford University Press, 1932; III, 165), quoted in *Wuthering Heights*, ed. William M. Sale (New York: Norton, 1963, 1972), p. 272.

10. U. C. Knoepflmacher has made a very similar point in a fine essay, "Genre

and the Integration of Gender: From Wordsworth to George Eliot to Virginia Woolf," in *Victorian Literature and Society: Essays Presented to Richard D. Altick*, ed. James R. Kincaid and Albert J. Kuhn (Columbus: Ohio State University Press, 1984).

11. Adrienne Rich, "Planetarium" (1968), *The Will to Change* (1971); reprinted in *Poems: Selected and New, 1950–1974* (New York: Norton, 1975), p. 146.

12. Luce Irigaray, "This Sex Which Is Not One," in *This Sex Which Is Not One*, trans. Catherine Porter with Carolyn Burke (Ithaca: Cornell University Press, 1985), p. 25.

13. Ibid., pp. 31–32.

14. The image in *Mary Barton* that suggests the unbridled anger of a revolution is the factory fire in which Jem Wilson proves himself a hero. That scene exists partly to establish Jem as the appropriate choice for Mary (appropriate in that his hidden passion matches hers; that his is the real courage [sexuality] of the novel) and also to deflect the need for a riot. It has the mob hysteria missing even from the strike in *North and South*. That fire scene is a corollary of the fire and destruction at the Randyvowse in *Sylvia's Lovers*—it is a false fire alarm that rouses the men who are subsequently unfairly impressed at the tavern—but Gaskell's use of fire suggests the subtler conservatism of her revolutionary anger: recall Elias Canetti's suggestion in *Crowds and Power* that fire, as a symbol for crowds, is important first because "fire is always the same." Here, Gaskell's interest in change again rehearses the idea of similarity—resemblance—amid difference. (See generally, *Crowds and Power*, trans. Carol Stewart [New York: Continuum, 1973 (1960)] and, for fire, pp. 75–80.) In Canetti's phrase, "The dangerous traits of the crowd are often pointed out and, among them, the most striking is the propensity to incendiarism" (p. 77). The crowd in *North and South*—and hence, the more amorphous threat in that novel of group power—is that of a sea. (See Canetti, 80–81.)

15. Arthur Pollard, *Mrs Gaskell: Novelist and Biographer* (Cambridge: Harvard University Press, 1966), p. 211; Eagleton, p. 18.

16. Silverman, pp. 154–158. See my discussion of pre-Oedipal language in chapter 1.

17. I see in Bella's departure a reference to the end of *The Scarlet Letter*, in which Pearl begins a new life but does so ambiguously, by going back to Europe and—presumably—marrying into the nobility, writing letters with "armorial seals" upon them, though they are seals "unknown to English heraldry." These letters may mark Hester as a love interest, and Pearl may have gone to an untimely "maiden grave," but the clearer suggestion of the novel is that the daughter has found her place by leaving the New World, while the mother makes her life there. In Hester Rose's life of service, we may see another echo of Hester Prynne's—and Bella, like Pearl, is unexpectedly left an heiress.

Gaskell was living near Nathaniel Hawthorne, whom she much admired, while writing *Sylvia's Lovers*. She wrote to George Smith, "Do *you* know what Hawthorne's tale [*The Marble Faun*] is about? *I* do; and I think it will perplex the English public pretty considerably." *GL* 441, 20 September 1859, p. 575.

18. Edgar Wright, *Mrs Gaskell: The Basis for Reassessment* (Oxford: Oxford University Press, 1963), p. 173. He, too, mentions Charles Eliot Norton, but only as an example of Gaskell's feeling of "anticlimax"; he does not relate the affair to narrative motivation. And, though this barely needs to be said, surely no critic would link narrative structure to a male writer's "change of life." Biology is brought in here to support more critical argument than it rightfully can, and brought in as literary destiny in a way it would not be in discussing anyone but a woman novelist, particularly one habitually relegated to the female realm.

19. *GL* 375, September 1857, pp. 476–477.

Chapter 6

1. See Edward W. Said, *Beginnings: Intention and Method* (Baltimore: Johns Hopkins University Press, 1975), especially chapter 3, "The Novel as Beginning Intention," with its helpful discussion of *Great Expectations.* Peter Brooks discusses the intersection of fairy tale and psychological narrative in "Repetition, Repression and Return: The Plotting of *Great Expectations,*" in *Reading for the Plot: Design and Intention in Narrative* (New York: Knopf, 1984), pp. 113–142.

2. Michel Foucault, *Les Mots et les Choses* (translated as *The Order of Things: An Archeology of the Human Sciences* [New York: Vintage, 1973], p. 132). All subsequent references are to this edition and are included in the text.

3. *Wives and Daughters*, ed. Laurence Lerner (Harmondsworth, England: Penguin Books, 1966), p. 35. All subsequent references are to this edition and are included in the text.

4. For a discussion of these issues, see Margaret Homans, *Bearing the Word: Language and Female Experience in Nineteenth-Century Women's Writing* (Chicago: University of Chicago Press, 1986), particularly chapter 10, "Mothers and Daughters II: *Wives and Daughters,* or 'Two Mothers,'" which discusses some of the same questions of Molly's reading and feminization, and the replacement of the lost mother with a man. Patsy Stoneman, in *Elizabeth Gaskell* (Bloomington: Indiana University Press, 1987), also discusses family relations in the novel, linking what I call systems of information with a specifically female (maternal) attentiveness to detail.

5. My discussion throughout owes much to Alexander Welsh's compelling book, *George Eliot and Blackmail* (Cambridge: Harvard University Press, 1985), which focuses on the technology and power of information in Victorian culture, and suggests much that is useful about blackmail as a "pathology" of information. Welsh's discussion of ideology is less focused than my treatment here, and he extends the central term of *blackmail* to cover all kinds of usurped knowledge, secrets, and curiosity; nor does he discuss a gendered notion of gossip. Neverthe-

less, we are clearly asking many of the same questions, and I find his treatment intriguing.

6. One would not be over-reading to place this emphasis on knowledge in the center of the debate over professional expertise and, further, in the intellectual imperialism of colonialism.

7. *GL* 550, 3 May 1864, p. 732.

8. My treatment throughout this chapter draws on Gillian Beer's brilliant *Darwin's Plots: Evolutionary Narrative in Darwin, George Eliot and Nineteenth-Century Fiction* (London: Routledge & Kegan Paul, 1983), which is the best discussion I know of the dependence of Darwinian "plots" on the norms of fiction. Gaskell was one of Darwin's favorite novelists, although neither Beer nor George Levine, in *Darwin and the Novelists* (Cambridge: Harvard University Press, 1988), connects these interesting insights on the way Darwinian plots shaped Victorian fiction to Gaskell's novels.

9. For a treatment of gossip and female texts, see Patricia Meyer Spacks, *Gossip* (New York: Knopf, 1985).

10. Susan Stewart, *On Longing: Narratives of the Miniature, the Gigantic, the Souvenir, the Collection* (Baltimore: Johns Hopkins University Press, 1984), pp. 161–162. The passage from Donato is from "The Museum's Furnace: Notes Toward a Contextual Reading of *Bouvard and Pécouchet*," in *Textual Strategies: Perspectives in Post-Structuralist Criticism*, ed. Josué Harari (Ithaca: Cornell University Press, 1979), pp. 213–238.

11. Homans discusses the relationship between *Wives and Daughters* and *Jane Eyre* in *Bearing the Word* (pp. 275–276) as an instance of the daughter's transmitting the father's word through the female text.

12. *GL* 431, 3 June 1850, p. 559.

13. Maria Edgeworth, *Helen* (London and New York: Pandora, 1987), p. 390.

14. Virginia Woolf, *A Room of One's Own* (New York and Burlingame: Harcourt, Brace & World, 1929), p. 3. All subsequent references are to this edition and are included in the text.

15. Beer, p. 42.

16. Sigmund Freud, *Civilization and Its Discontents* (New York: Norton, 1961), p. 24. All subsequent references are to this edition and are included in the text.

17. Beer, p. 48.

Index